HOPE FAITH AND CHARLIE

An inspirational journey
of a child's courageous battle with cancer,
his family's fight to save his life,
and the blessings that happened along the way.

A True Story
A True Miracle

by

Deirdre Carey

authorHOUSE®

10% of all proceeds from the sale of *Hope, Faith and Charlie* will be donated directly to The Floating Hospital for Children's Cancer Center at Tufts-New England Medical Center.

AuthorHouse™
1663 Liberty Drive, Suite 200
Bloomington, IN 47403
www.authorhouse.com
Phone: 1-800-839-8640

This book is a work of non-fiction. Unless otherwise noted, the author
and the publisher make no explicit guarantees as to the accuracy of
the information contained in this book and in some cases, names of
people and places have been altered to protect their privacy.

First published by AuthorHouse 10/25/2007

ISBN: 978-1-4343-3163-2 (sc)

Library of Congress Control Number: 2007906674

Printed in the United States of America
Bloomington, Indiana

This book is printed on acid-free paper.

Cover Design by Erin Johnson

Designer
Kel & Partners
69 Milk Street
Westborough, MA 01581
508-366-2099
www.kelandpartners.com

This book is dedicated to my two beautiful sons
Jay and Charlie Capodanno.

I love you.
Mommy

"I hope you still feel small when you stand beside the ocean,
Whenever one door closes I hope one more opens,
Promise me that you'll give faith a fighting chance,
And when you get the choice to sit it out or dance,
I hope you dance!"

- Lee Ann Womack

Author's Note

This is a work of nonfiction. I have rendered the events truthfully and honestly just as I have recalled them. Some names of individuals have been changed in order to respect their privacy. While circumstances, events and conversations depicted herein come from my own personal recollection, they are not meant to represent precise time lines of events or the exact word-for-word reenactments. They are told in a way that evokes the real feelings and meanings of what was said and my view of what happened at that time.

Contents

Chapter 1
A Mother's Instinct

Trying to Be Supermom

"Cripes! Don't do this to me, Brian!" I pleaded into the phone, slapping my hand against my forehead. "We've been talking about this project for weeks. You're telling me, NOW, *two* days before the materials are to ship to Las Vegas, that you don't have the signage printed yet! I don't believe this," I growled, pushing back in my office chair with a harsh thrust.

As a 33-year-old supervisor at a Newton, Massachusetts-based marketing agency, I had been working on the deliverables for a trade show for months, and at the eleventh hour, the last-minute details were not falling into place. In my career, I had orchestrated many trade shows, but I was particularly stressed out about this one; I had to prove to my managers (and to myself) that I could work the flexible schedule I had negotiated upon returning from my recent maternity leave, and produce like any other 8:00 a.m. to 8:00 p.m. full-time employee. This, of course, was in addition to my other priorities including, but not limited to, raising two boys, one an infant, as well as the cooking, cleaning, shopping and other assorted married and motherly tasks.

I'd gone back to work less than three months after the birth of my second child, Charlie. My goal was simple: I would prove to myself and my new employer that I could handle my new position and my family with ease. I was pretty confident that I could be one of those "supermoms." Fortunately, my new boss Patty, a working mom herself, knew that my children came first. Granted, I was considered a very dedicated and loyal employee, but it was absolutely evident that my number one devotion was to my family. In fact, I was passed over for two promotions while I was out on maternity leave. The promotions would have required more travel, and I was not going to leave my children for long periods of time, regardless of what the salary increase would mean to us. Still, I take pride in all that I do, and if I was going to be the only one at my company with a flex schedule, I was going to make darn sure it worked. So, given that I was a multitasker by nature, I should have had no problem balancing my job, our precious five-month-old Charlie, my supportive and handsome husband John, and our beautiful two-year-old son Jay.

This trade show was a big deal for me. Regrettably, it was the first time I would have to travel in my new position, which I dreaded. I hated the thought of leaving the kids. I knew that John was completely capable of handling things at home, but we were all still adjusting to my returning to work from my maternity leave, and even more important, Charlie was still so young, and he hadn't been feeling that great over the last few weeks. It was early February, and I'd been to the pediatrician's office at least once or twice a week since Christmas morning when Charlie had spiked his first high fever of 103. The doctor on call Christmas morning checked Charlie's chart and determined that the fever was more than likely the result of an ear infection that he'd been battling. We'd tried five different antibiotics in five weeks, but nothing had cleared it up.

"Give him some Tylenol, and if the fever doesn't break, bring him to the ER at Children's," the on-call pediatrician instructed us. Children's Hospital was just about the *last* place we wanted to spend our Christmas! Fortunately, the fever broke.

A few weeks passed. On the night before I was scheduled to go on a company "team building" ski trip, Charlie had another fever. In fact, both Charlie and Jay were up vomiting. I was furious that I had to leave my children, especially when they weren't feeling well, but this trip was mandatory. John made it out to be no big deal, and his mom and dad came over to help out, so I reluctantly packed my bag and headed north for a two-day, work/play adult sleep-over party at the beautiful Mount Washington Inn in New Hampshire.

After I checked into the hotel, I immediately threw down my bags and raced to the phone to call home. No answer. Never a good sign when children are sick. I tried unsuccessfully to reach John and the kids for the next two hours. I even called my neighbors to help track my family down. Concern quickly turned to panic. "Where could they be on a freezing February night?" I demanded of myself, as my nerves grew uneasy. Finally at about 8:30 that night, I tracked John and the boys down at home. He'd taken Charlie to Urgent Care at our pediatric facility because he'd had another fever of 102. I felt a pit in my stomach. It was a horrible feeling to be so far away when my poor baby was sick. As always, John downplayed the situation, informing me the doctor thought it was just the bug he and Jay must have caught. Skiing was now the farthest thing from my mind.

The next day, I made a presentation at our company meeting, and I was thrilled with the applause I received after my speech, which fed my lingering hope that I could master this working-mom gig.

After the meetings were over, we had time to ski, go shopping or just hang out, followed by a company dinner that night. The next morning after breakfast, my friend Amy and I hit the road for home. We were about three minutes down the road, when I grabbed her arm and motioned for her to pull over. *Blahh!* I got violently ill right there in a snow bank. It was quite embarrassing because half the people from my company were driving by honking and waving; obviously thinking I had had too much to drink the night before. The fact of the matter, though, is that I hadn't had anything to drink the night before, and here I was looking like a lush tossing my Eggs Benedict all over the shimmering, snow-blanketed front lawn of the Mt. Washington Inn. I dragged my pale, limp body back into the car, looked at Amy, who was horrified, and told her I must have caught the bug that the kids had. She passed me a piece of gum, and we headed home! When I arrived, the first order of duty was to brush my teeth. Then I checked on the boys, kissed my husband and went to bed for an entire day to recover from whatever stomach flu had taken hold of me and my children. Fortunately, like Jay and Charlie, recovery was less than 24 hours away.

Pushing for Answers

Now here I was two weeks later in a screaming match with the sales representative at our exhibit house. I was livid that he didn't have everything he needed to complete the signage in time to make the freight truck out to Vegas. This meant we'd have to overnight them out, which would cost a fortune and completely throw off my budget, which I was meticulous about.

"Well, if we don't have the right graphics by the end of today," Brian said, trying to soften the blow, "I guess, ah, it's not going to make the truck, Dee."

"AARRG!" I slammed down the phone. I could see the young account manager who worked outside my office door as he looked up at me, caught a glimpse of my angry expression, and then immediately looked back down at his desk. I took a long, cleansing breath. I needed to regain my composure before I went to fill Patty in on our little problem. Suddenly, the phone rang.

"Deirdre, it is Kristine from the Barn Yard." Kristine was not only Charlie's day care teacher, but she was also our neighbor and my very dear friend. "Everything is okay," she tried to reassure me, "but, I hate to say it, Charlie's got another fever." My emotions shifted instantly from a frustrated supervisor to a worried mommy. "What is *up* with these fevers?" I mumbled into the phone. Charlie had another appointment with the pediatrician scheduled for the next day because of a slight cough he was courting and the beginning stages of a runny nose. He'd also continued to throw up a few of his morning bottles, which the doctor believed was just the stomach bug lingering in him because he was an infant. "Ooohhh, my poor little man. Give him a kiss for me and I'll be right over to pick him up," I said.

I logged off from my laptop and racing down to Patty's office. Now I needed to tell her that, not only did we have major issues with the trade show signage, but also I had to leave that minute to pick the baby up and bring him to the doctor's office – again! Patty is a working mom too, and was very supportive of me. She was confident that I'd get my job taken care of somehow.

"I'll call you from the car right after I get through to the pediatrician," I yelled as I headed out the door with my briefcase and laptop.

Dr. Lilia Cuozzo has been our pediatrician since our first child, Jay, was born. We adore her. She gently guided us through Jay's four months of colic and acid reflux disease. On more than one occasion she dried my tears when I'd call her bleary-eyed every morning to let her know Jay cried 20 out of 24 hours a day due to the burning from the reflux. She is young, sweet, smart, and most important to me, she's a mom too. Here I was back again with Charlie for about the seventh time that month – for everything from ear infections to vomiting episodes and congestion. You name it, poor Charlie had had it.

"He's got another fever, and we've noticed a slight cough," I explained with concern. "At least the vomiting has stopped," I added, trying to sound optimistic. As she examined Charlie, we noted that it was February and every kid in day care had a cold.

"That ear is still infected, and his lungs sound junky. I think he's got RSV, which is an upper respiratory virus," she said as she methodically listened to his tiny chest.

Charlie giggled and cooed as Dr. Cuozzo explained RSV while her nurse showed me how to use a contraption known as a nebulizer. He'd need the treatments twice a day. I shook my head in disbelief. Had my son been bathed in a tub filled with every germ and virus known to mankind? "I don't freakin' believe this," I mumbled as I scooped Charlie up off the exam table, threw the diaper bag over my shoulder, which at first got caught on my neck, and grabbed this nebulizer contraption with my free hand.

As I drove away, I started to think about the fact that, at five months old, Charlie just seemed to have a lot of little illnesses. But when your child is in day care, regardless of how squeaky clean the center is (and ours was more like a country club), those little germs rear their ugly heads everywhere.

I was nervous about telling Patty the news. I was supposed to be boarding a plane for Las Vegas in less than ten days. But, as always, Patty reassured me that the work would get done, and that I should just be concerned with taking care of Charlie. Still, I was concerned with losing my job, which I'd only had for less than a year.

To put it mildly, the nebulizer-thing was nothing short of a pain in the ass! I was instructed to get my squirmy little five-month-old to suck on the end of a tube that was blowing white fumes into his face! Needless to say, his first few treatments were a little ridiculous.

For the next few days, I continued to work from home, and checked in with Patty hourly. Fortunately, the details of the event were finally coming together. After three days of being home with Charlie and semi-mastering the nebulizer, I felt I should really get back into the office, since we had four days left until the show. But in the back of my mind I kept thinking, "I'm never going to get on that plane." I just couldn't bear the thought of leaving the baby at home when he wasn't feeling well. Despite my worries, Charlie maintained a good appetite and was still smiling and giggling. Even with RSV, he was sleeping through the night. Beyond this all of his ailments over the past five months had been attributed to normal childhood illnesses.

But I just didn't feel comfortable sending Charlie to day care with a nebulizer, even though Kristine and all the teachers had years of experience with them and one child in Charlie's class had even been on one permanently.

"We can absolutely handle it, Deirdre," Kristine reassured me. I felt a tremendous tug at my heart. I should be taking care of him. I'm his mommy! And when you're sick, who else do you want to take care of you but your mom? Although I tried to suppress it, in the back of my mind, something just didn't feel right to me.

After three days, I brought Charlie back to the pediatrician to see if his lungs were improving with the nebulizer. I mentioned that I was aware of another child with RSV who had been admitted to the hospital and I wanted to know if she felt Charlie should be admitted as well. Dr. Cuozzo listened to his chest and said he sounded better, but that I should keep him on the nebulizer for two more days. Then she'd check him out again, and if he wasn't better, she'd have to draw some blood to probe further.

That afternoon, the phone rang. It was Patty. I was kneeling down next to Charlie, stroking his thick, jet-black hair as he sat in his bouncy chair.

"I'm trying to decide whether I should come in tomorrow, even for a few hours to print off some stuff I've been working on," I told her. "But I'd have to leave Charlie at day care with the nebulizer." My voice cracked and I held my breath for a moment.

When I opened my mouth to try to form a sentence, I lost all self-control, and began to sob. I'm not sure if it was a combination of everything happening at once – postpartum exhaustion, frustration, and fear – but I was overwhelmed with emotion.

"Patty," I cried, choking on my tears, "something just doesn't seem right, and he's not getting any better. What could be wrong with him, why can't he just be healthy?"

"I don't know, Deirdre, but I don't think you should come in. I know you want to be there with Charlie. Just take care of him. We both know that's what's most important."

Of course it was. Something was scaring me and I wasn't sure what it was or if I should actually mention it out loud.

"What does the doctor say?" Patty asked softly.

"He should be off the nebulizer in a few days," I sniffed, "and hopefully this new antibiotic will clear that damned, everlasting ear infection. But I don't know, Patty, something's just not right…something's just not right," I repeated over again. With those words, I stopped crying, trying to swallow the enormous lump in my throat that was preventing me from taking in a full breath.

"Would you feel better if you went back to the doctor tomorrow?" Patty asked.

"I just don't know what else she can say. Everything he has sounds legitimate, every kid gets ear infections, has runny noses and pukes. I trust Dr. Cuozzo completely, and I know she knows her stuff. But, I just don't know…this has been going on for a while. I mean, I guess it could be he just comes down with everything because he's in day care. But he's only five months old and he's had this ear infection and the throwing up bug, now the RSV!"

Patty reassured me she was completely fine with me working from home another few days, and she actually took some work off my plate to relieve some of the stress. I hung up the phone, fixed Charlie a bottle and cuddled him on the couch. It was Tuesday. Dr. Cuozzo doesn't work on Wednesdays. That was okay, because if I brought him in tomorrow, I could at least have another set of eyes look at him — just to be sure. That was my plan. Charlie began stroking the left side of his head as he drank his bottle. He always did that — it seemed to be soothing for him. As he rubbed, I buried my head into one of the tiny little rolls on the side of his precious little neck and took in the sweet smell of his delicious skin. He kicked his tiny little legs with excitement. "I love you so much, my little man," I said, placing a kiss on his chunky cheek.

Kristine dropped my energetic and wide-eyed son Jay off that evening, and he came barreling in the door to tell me about his day, and how he played with his best friend Jacob.

"Jake and me played on the structure," he exclaimed. Jay, with his feather-light, fuzzy-duckling, light blond hair and his welcoming warm brown eyes, beamed with joy.

"Come here, you," I said as I motioned for him to jump up into my arms. "I could kiss this face one million times a day, and I'd still want more," I said as I squeezed him tightly. He wrapped his arms around my neck. It was 5:00 p.m. and I was just about to start dinner. I put on *Sesame Street* and helped Jay climb up on the couch with a sippy cup of milk. I picked Charlie up from under his play gym and placed him in his Exersaucer.

As I began to turn my back to head to the stove, I noticed out of the corner of my eye that Charlie immediately slumped completely forward, planting his head on the side of the saucer as if it was just too heavy for him to hold up. I was completely taken aback by his action. He didn't appear to be in any pain or distress. He was breathing with no problem, and even had a little smile on his face. But he seemed tired and weak – too weak to balance himself in an upright position. And it appeared the only comfortable position for him was resting his head on one side. Without hesitation, I rushed to his side, and quickly scooped him up and began pacing up and down the kitchen floor. That was it! My heart was beating so fast, I thought it would burst right through my chest. My hands began to tremble. "Enough is enough!" I proclaimed loudly, breaking Jay's concentration from the television. I began devising my plan. I was going to take him to the hospital tomorrow and I was going to demand that he be admitted for tests.

"Yeah, that's exactly what I'm going to do," I told myself. I wanted answers! If I thought it was urgent, I would have taken him to the ER that night. But Charlie didn't appear to be in any grave danger. He ate his dinner, giggled at the faces his big brother made to make him smile, rolled around a bit on his belly, and went to bed without any fussing at all.

When John got home, I told him about my plan. He agreed. Enough was enough. Deep down I believed something was wrong with my son, and I needed to get some answers. As for John, I think he felt if I didn't take Charlie back in, I wouldn't stop talking about it! My mind was racing and I hardly slept a wink that night. I must have checked on Charlie fifty times. He slept…well…just like a baby.

The Sign of the Cross

On Wednesday morning, John left to drop a blissful Jay off at The Barn Yard at 7:00 a.m. I knew if I drove directly to the Emergency Room at Newton-Wellesley I'd sit there for hours. So I decided to call and ask to see Dr. Fox, the head of the Pediatric Department at Dedham Medical Associates. All my girlfriends think Dr. Fox is God! I was on a first-name basis with Dr. Cuozzo's secretary Cathy. My plan was to call Cathy right when the office opened. I'd have her get me in to see Dr. Fox right away. I figured I'd have Dr. Fox pave the way to the hospital for us so we could avoid having to hang around the ER before we'd be seen.

Charlie was still in bed sleeping, so I had time to start thinking things over again. I called my friend Jane to ask her if she thought I was crazy and overreacting. She has an infant daughter, Susie, with a severe heart condition. Jane agreed that, if nothing else, seeing Dr. Fox would just make me feel better. I paged John to ask him again what he thought. John hesitated, but he knew I was really concerned at this point and said, "Just bring him in."

I was sitting on my bed. I hung up the phone and slowly reclined backwards onto the upright pillows. I glanced down the short hallway to Charlie's room, noticing the door to his room was three-quarters of the way shut. I found myself staring at the six-panel door, becoming fixated on it. My eyes wandered across every inch, every corner, and every piece of grain in the wood as I studied the door. Slowly, the sun's rays began reflecting on the door. I adjusted my position on the bed, and with that, my eyes began to trace the form of a cross around the reflection created within the outline of the six panels. I felt the blood draw from my face and for a moment, my body froze. I then slowly shook my head to try to arouse myself, but knew I was not sleeping. I felt chills through my entire body.

Instantly, I sprang from my bed in a complete panic. My eyes darted for the clock. It was 9:17 a.m. on February 23. Charlie was still asleep, and it was three hours past his normal waking hour. I had checked on him six times that morning, just to make sure he was okay. I figured since he wasn't feeling well, his body required more sleep. My heart was pounding violently against the walls of my chest as my trembling hands tried frantically to dial the number for the pediatrician's office.

"Dr. Cuozzo's office," the familiar voice stated, "this is…" I cut the doctor's assistant off immediately. "Cathy, it's Deirdre…Capodanno… Jay and Charlie's mom. I need to see Dr. Fox immediately. It's Charlie. Something is just not right, and if the doctor can't see me right away, I'm heading straight for the hospital," I blurted out while choking back tears and pacing back and forth. Working her magic, she told me to come right in. I knew God had just given me a sign to get Charlie to the doctor immediately.

I scooped my sleeping child up and got him dressed in about thirty seconds. I tried to compose myself, sitting for a minute at the top of the carpeted staircase holding Charlie. He had awakened with a huge grin on his face, but he still appeared limp and weak. I kissed his little cheek and told him he'd be feeling better soon, and I promised him, my little Charlie-Bear, that we'd get some answers TODAY. As we sat there at eye level with each other, I noticed that his forehead, which was covered with thick curly black hair, seemed to be pulsating. At this point, I seriously thought my mind was playing tricks on me, so I jumped up and ran him into the light. The pulsating was gone. I shook my head. I wondered if something was actually wrong with me.

An Ear Infection Gone Awry

I flew down Route 1 from Franklin to Norwood, weaving in and out of traffic like a lunatic. Charlie was quiet in his car seat, and he seemed to be feeling okay. It took me twenty minutes to get to Dedham Medical, which should normally take me at least a half hour — especially at that time of day. I managed to calm myself down as I sat in the waiting room. I was still shaken by the cross-sighting episode, but I knew I was doing the right thing. "Relax," I instructed myself, taking a deep breath and planting a pleasant but forced smile on my face to draw attention away from my shaking knees and frantic toe tapping.

"God's making sure we get some answers today!" I proclaimed louder than I should have, soliciting a few odd looks from other parents. I shrugged my shoulder as if to say "oops" and started kissing Charlie's head as I fed him a bottle and snuggled him tightly in my lap.

Dr. Fox's nurse shuffled us to an exam room. Before she had time to shut the door behind us, I began spewing off why I was back in again today.

"Something's just not right," I blurted out. "He seemed okay this morning, but he's actually only been awake for a half hour, so I can't *really* say how he's doing *exactly*, but I can say he doesn't have much energy." I gave her the history of the five-week ear infection, the three high fevers, the tummy bug, and the RSV. I told her I grew increasingly concerned when he slumped over in the Exersaucer. I just kept repeating, "Something's just not right, I don't know what it is, but something's not right with him." It was evident in the tone of my voice I was anxious to have further tests done. I unzipped Charlie from his snowsuit and immediately noticed he was in a pool of sweat.

"Hmm," the nurse pursed her lips while taking the baby's temperature, "103."

"You're kidding me?" I said with a blink. "That's the fourth high fever in two months. But he hasn't had one in a few weeks." Her facial expression changed and I could see the concern in her eyes.

"Let me get Dr. Fox right away."

13

At this point, Charlie was just a limp little ball in my arms as I cradled him. Still, he was breathing normally, but he just seemed to have very little energy. He looked up into my eyes and gave me a precious little smile. It appeared it was too much for him to lift his head off my arm. But he wasn't crying and didn't appear to be in any pain or discomfort at all.

Dr. Fox made his way into the room, washed his hands, and shook mine. I immediately began blurting out my thoughts. "Something's just not right with my baby. I really want him admitted to the hospital. As a mom, I know something is wrong. Look at him!" I yelped, and then bit my bottom lip to prevent myself from choking up. The pediatrician turned and looked down at Charlie. The doctor didn't even lay a hand on him. "I can see just by the way you're holding him and the way he is laying so limp in your arms that you're right. I'm sure he just needs some IV fluids to get his energy back. I'll give Children's Hospital emergency room the heads-up that you're coming."

"Children's?" I questioned.

Now, Boston's Children's Hospital is one of the finest pediatric hospitals in the world. But the thought of waiting for hours in the emergency room there just to get hooked up to IV fluids was not going to fly with me. We took Jay there once for dehydration and we waited close to four and a half hours, only to get one hour of fluid!

"Dr. Fox, is there any way I can take him to Newton-Wellesley Hospital? We're very happy with that hospital; Charlie was born there just five months ago. And if we're thinking he just needs fluids and some tests, I'm sure they'll be able to see us right away and give him full attention."

"Well," the doctor said, scratching his chin, "normally I'd insist on Children's, but I know you're right about the wait. I just sent someone to the ER and they've been waiting two hours already. Charlie does look like he needs immediate hydration, but let me call over there first. I want to be comfortable with the pediatric emergency room doctor first."

"Okay, good," I nodded in agreement. My nervousness began to subside because I thought that if things were really serious, he'd insist on Children's. What I wanted most was for Charlie to be seen right away and have undivided attention.

Dr. Fox came back minutes later and informed me he'd spoken to a Dr. Weltman, who was the head of pediatrics at Newton-Wellesley, and he felt comfortable sending us there.

"Good luck," he said as he placed his hand on my shoulder. "Please call me this afternoon to let me know how things are going." I thought that was extremely nice since Charlie wasn't one of his regular patients. "Mrs. Capodanno, I've always said moms know best, they really do," he said as we left the room.

I paged John to let him know that the plan was in action. He didn't respond. I wanted to get to the hospital as soon as possible. I was not anxious any more; I was actually really happy that we were finally getting somewhere. I called Kristine at the Barn Yard to let her know we were heading to Newton-Wellesley, and to have her let John, if he called there first, know in case he could get out of work early to meet us. As a driver for UPS, getting out early or taking a day off was basically impossible. But knowing my husband and how much he loves his children, he'd risk a fight with any manager to be with us.

"One of us will pick Jay up by four I'm sure," I informed her.

Making Headway Toward Disaster

I strapped Charlie back into his seat and pulled onto Rt. 128 heading for the hospital. Although it was late February, it was a brilliant, sunny morning.

15

"Now we're going to get somewhere, Charlie Bear!" I smiled triumphantly as I snuck a peek at Charlie in the rear view mirror. I dialed Patty on my cell phone to fill her in.

"I'm so glad you decided to take him back today, Dee. I was really worried," she admitted. "At least maybe we'll get some answers."

"Patty," I said quietly, preparing to tell her there was no way I could go to Las Vegas now.

She sensed what was coming and immediately chimed in. "Deirdre, Sweetie, I know what you're going to say, and don't even think twice about it. I had my flight changed yesterday so I can go out to the show early and handle all your stuff. Don't give it another thought." I assured her that I'd somehow get my laptop to her that day with all my notes, charts, etc. so she could have everything she needed. "Just get that baby boy better," Patty said gently as she hung up the phone.

As expected, the neatly organized ER at Newton-Wellesley was quiet, clean and orderly. There were only two adults in the waiting room. Charlie was the only pediatric patient. A nurse immediately checked us in and commented on what a beautiful baby he was. "His eyelashes are so long!" she said. She escorted us to an examining room where two older nurses joined us. Charlie was still pretty lethargic, but responsive. "Oh, we never get to see the babies. He's so precious!" she squealed.

I could see John frantically racing toward our exam room. I waved to catch his attention. Right behind him was Dr. Weltman. She was an attractive woman, with a slender build, curly black hair and a very gentle smile and demeanor.

"Hi. I'm Liz Weltman. I had a chat with Dr. Fox regarding Charlie," she said, reaching over to touch his shoulder. "Our plan is to hook Charlie up to some IV fluids so he can get some hydration, then we'll run a series of tests to see what may be going on with him. Now, we're going to have to put an IV line in his arm, which won't be too fun for him or for you guys."

"We've gone through this before with our older son and it took them trying both arms and both ankles to get it in. I'm sure it couldn't be worse than that," I said nervously.

John and I both climbed up on the ER gurney to cuddle with Charlie. Charlie was alert, smiling at the nurses, but just seemed beat. As they began the procedure, I described, again, the history of Charlie's illnesses. But for the first time, I mentioned that he scratched the left side of his head a lot. Dr. Weltman listened intently as the needle was inserted into his tiny little arm. Charlie did not even flinch as he was stuck with the needle.

"Oh, you're so brave, little man," I said proudly. I kissed his face as John stroked his head. I could see the two nurses look at each other with visible concern on their faces, and then at Dr. Weltman. For a moment, no one spoke a word. My stomach tightened, and I reached for John's hand.

"What's wrong?" I asked nervously.

"I'll be honest with you," Dr. Weltman said, clasping her hands together. "It's not necessarily a good sign for a baby not to respond to the pain of a needle. He does seem to be in pretty rough shape." With that her tone changed and there appeared to be a sense of urgency to get moving. "What we're going to do now is draw blood from the line, and give him a spinal tap. I'm afraid this will be pretty invasive, and for the baby's safety, as well as your own, we can't have you in the room with us. I promise you he'll be in the best hands possible."

"No, I can't leave him!" I protested. I felt comfortable with Dr. Weltman and both nurses, but still, he was our baby and he needed us.

"Please, Mrs. Capodanno, let us just get this done quickly. You and Mr. Capodanno can go down to the cafeteria, grab a drink, and give us about fifteen minutes. By the time you come back up, we'll be done."

"Will someone kiss him for me?" I asked, choking back tears. The thought of leaving his side for a minute tore me apart. "I promise," Dr. Weltman said.

With tremendous hesitation, John and I obeyed her request and made our way down to the cafeteria where we each grabbed a cookie and a drink. As we started to seat ourselves at a table, an older gentleman entered the cafeteria. "Capodanno...Capodanno?" he bellowed out randomly. The fright that overtook our faces made us easily identifiable to the entire room.

His badge read "Volunteer." "Are you Mr. and Mrs. Capodanno?"

"*Yes!*" we both answered as we jumped to our feet, spilling the tea that I had yet to take a sip of.

"What's wrong?" I screamed, searching the man's face frantically for an answer.

"I don't know, Miss, they don't tell us these things. I just got orders to find you folks and bring you back to the ER immediately." I felt all the blood drain from my head. We'd been gone for all of about six minutes. I sprinted to the elevator as John tried to calm me down. "I'm sure she just has more questions for us. Relax, Honey — you always think the worst."

It seemed like an eternity for the elevator to arrive. We raced to the exam room where we had left Charlie, but it was empty. Across the hall there was a huge commotion under a sign that read "Trauma Unit." There must have been at least 12 doctors, nurses and technicians frantically racing back and forth, shouting orders to one another, and hovering over the gurney. Instantly, I could hear a baby's weak and wounded cry. It took a second for my brain to process that it was my

18

own son's cry, because it was not his usual cry – it was a cry that slashed right through my entire body. I caught a glimpse of Dr. Weltman. She saw the panic in our eyes, as we pushed and shoved ourselves through the doctors and nurses surrounding our frightened baby.

"What's going on?" I screamed.

Dr. Weltman had an extremely calm demeanor, and even in the middle of what was surely a crisis, she remained soft-spoken.

"Well," she took a deep breath, "when we inserted the needle in his spine, and pulled back to draw the fluid, he had, ah, an apnea episode," she explained, choosing her words precisely.

"Apnea!? You mean he stopped *breathing?*" I screeched, and with that, my body began to tremble out of control.

"Yes. But he's stable now." She tried to sound reassuring. But I could see in her eyes something was drastically wrong. John looked petrified, but didn't say a word. I was hysterically crying but somehow managed to squeeze in next to Charlie to kiss him as a respiratory technician held an oxygen mask over his face. He was very frightened and his crying was heartbreaking. I buried my face in his tiny shoulder and kissed his cheek to let him know we were there with him. John draped himself over Charlie's tiny legs, and stroked my back as we both wept in fear.

Diagnosis: Meningitis

Once we could see Charlie had quieted down, Dr. Weltman pulled us aside and very slowly and graciously explained, "Mr. and Mrs. Capodanno, we believe that Charlie is very ill, and this facility isn't capable of treating him. He needs to be transported to Children's immediately. His counts are very high. We think he could have encephalitis or meningitis."

"What are counts?" I wondered in my panicked state of mind.

"I was concerned when you mentioned Charlie rubbed the side of his head, and upon feeling his skull, it's quite evident that there is swelling around his fontanel," Dr. Weltman said.

John and I were terrified. We knew Charlie must be in very bad condition to hear this very well known hospital "couldn't care for him."

"Are these diseases treatable...curable?" I gasped, barely able to stand up straight.

"Yes, both are very treatable *and* curable. We believe it is meningitis, but we're not sure if it's bacterial or viral meningitis, and there's a big difference. He needs to be admitted to the ICU at Children's immediately."

Everything was happening so frantically, it was hard to comprehend the magnitude of the crisis that had just crashed down on us. We could hear ambulance sirens coming closer and closer. We didn't realize at first the ambulance was for us! Within minutes, Charlie was strapped into an ambulance car seat, which was placed onto the transporting gurney. Because the EMT was hovering over his little body, I was only able to catch a tiny glimpse of his face, noticing his beautiful little eyes were floating in pools of his own tears.

"Only one of you can ride with us," the polite EMT told us.

"I'm going with Charlie," I told John, not giving him a choice in the matter. John would have to drive our car. I attempted to climb into the back of the ambulance with Charlie, but that idea was quickly squashed when the EMT grabbed my arm.

"Sorry. You can only come if you ride up front with me," said the driver.

"Fine, let's just hurry!" I hoisted myself up into the passenger's seat. "God, *please* help us," I prayed out loud. "Please let Charlie be okay, we love him so much, we love him so much!" I repeated over and over again.

As we darted through the streets of Boston, my mood changed from panic to anger. I became irate at seeing how many idiot drivers just don't get out of the way of a racing ambulance.

"This is unbelievable! Look at these jerks!" I yelled, slamming my fist on the dashboard. I picked up my cell phone and dialed Patty. No answer. So I called one of the people who worked for me.

"Jim," I hollered, trying to be louder than the sirens, "we're in an ambulance heading for Children's Hospital. I don't think you guys will be hearing from me for a while. Please ask everyone to say a prayer for Charlie." I couldn't even hear his response. The next call I placed was to my father. He had known of my plan to get Charlie admitted to the hospital that day. "Hello," he answered. "Dad!" I yelled frantically into the phone, "I'm scared; we're on our way to Children's. It might be meningitis." I couldn't hear his response either. My voice cracked. "Dad, please say a prayer for our baby." I hung up the phone, turned my head toward the window and felt the warm tears stream down my face.

As I exited the ambulance, I ran over to the gurney to be with Charlie. They had his entire body and the car seat wrapped in a white sheet. All that was visible were his big hazel eyes peering out at me. I could tell he was so frightened. The EMTs and I dashed through the halls of the hospital, bypassing the dreaded Emergency Room.

"Well, Charlie knows one way to cut the line in the ER waiting room," I joked nervously to the transport nurse.

Intensive Care

We were immediately admitted to the Intensive Care Unit. Charlie was hooked up to a bunch of machines and looked so tiny in the little hospital crib. A steady flow of doctors and nurses introduced themselves. An extremely young-looking doctor approached and extended her hand.

"I'm Dr. so-and-so, the fellow in ICU." "What's a fellow?" I questioned. She went on to explain how the doctors are "ranked" by the number of years they'd been in school, and doing their residency blah, blah, blah. I wasn't really interested. I just wanted to know who the top doctor was, and who would be in charge. John appeared red-faced, out of breath and visibly shaken.

"I couldn't keep…" he stopped to catch his breath, "couldn't keep up with the ambulance, and had no idea where I was!" He sank into the reclining chair next to the crib. I introduced him to the fellow. He had that same "How old could she be?" look on his face. Some of these doctors didn't look old enough to be doctors. The fellow explained that they were going to run more tests on Charlie's blood, urine – pretty much every fluid they could extract from his body they could test, they would test. It appeared that Children's was in agreement with Dr. Weltman that it was more than likely meningitis — which she described as a swelling or inflammation of the brain usually caused by infection. It could be viral, meaning in his blood, or bacterial. One could be treated with antibiotics; the other would have to work itself out. Because he'd been on antibiotics for five weeks for the ear infection, they were just going to go with IV antibiotics immediately.

The ICU was an enormous room with about 10 beds. Every bed was exposed so you could see what was going on with every child. Although it was a busy place, it was a very controlled environment. Moments later the phone rang, and I heard the nurse say, "She's right here!" It was Dr. Cuozzo. I quickly grabbed the phone. "I'm glad you brought Charlie back in. Thank God you did. I'm sorry for all that you've gone through today. I've reviewed all my notes, and I've ordered the hospital to do a CT scan on Charlie just to rule anything else out." I had no idea what "things" she wanted to rule out. I'm not a doctor, but John and I certainly wanted every test done to make sure we knew exactly what we were dealing with! She informed me she'd check back in with us the next morning.

John and I were both completely exhausted from the emotional nightmare we'd been through that day. We were nervous that Charlie had a serious illness, but we found great comfort in knowing that we were in the best possible care at one of the finest pediatric hospitals in the world. We remained calm and listened intently to whatever the doctors and nurses told us. Everything seemed to be under control.

I called Kristine at the day care to update her on what had transpired. She was speechless. She needed to know as soon as possible if they thought it was meningitis, because they had about fifty other children at day care who could now have been exposed to the virus. She volunteered to take Jay home and feed him dinner until John got back to Franklin. We didn't want to frighten Jay. We agreed that it would be best for John to go home to be with him and that I would stay with Charlie.

Only one of us could stay by Charlie's bedside anyway. The "parent bed" that was next to Charlie's crib was about the most uncomfortable thing I'd ever laid down on in my entire life. I gave up trying to sleep almost immediately. I just sat there and stared at Charlie, gently stroking his little arm. The nurse assigned to him that night was right outside the curtain at all times. Although we were safe, I didn't take my eyes off of my son for one minute the entire night.

We only spent one night in ICU and were then moved to another floor. The plan was to administer IV antibiotics into Charlie for five straight days. Nothing appeared to be life threatening. We were all comfortable with the doctors' diagnosis and treatment plan.

Dr. Cuozzo called first thing in the morning. "Have they done a scan?" she asked.

"No, and from what I can gather, they don't seem to be planning to do one either," I informed her. They felt the swelling had gone down already.

"Oh no, we're going to get that scan done today," she insisted. I had no idea what a CT scan was, or what they look for, nor did I give it too much thought. So I agreed with whatever Dr. Cuozzo wanted to have done.

Chapter 2
The Sky Falls In

Roommate from Hell

Charlie and I spent the second night in the hospital sharing a room with another sick child, baby Joshua, and his extremely loud and obnoxious mother. Joshua was having a bad bout of diarrhea. His mom was the type who spoke out loud even though she was only talking to herself. "Oh Joshua, Joshua, look at the poopy mess you made. Now mommy needs to clean you all off again, for Christ sake," she snapped. At midnight, the phone rang. It was Joshua's mommy's boyfriend. They were devising a plan so that he could avoid paying child support for his kids. How did I know all this information? Because she was ranting and raving at the top of her lungs. "Pretend you're insane in front of the judge," she declared. This entertaining but extremely annoying conversation went on for about a half hour. Finally I got up, pulled the curtain between the two beds to one side with a snap, spoke not one single word, but shot her a look that could have sliced her in half. She finally got the message. This woman was easily three times my size and girth, but given the lack of sleep I had gotten the night before, and the fact that her voice was grating on me with every rotten syllable, I was up for anything at that point. She hung up.

The next morning, a very young doctor with a Jamaican accent and dreadlocks appeared. He checked Charlie out from head to toe, and we both agreed he finally looked like he had color back in his cheeks and a bit more energy.

"Well, Dr. Cuozzo is adamant that we do a scan on Charlie," he said. "We decided not to do an actual CT scan. Instead, we are going to do an ultrasound of his head. It is scheduled for 9 a.m. He won't need to be sedated, and you'll be with him the whole time. The nurse will give you Charlie's file and you can bring it downstairs."

I was glad to hear we were going to do some kind of scan, and happy that Dr. Cuozzo was so persistent. Better to be safe than sorry.

Charlie was unhooked from his IV bag, and I carried him downstairs. I was still in my pajamas and slippers.

Our World Turns Upside Down

The ultrasound room was very dark and quiet. The technician was exceptionally quiet too. She instructed me to place Charlie flat on his back on the table. He was a bit squeamish at first, but managed to settle down. During both my pregnancy ultrasounds, I'd lay there desperately trying to identify what baby body parts were what. This day was a bit different. It wasn't me lying on the table; it was my five-month-old son. I was still watching intently as the technician carefully moved the jellied wand over Charlie's head. Basically, I couldn't make out a darn thing nor did I have any idea what they might be looking for! Things seemed to be going smoothly until at one point the technician just stopped. She frantically started typing into the keyboard without removing her eyes from the screen. She waved the wand over his head again, and again.

"Has the baby's head been struck with a blunt object…has he taken a blow to the head?" she asked me matter-of-factly, never making eye contact with me.

"Excuse me?" I asked, trying to comprehend her question.

"Has he experienced any head trauma?"

"No!" I shouted at her. "Why are you asking me that?" My mind began to race. Could he have fallen at day care? How could he fall? He can't even stand up yet! Could one of the other babies have hit him with something by mistake? Could one of our beagles, Fred or Ginger, have knocked him over accidentally? None of these things could have happened because he's never without adult supervision. And I would *know* if he'd been harmed or injured in any way! My head was reeling with questions and fear. What the hell could have provoked her to ask such a harsh question? What was she seeing on that scan? The technician didn't speak another word. She got up, grabbed Charlie's file, and instructed me to wait right there. Her head dropped as she passed me, and her eyes were focused on the ground.

It was still pitch-dark in the room, and the only light that showed was from the ultrasound monitor screen. I clutched Charlie tightly in my arms and searched with my other hand to find a phone on the wall. It was a hospital phone, but I dialed 0 and begged for an outside line.

"Operator," the voice on the other end said.

"Yes," I pleaded, "I need you to help me, can you please connect me to, to………oh my God, wait, I can't remember my husband's pager number. Hold on. No, help me. This is an emergency!" I was screaming into the phone. "Okay," I said, trying to collect my thoughts, "my husband, he ah, works for UPS out of Norwood, Massachusetts. Can you look up that number for me?" I begged.

"M'am, I have a 1-800 national number for UPS listed; would you like that?" the operator offered.

"No, no, not a national number....no, can you please check again to see if you can get me a direct number for the facility in Norwood, Massachusetts?"

The poor operator knew I was completely panicking, but she couldn't help me. That was the only number she had on file for UPS. John had worked for them for twelve years. He'd had the same pager number for many of those years. But at this crucial moment, in sheer panic, I could not remember a single digit of the number to save my life!

"Wait, wait, please, please don't hang up....I need you...can you dial this number for me?" I asked. "Try..." Just then one of the ultrasound supervisors entered the room, which was still in darkness. I dropped the phone, and it dangled there until this stranger hung it back up for me. He could tell I was in complete despair, and he spoke very calmly to me.

"Please put the baby down on the table again," he asked politely. He rubbed Charlie's belly while he performed the ultrasound. Again, the wand glided across Charlie's head, and then the tap, tap, tapping on the keyboard. Then he gently placed Charlie back in my arms, and stood right next to me, almost leaning against my left side.

"Mrs. Capodanno, it looks as if the baby has bleeding on his brain, ah, hemorrhaging. It appears he may have taken a blow to the head. We've ordered an immediate CT scan. Are you okay to walk the baby over to the scan area by yourself or would you like some assistance?" Of course I was in no condition to do so, but I answered "yes" weakly.

"How...what causes...how does your brain hemorrhage?" I asked in a ghostlike state.

"It could be caused by many things. He may have been struck in the head, or banged it somehow. We can see there is evidence of bleeding. They'll give you more information after the CT scan, okay?"

He responded as mildly as he could. He said to wait about five minutes and then walk across the hall to the CT scan area.

When he left the room, I clung to Charlie with one arm and held myself up to the wall with the other. My knees were shaking, and I almost lost my balance. It felt as if the room was spinning around and objects appeared to be flying by me. What was going on? I was alone and terrified. I again grabbed for the phone and dialed the operator.

"Please, it's an emergency. I need to reach my husband; he works for UPS in Norwood, and I need to get in touch with him immediately! Please don't give me the national number." But again, the only number they had was the national 1-800 number.

"No!" I screamed. "Wait...wait...here...here...I just remembered another number...dial my sister's number at work," and I gave the operator the number. I have absolutely, positively no idea how I could remember my sister Kel's number at her new job. She'd only been with this new company a few short months. But somehow, it was the only number I could recollect at the time.

"Kel Kelly," she answered cheerfully.

"Kel, oh my God, help! Kel, something is wrong, really wrong. They're asking me if Charlie's been struck on the head. They said his brain is bleeding; I need John here right now. I need him. I can't think of what his phone number is. Why can't I remember his number? Please, please find him and tell him to get here right now. *Please!*" I screamed frantically into the phone. My entire body was trembling. I felt dizzy and nauseous. It was difficult to focus, and it took all of my strength to hold my own body up, as well as Charlie.

"Okay, Dee, calm down. What's going on," she tried to be comforting so she could better assess the situation.

"Charlie...his head...they say he's got bleeding on his brain." I could barely get the words out through my gasps. "Please find John, please! I need him here *now*!" I cried.

"Let me come over there," Kel offered.

"No! Right now what I need you to do is find John. Please hurry." I don't remember hanging up the phone.

It felt as if I was walking in slow motion down the hall, dragging my feet, which were still in my slippers, clinging to Charlie as tightly as I could. People were walking by, I could see their movements and motions, their lips moving in conversation, but I couldn't hear them or any other noises. Shock had created a barrier between me and everything else around me.

When we finally reached the CT room, I tried to compose myself so I could comprehend what the nurse was trying to explain to me. They gave Charlie IV sedation. A very pleasant technician with straight blond hair came over to my side. She explained what the CT machine does, and that she'd be right behind the glass wall with the other technicians. She told me to stand in the corner, and placed a large vest over my shoulders. She smiled at me and disappeared.

I saw the table Charlie's body was strapped to slowly enter the CT machine. He looked so incredibly small and helpless. I wanted to rip him off the table and hold him. Just as the scan started, the phone in the room rang. The nice nurse pointed to the phone. I couldn't understand what she was telling me to do. She opened the door and said politely, "You have a phone call."

My sister must have been able to track him down. John was delivering packages to the outlet mall near our home when he received the frantic page from his office to call in immediately. Upon learning that he needed to return to the hospital right away because of an emergency, his face went ashen. The clerk in the store he was in saw the panic in his eyes, and asked what was wrong. He explained what he knew, which was very little.

"Mrs. Capodanno, the phone is for you," the nurse repeated. It's got to be John. Please God, let it be John. I tried to tell myself to be calm and not to freak him out. I picked up the receiver.

"Honey, Honey, Deirdre?" the voice questioned.

"Yes, it's me. You need to get here immediately. They think Charlie has some hemorrhaging in his brain. He's having a CT scan right now! Please get here as soon as you can. I need you here. I love Charlie so much. John, what could have happened?" I began to cry.

"Wait, what do you mean hemorrhaging?" John said in a frantic voice. "Where is he, how is he now?" John asked, obviously trying to get an understanding of where I was and what was happening to Charlie.

"John, he's in the machine right now, the cat-scan thing. He looks so lifeless," I sputtered into the phone. "Just get here, please hurry!"

"Wait, Honey, wait...I don't know...where...how do I get there?" John asked, obviously completely overwhelmed and panic-stricken to be asking me to give him directions on how to get to the hospital.

"John, I don't know...get on the VFW Parkway, you know where this hospital is, it's in Boston, and you were here last night!" I snapped unintentionally at him.

The scan took only a matter of minutes.

"Was that your husband on the phone?" the nurse asked.

"Yes," I answered. "Can you tell me what the scan said?"

"I really don't read the scans. The doctor will meet you upstairs. Here, is it okay if I walk back up with you?" she asked. She tried to make small talk as she escorted me back to our room. I was clinging to Charlie as tightly as I could. I was completely numb, shuffling along cradling my limp, sedated, baby boy in my arms. And this complete stranger was cradling my own limp body in hers.

"Is Charlie your only child," she asked softly.

"No," I shook my head slowly from side to side, and then dropped it onto her waiting shoulder.

The Discovery: Brain Tumor

Back in the room, Momzilla (Joshua's mom) was verbally concocting another one of her government scams, and I couldn't even make eye contact with her. Charlie's nurse came over to me immediately and whisked Charlie from my arms. She placed him gently on his bed, and hooked him back up to the IV. Within a minute, a doctor I'd never met before entered the room and introduced himself. My hand was limp as I shook his. He was extremely soft spoken, to the point I could barely hear him. I leaned closer to him.

"What did you say?" I asked, staring directly into his eyes.

"Yes, well, um..." his nervousness was evident. "Um, Mrs. Capodanno, you see, the CT scan has discovered that Charlie has a large mass in his brain," he uttered softly.

"Mass? What's a mass? A tumor? Is that what a mass is, a tumor?" I asked grabbing hold of his arm.

"Yes," he whispered. "It's really rather large. In fact, they couldn't even see the whole mass on the ultrasound screen. Anyway, Mrs. Capodanno, we have paged the neurosurgeon to come down and speak with you immediately. Are you alone?" he asked.

"Yes, but my husband is on his way. Neurosurgeon...I mean...wait, wait a minute," I pleaded, still trying to comprehend his words. "Oh my God, could it be cancer?"

"It's impossible to tell without a biopsy. The neurosurgeon can discuss that with you in more detail, okay?" It was obvious this young doctor in training had never had to deliver that kind of news before, and it was pretty tough for him to handle.

"All right, as soon as the neurosurgeon is available, she'll be down to see you immediately…I…I'm," he stopped to clear his throat, "I'm truly sorry," he added shyly. "Is there anything you need, anything I can do for you right now?"

"Yes. Is there a priest or someone here who can come and pray with me?" I asked calmly.

"I'll page the chaplain for you immediately," and with that the young doctor exited the room.

I wasn't crying. I wasn't screaming. I was frozen. I was completely numb. Shock had taken complete hold of my body and mind. My beautiful, precious child, who was just days shy of turning six months old, had a massive tumor in his brain.

Before I even had time to turn around, a sweet nun, who was all of about 80 pounds, came racing through the door. She had on a gray suit and a gigantic cross around her neck. Before she said a word, I grabbed both her hands in mine.

"My son has a brain tumor, a mass, in his brain," I said, squeezing her delicate hands.

"Dear Jesus," she replied, closing her eyes for a moment. Then we stood there, praying with each other, asking Jesus to give us the strength to see Charlie through this difficult time, and to heal his precious body. Her name was Sister Carlotta and as tiny as she was, she was an enormous support for me at that very moment.

The nurse had gotten Charlie to sleep again. I could hear John's heavy work boots barreling down the hall. "What the…what the hell's going on?" John asked breathlessly as he witnessed Sister Carlotta and me huddled close to each other holding hands and praying.

My throat was completely dry as I tried to swallow, to no avail. The nun quietly excused herself and said she'd be right outside if we needed her. I swallowed hard again. I took a deep and deliberate breath in as I prepared myself to deliver the shocking news.

"Honey," I said gently taking John's hand into mine. I spoke as softly and as slowly as I could. "Charlie has a brain tumor. The doctor said there is a large tumor in his brain." I was remarkably calm in my delivery. Yet, it was at that moment when my entire world began to crash and crumble all around me. My handsome, strong, burly husband fell to a million pieces in front of my eyes. He fell back onto the parent bed and began sobbing uncontrollably. His wails were ripping my heart right out of my chest. He grabbed a towel from the bed and buried his face in it. He was at my knees, and I tried to catch him as he crumbled, but the weight of his body slipped right through my hands, and he slid to the floor. I began to stroke his thick, jet-black hair.

"What did I do? What did I do?" he sobbed openly. With every wail I held his head tighter and tighter against my legs. "What did I do to have this happen to my little boy? I did this…." he cried.

At that moment, from somewhere deep inside me, I found strength extremely uncharacteristic of me.

"Listen," I said with conviction, as I grabbed his face in my hands, "Charlie's going to make it. You didn't do *anything* to make this happen. God doesn't work like that. He doesn't punish people. And He wouldn't punish Charlie. He's going to survive. I know he will. We need to be strong for him."

John continued to sob loudly, but managed to walk over to Charlie and lean over him and began kissing his entire little body. His tears drenched the baby's blanket. Charlie looked up happy to see his daddy was there and reached out with his tiny finger and touched John's nose.

"We love you, Charlie, we love you so much, baby. You're our little baby boy." John scooped Charlie up and held him as if he'd never let him down again.

My heart was feeling a pain too excruciating to bear. Yet somehow, I was still in control. But I didn't want to be in control. I wanted to fall apart. I wanted to obey my body and let it shatter into a million tiny splinters, because that's what I felt was happening inside me. But I needed to be strong for Charlie and for us. I was in such a state of shock that my mind went into autopilot. We were in the middle of an enormous crisis, and one of us had to stay on alert and focused. I just didn't want it to be me.

John placed Charlie gently on the bed and turned to call his brother.

"Doug," he said through his tears, "it's not good. Charlie's got a brain tumor. Can you come here?" He dropped the phone. I called Kristine at day care.

"Kristine," I said directly and methodically, "it's not meningitis. It's a brain tumor. Charlie has a massive brain tumor." I quickly orchestrated a plan. "I'll call Jill, my sister-in-law, and have her pick Jay up. Please, Kristine, do me one favor. Ask everyone you know to pray for Charlie." My voice was shaking. Kristine was utterly speechless and crying on the other end.

Meeting the Neurosurgeon

Dr. Liliana Goumnerova calmly entered the room. She was a very attractive woman with jet-black hair, beautiful skin, and a pretty smile. She was about my height, and couldn't weigh more than 100 pounds soaking wet. She looked to be in her early forties, if that. I was nervous she was so young. She smiled, shook our hands, and escorted us to a private consultation room.

John sank into the couch, as did I beside him. He still had his face buried in the towel as if he was suffering from a toothache. He continued to sob openly. His legs were shaking. We did not say a word, but just sat there staring as the doctor smiled gently at us and began to explain what she knew.

"I understand that Charlie has a massive brain tumor. It's quite impressive in size." Her words were just swirling around in our heads, and it was impossible to comprehend what she was telling us. She continued on, and we absorbed what we could. "The tumor was located in the left frontal lobe of his brain...an MRI would further define more specifics about the size and location...the tumor would need to be removed immediately...as with any brain surgery, it would be a very delicate and invasive procedure." She couldn't tell us much more than that until she was "inside" his brain.

This woman was a complete stranger, whom we'd met only minutes earlier. She had a confidence about her that John liked immediately. To us, she made it very clear she was an expert in her field, and she knew exactly what needed to be done. She was not the "warm and fuzzy" type of doctor I had grown accustomed to dealing with, like Dr. Cuozzo. But she performed brain surgery for a living. Even so, Dr. Goumnerova never made it appear that Charlie's life was in complete danger. She made it sound as if she'd seen a million brain tumors in her day. But this tumor was different. It was in my son's brain.

She assured us she would perform the delicate procedure and remove what she could of Charlie's tumor. We hung on her every word.

"Will he live?" John asked, finally breaking his silence. "Do kids survive these types of tumors?" I interrupted.

"Oh sure, sure they do. Even if it's cancerous, some children do very well for a while," she added. *For a while … what the hell did that* mean? I wondered.

That was it. This person would be opening our son's skull and removing a massive tumor from his brain. We had no other options. There were no decisions to be made. Simply put, our son's life was in this woman's hands.

As we sat there, listening to her words, it was still inconceivable to think of the complicated operation she would perform on our six-month-old baby boy. My mind wandered for a moment, pondering the thought that this doctor would be drilling into my son's skull and cutting into his tiny brain. I quickly shook my head from side to side to erase the thought…not allowing myself to think that way again.

It was Friday afternoon, and she'd be performing the surgery first thing Monday morning. She gave us her card with her beeper number on it in case we had any questions. She was on call that weekend, so we could get a hold of her at any time.

In a daze, we walked in slow motion back to Charlie's room. Our minds were racing with what the neurosurgeon had just told us she'd be doing to our son. Although the hospital halls were buzzing with doctors, nurses, and patients, alarms were going off, and carts were being wheeled by, we were engulfed in utter, eerie silence the entire walk back.

Charlie was playful and cheery as he was being prepped for his MRI. John and I helped wheel his crib down to the MRI area where our family began to gather. Doug, Kel, my dad, and my brother-in-law Matt (Jill's husband) had already arrived. It was too much for my mother to comprehend, and rather than drive herself to the hospital in shock, she stayed at home and prayed.

John was still crying, and I was still on autopilot cradling Charlie and singing to him as they administered the anesthesia into his line. John's parents, Joan and Frank, had left a few days before to drive down to Naples, Florida, to golf and visit friends. Surprisingly, they had not left a phone number where they could be reached. So there we all were, jammed into this tiny, dark "holding" room. It was quiet except for the sniffling. I was humming a song into Charlie's ear as I cradled him in my arms. I didn't want him to see how scared we all were. I wanted him to feel safe.

The First MRI and a Family Unites

I was allowed to go into the MRI room with Charlie. John stayed outside with the others. As I left, Doug was cradling John's head against his own neck, with my dad rubbing John's back. It was a heart-wrenching sight.

The MRI room was just like the ultrasound room, dark and scary. I watched as they slid Charlie, who was limp and strapped to a table, into the tunnel. I was told that once it started, I couldn't change my mind and decide to leave. I wasn't going to leave the room without Charlie. I sat outside the MRI machine in a rocking chair clutching my knees to my cheek. The noise from the tunnel was loud and penetrating. At first it was like a jackhammer, then a laser gun. Bang, bang, bang. Dit, dit, dit. Bang, bang, bang. As the noise and the beat grew louder and stronger, I rocked harder and faster to the point of almost flipping over. It was as if I was in the twilight zone. I wanted to send Charlie positive energy. Even if he was under full sedation, I didn't want him to be scared. I wanted to climb in there with him and hold him. I rocked and prayed, and rocked and prayed.

The entire scan lasted about 1½ hours. When it was over, a heavyset technician with curly, frizzy red hair opened the door. She smiled at me, but she had a hard time making eye contact. She moved Charlie from the chamber table to the portable gurney. I searched her face for some sign, anything that would tell me what they saw on the scan. She just kept that half smile on her face.

"He's so beautiful," she said.

"I know he is, and he's so brave, isn't he?" She patted my shoulder but didn't answer me.

Our entire family jumped to their feet as we exited the room. I walked over to John and hugged him. I then slowly turned around, and began walking…just walking…aimlessly…trying to find a way out…a door…something…some way to escape. I ended up walking into the corner of a wall, bumping my head. With my cheek pressed hard against the wall, I slowly slid to the floor. I began to weep quietly. I felt John grab me from behind and lift me into his arms.

We stayed by Charlie's side until he came out of his sedation. The entire herd of us helped the doctor push Charlie's hospital crib back to the elevators. We thought we'd be returning to the Joshua room. But when you're categorized as a neurosurgery patient, you're taken to 9 North.

When we arrived on the floor a nurse escorted us to Charlie's new room. We were just getting settled when a distinguished-looking man entered the room.

"Mr. and Mrs. Capodanno?" he asked.

"Yup," I said as I stood up from the chair, realizing I was still in my PJs and it was late in the afternoon of Friday, February 23.

"I'm Dr. Wiener, the CEO here at Children's Hospital. You've got a good friend in Jack Connors, who just called me to make 100 percent certain that you and your little Charlie are well taken care of while you're here at Children's. Jack was very upset when I took his call. Here is my telephone number if you need to reach me. Call anytime. You know, you're at one of the finest hospitals with some of the best neurosurgeons in the world right here. Call me if you need me." And with that, he shook our hands and left.

I'm pretty sure all of our jaws were on the floor. Jack Connors was a very powerful and influential businessman in Boston. He owned New England's largest advertising agency, known as Hill, Holliday. I had worked for him from 1989 to 1995. He served on many hospital and health care boards in and around the Boston area. My sister-in-law Suzanne still worked at the agency and she had contacted him immediately upon hearing of Charlie's grave situation. Everyone wanted to be sure Charlie was in the best possible hands, with only the best doctors treating him. "Jack is so amazing," I said. "I can't believe he made that call for us."

Face to Face with the Grim Reaper

It seemed like a hundred different doctors and nurses came and went. We couldn't remember what all their names were, and who was who. But one group caught my attention immediately. Five doctors entered the room wearing their white lab coats. Embroidered on each of their coats was the word "Oncology." Like little ducklings, they walked in perfect formation one behind the other. Children's is a teaching facility, and you could immediately tell the attending doctor, fellow, and the resident doctor by the order in which they entered a room. The head duck was a short man, not much taller than me. His white lab coat had "Dr. XXX, MD Neuro/Oncology" embroidered across the chest pocket. John and I stood up.

"Oncology, doesn't that mean cancer?" I whispered. Why did we need to meet these people? We don't even know if Charlie has cancer! I was scared.

"Mr. and Mrs. Capodanno, I'm Dr. XXX," he said, extending his hand. "I work in pediatric neuro-oncology here at Dana-Farber," he continued in his raspy voice. The Dana-Farber Cancer Institute is a world-renowned cancer institution. People come from all over the world to be treated there. It's actually attached to Children's. "If the baby's tumor is malignant, cancerous, we will be the team overseeing his care," he continued very matter-of-factly. He glanced over at Charlie in the crib, not really acknowledging him.

"As you know, they'll do a biopsy of the mass right in the OR. If it is malignant, we will still need to do further tests and won't know the results for a few days," he informed us. Behind him all the ducklings were listening intently.

Dr. XXX said he'd check in with us periodically, and turned to head out the door. And falling into perfect formation again, the ducklings followed him.

"I don't like him," I told John.

"Probably because he's a cancer doctor," John replied. But I could tell John didn't like him either.

"No," I replied, "probably because he has zero personality or bedside manner. He never called Charlie by name, not once. And he barely even acknowledged Charlie at all! I don't like him," I complained. "Let's make sure he's the best, 'cause I don't like him. And if he's not, I want another doctor."

We asked a friend at Hill, Holliday who works in the research department to do a search on his credentials. There was no denying it; he *was* the best doctor we could have on Charlie's case, *if* it was in fact cancer.

"Well, we won't need him anyway." John tried to sound reassuring.

We bonded immediately with our nursing team. They were extremely professional, but you could tell they were in love with Charlie instantly.

I watched them like a hawk and questioned everything they gave him.
I also drilled them with questions. I'd ask them a hundred times a day,
"Do you see kids with brain tumors a lot? Do they do well? Are they
ever not cancerous?" I would dig for any positive, hopeful information
they'd give us.

"Kids are very resilient! They do very well," they'd say with big
smiles.

Wandering Aimlessly

Every now and again I'd need to take a minute to get out of the room
alone. I would stroll the halls and look at the hundreds of pictures of
all the past patients who had sent in updated photos. I noticed that the
majority of the kids were cross-eyed. This really struck me as unusual.
When I returned to the room, I began questioning John.

"Did the surgeon mention Charlie might be cross-eyed after his
surgery?" I asked curiously.

He laughed. "Why do you ask?"

"Because, every one of the kids in those pictures hanging on the wall
is cross-eyed!" I exclaimed.

"You're nuts," John laughed. So, I grabbed his hand and I dragged
him down the hall to prove my point. It would not matter if Charlie was
cross-eyed or blind, or deaf. We wanted him in whatever condition we
could have him. But in my crazy state of mind, I found it so strange to
see a wall of cross-eyed kids hanging in the neurosurgery ward. "See," I
proclaimed pointing at specific pictures. John looked at me cross-eyed as
he walked back to the room. "Who cares?" John laughed.

I'd read all the lovely thank-you notes parents wrote. I'd absorbed
all the beautiful poems. One struck me immediately, and I ripped it off
the wall and had a nurse make a copy of it for me. I marched back to

Charlie's room and gave a copy to everyone who was there. It reminded me that God was by our side for this entire journey. However, I didn't like how the poem ended (it was not a happy outcome) so I rewrote it to make it a happy ending.

As parents of a challenged child,
We have those days
When our hearts seem too heavy to hold
Those are the days when God's holding our hands
Showing us our soul.
As parents of a challenged child,
We have those days
When all we can do is cry.
That's God's way of clearing our eyes
So we may clearly see
How bright and shiny tomorrow's going to be.
If ever our child should have to go away
For even just a short stay
That's God's way of saying
It's His turn to help today.
Now we believe when all is said and done,
It matters not what material things were lost
Nor what were won
For God saw in our hearts a special love
Second to none.
As parents of a challenged child
We've come to love the simple things in life
Like a smile or a touch
For within our child's smile
God is saying we're doing just fine
And for our child's loving touch
We thank God so very much!

Our Quest for Prayers Begins

We spent a majority of the evening calling everyone we knew — friends, neighbors, relatives, co-workers — to ask them to spread the word: pray for Charlie. Yet by the time we reached most of them, the word had preceded us and just about every person was crying into the phone, or just completely speechless. I was teary, but somehow remained composed. Our request to everyone was the same: "Please call everyone you know and ask them to pray for the success of Charlie's surgery." I'm sure the phone lines must have lit up clear across the country. John and I are blessed with many dear friends and not one of them was going to turn down our desperate and dire request for divine intervention from heaven above!

Kristine and our dear friend and neighbor Anne went door to door in our neighborhood alerting everyone of Charlie's illness and asking for their prayers. Family and friends got on-line to spread the word and get Charlie's name on on-line prayer lists. I called the pastor at our church, Father Tom Walsh. When he got on the line, I completely lost it.

"Father Tom, this is Deirdre Capodanno from Crossfield Road. Our six-month-old son Charlie was diagnosed with a massive brain tumor."

"Dear God," he gasped.

"Could you please ask the congregation to remember Charlie in their prayers?" I pleaded, fighting back a sea of tears. He said he'd add Charlie to the prayer list for every single mass.

What Charlie was going though was far beyond my mother, Joanne's, comprehension. I believe it was a combination of sheer shock, the fact that she would not allow herself to conceive that her beloved grandson had a brain tumor and her "everything will be fine" mentality of coping with a crisis. Instead, she took on the tremendous responsibility of spreading the news of Charlie's situation across the country through phone calls, emails and prayer groups to get as many people as humanly possible to pray for Charlie and our family.

We called, and called, and called. And we begged for prayers. Our tearful friends would ask, "What can we do?" and "How can we help?"

"All we ask is for your prayers. That's all we want from anyone. That's all that matters to us right now."

Late that afternoon, I was alone for the first time in the hospital. I sat down in a chair in the hallway and stared out the window. Sitting there, I felt a great sense of peace knowing we had friends from every corner of the country praying for our son. I felt comfort in knowing we were in one of the best hospitals in the country. And I felt so blessed that my child was still alive, and that we had received the sign to get him to the hospital before it was too late. But was it already too late? We just didn't know the answer. And we wouldn't know — until the doctor was "inside" his brain.

Tracking Down John's Parents

We were surrounded by visitors during the first few days in the hospital. It was actually very distracting for us, which is exactly what we needed. My sister-in-law Beth and her husband Rob arrived from New Jersey. So, between Beth, Rob, Jill and Matt, and our extended family at day care, taking care of Jay during those first few days was like a well-orchestrated event. My girlfriend Amy came in and she was a wreck. The room was full of people, and my dad summoned me to his side.

"Poor Amy can't even catch her breath," he said. I put my arm around her and took her to one of the consulting rooms. There I comforted her. What was going on was inconceivable to her.

"Why you guys?" she sobbed, trying to control her tears.

"You know what, Amy?" I began. "I can't waste a minute of my time trying to think about 'why us' because who knows why? It is what it is. He's going to make it, Amy; I just feel it in my heart."

Later that afternoon, John and I discussed how we actually did most of the consoling to those who came to comfort us! What an odd role-reversal, but it kept John and I focused. I think our bodies and minds just went into survival mode, or just major denial; whichever, it kept our minds occupied, preventing us from allowing our thoughts to cross over to the dark side.

Jill frantically tried to track down my in-laws. She called every one of their friends who might have been able to help us connect with them. The problem was we didn't even know if they had made it to Florida yet. "Hi, it's Jill Petrie, have you heard from my parents?" she'd asked nervously with every phone call.

Late Saturday evening while we were all out in the hallway taking Charlie for a stroll, Jill continued to dial her cell phone. She had left a trail of family and friends from Massachusetts to Florida distraught with the news of Charlie's dire condition. As we headed for the windows, we heard Jill yell.

"Mom, Mom…It's not good," she wept, pressing the cell phone tightly to her ear.

"It's a brain tumor, Mom," she cried, visibly cringing at my mother-in-law's verbal reaction.

"Oh my God, oh my God! NO!!!" my mother-in-law yelled in despair. Jill could not regain her composure, and handed the phone to John. He kept his cool and tried to explain as best he could what had transpired over the last few days. After a minute, he too had lost it, and handed me the phone.

"My dad wants to talk to you," John said softly as he wiped his eyes with his sleeve.

"Hi, Papa," I said weakly.

"We love you, Sweetheart," he said, choking back tears. "We're coming right home. We love you." And then he too broke down.

"He's going to make it....he will...I believe it in my heart...we all want you here. Just make it home safely, please," was all I could say. They immediately packed their bags, turned the car around, and drove 27 hours back, stopping only once. I could not imagine the pain and fear they must have endured during the long and grueling ride home. They arrived at the hospital, drained and terrified.

At one point I realized I'd been in the same PJs for two straight days! And I smelled pretty ripe! Somehow a fresh set of my clothes appeared in our room. Sunday morning I decided it was time to take a shower. I hated leaving Charlie's side even for 10 minutes, but this was a must for me and everyone around me! Especially in such close quarters! As aunts, uncles, and friends came to visit, I snuck out to the "community tub room" to shower. The drain didn't work properly, so there I stood, knee deep in other people's water, hair and soap scum. I took about a 30-second shower and jumped out. I got dressed in my overalls and white shirt and turned to look at myself in the mirror. I was frightening. The dark circles under my eyes were horrifying. And since I hadn't eaten in days, my face looked very drawn and my clothes actually dangled off my bones. I looked like I'd been to hell and back – and I suppose I actually had.

Baskets of flowers and food kept arriving. But the thought of putting food anywhere near my mouth turned my stomach. The phone rang off the hook; it was like Grand Central Station. The commotion of continuous visitors really was a welcome distraction for the day that lay ahead of us.

Kristine came in on Sunday, along with Charlie's adoring teachers from the Barn Yard. She had a huge bowl of fruit salad in tow. While sitting there chatting, I began to feel weak. Kristine filled a paper cup with some of the fruit, and I devoured it. I realized it was the first thing I'd eaten in five days.

I looked up at the clock and realized it was almost 10:00 a.m. I desperately wanted to make the Sunday Mass being conducted in the hospital's theater. My mother-in-law offered to join me. Sister Carlotta was saying Mass that morning. We seated ourselves in the front row. There were about 20 people in attendance. When Sister Carlotta asked if there were any special intentions, my mother-in-law lifted her hand ever so slightly, and struggled to form the sentence, "Please pray for the success of Charlie's surgery tomorrow." Hearing her desperate plea broke my heart. I began to cry and so did every single person sitting in that theater. None of these complete strangers knew who we were, or who Charlie was, or what surgery we were talking about. But they must have seen the sheer agony on our faces. They witnessed the condition we were in physically. They could hear the desperation in our voices. And they all wept openly with us.

I hadn't been home. John went home a few times to sleep with Jay. Each time he went home, I'd ask him to bring me some clothes, specifically underwear. For some strange reason, he'd only bring me in one pair at a time! A concerned friend had called to say she was praying for Charlie and asked if there was anything else I needed. "Yes! Clean underwear," I replied in jest. She thought this was hysterical. She took my joke literally. That morning after we returned from Mass, a beautifully packaged Victoria's Secret box was delivered. Inside were three new pairs of pretty undies. It definitely was a pick-me-up! It's the little things in life, like clean underwear, that can brighten even the darkest days.

The Painful Walk in the Garden

That afternoon when Charlie's room was seriously overflowing with visitors and hospital staff, John and I decided to take a walk down to the hospital's outdoor garden. We held hands as we walked, and found a cold stone bench to sit down on. There we sat in silence, falling to pieces in each other's arms. We still couldn't even grasp the concept that the following day our precious child was having major brain surgery to remove a large tumor that could be deadly cancerous. We talked at length about not trying to focus on why us or why Charlie. We just opened our hearts to each other and drowned in each other's tears.

We shared our fear in not knowing what was ahead of us. Was it cancer? Would the doctor be able to remove it all? Would his tiny body be able to survive the surgery? Would he ever be able to walk, talk and play with his brother? Would he grow up? Would he suffer? *Would he live?* These unanswered questions were ripping us apart. The fear of not knowing what would happen was beyond excruciating, beyond words, and beyond comprehension. What stuck in my own mind the most is that I didn't care how Charlie would come back to us from the surgery, maybe not being able to hear, see or walk. I just remember begging God to at least allow Charlie to be able to smile. It was so important to me that he could smile because his little smile was so beautiful.

We sat in that courtyard and begged and pleaded with God to save our son's life. We'd do anything He asked. We so desperately wanted our little baby boy to live. We wanted him to grow up with his brother. Jay deserved to have his best friend with him throughout his life. Charlie deserved to learn how to walk, talk and run. Six months old was just not long enough to live. We couldn't even fathom the idea of losing him.

John admitted, as he buried his face in his hands, that in his mind, he had begun to script a eulogy for Charlie at his funeral. This was the most painful thing I'd ever heard in my entire life. It brought me to the verge of vomiting in my mouth. The agony we endured that afternoon, with the fear that we could lose our son on the operating table the next day, was unbearable. It was as if we were no longer whole. Our bodies and our minds had shattered into sharp, broken, splintered pieces.

At one point that afternoon I, too, thought about Charlie's funeral. But I just erased it from my mind. I'd gotten this advice from my dear friend Jane days earlier when she called to give me support. Her gorgeous little daughter Susie was born with a rare, life-threatening heart condition. Jane's advice to me that morning in February was what helped me stay focused.

"The minute a horrible thought enters your mind, erase it. Just don't even think about it. You can't live like that. Charlie needs you to stay positive regardless of how long he's here on earth with us." Her voice cracked, and she cleared her throat. "Take every day as a gift." I took Jane's words to heart.

Jane is one of my best friends from college. Coincidentally, she met and married my childhood friend and neighbor Paul McCarthy. Paul is a Massachusetts State Trooper. He can appear gruff, but he's really a softy. Jane told me that Paul had been flipping through *People Magazine* that afternoon and there was a small article about a well-known actor commenting on how another actor was his hero. Jane said Paul got angry reading this and said, "These jackasses. They don't know what a real hero is in their self-centered little worlds. A real hero is the doctor who is going to remove Charlie's tumor tomorrow."

Visiting hours were almost over, and slowly everyone began to grab his or her belongings to leave. The lights had been dimmed in the hallway so that the patients and their parents would start settling in. At that point there was a gentle knock at our door. It was Dr. Cuozzo. Here she was on a freezing February night, seven months pregnant, hauling herself into the hospital to see Charlie the night before his surgery. She came in with a half smile on her face, and gave John and me each a hug. She appeared visibly shaken. I scooped Charlie up from his crib, and placed him in her arms. I saw a tear well up in her eye.

"Thank you for coming in," I said, kneeling next to her. "We understand this is very hard for you, too." I squeezed her shoulder. She shook her head in agreement, but didn't say a word. This child was her patient. He was only six months old and he was having brain surgery the next morning. This was painful for everyone who knew and loved Charlie, and knew and loved us.

The Night before Surgery

That night, after everyone left, John and I were alone. I confessed that I was too afraid for the morning to come. He disagreed, stating that he wanted to get the tumor out of Charlie. That was my husband, back to his brave self. He wanted the surgery done, so we could move on. To try to ease his mind, he picked up a sports magazine, flipped through it for two minutes, and tossed it. He shuffled around the room retrieving a notepad and pen from the nightstand and without saying a word he began writing:

February 27, 2000

As I sit here in room 919N at Children's Hospital with my beautiful wife and my sick but always beautiful son, I think of all the things that are wrong with this world. Before I sat down to jot some notes, I was flipping through Sports Illustrated with an NBA player on the cover who is making 9 million dollars a year. And I am less than 12 hours away from a neurosurgeon taking apart my son's brain to remove a tumor. I think she should be on a cover of a magazine that sells 10 million subscriptions a week. I am no longer going to have conversations with my father-in-law saying Michael Jordan or

Tiger Woods is God. Dr. Goumnerova is our God. She has my son and my family in her hands.

We have had so many questions go unanswered. Questions about the surgery, but we know it's going to be all right. My priorities in life are going to change. It took an awful event for me to put my life in perspective but everyone over the age of 18 should spend a night on 9 North. I sit here listening to the boy in the next room yelling over and over, "Make it stop." He has cried non-stop since we got here. And in the room next to him is Jennifer who is 24 years old and has spent 22 years of her life in and out of this hospital.

My son will walk and talk and do all the things little boys should do. He will also do charity work with his brother and parents. He is a miracle baby. We love our two boys more than anything in the whole world. I sit here and stare at the most beautiful boy that people have ever laid eyes on. And think about his first T-ball game, his first hoop game. The first time we come back to Children's to show other patients that, yes, you too can overcome brain surgery and lead a normal life.

I want to pick my son up, rip off all his tubes and cuddle him in my arms for eternity. I don't want February 28th to come. I need my son. Although I have great confidence that February 28, 2000, will be the single best day of my life when Dr. G. comes out of the surgery with a smile. She is our God. And he is our miracle. We love Charlie and so do hundreds of people. It amazes me how many people love this little six-month-old boy. People have shown us so much compassion – from his wonderful teachers at the Barn Yard, to Gina's husband David who gave us their precious "St. Michael" medal their son wore when he spent five weeks in ICU. So many people have bonded together in tough times; people you would never expect to hear from have called and prayed.

My son is going to be all right. He's a miracle child.

So the next time I have a bad day at work and I'm tired and just want to relax and veg in front of the TV, I will sit in my son's room and veg out in front of his crib. Time to get some rest. Will finish writing tomorrow night with wonderful news. We love you Charlie so much. God bless you.

As hard as I fought that night to stay awake, fearing what the next day would bring, sheer exhaustion must have taken control, and we both fell asleep sometime around 3:30 a.m.

Chapter 3
Life in a Surgeon's Hands

....

Heavy Hearts

The door to Charlie's room swung open with a bang. John and I had to peel ourselves off the ceiling from being awakened so abruptly. It was pitch black in our room and, outside, the city streetlights were still on. It must have been roughly between 5:30-6:00 a.m. because that was when the neurosurgery team rounded each morning.

"Good morning, Capodannos!!!! Big day today!" a loud, cheerful voice boomed. It was Dr. Jody Smith, the neurosurgery fellow. She had the best bubbly personality and was always so upbeat, even when talking about potentially malignant brain tumors. "How's my handsome boy today?" she said, leaning over to rub Charlie's back. Charlie smiled at her and began kicking his legs. He liked her too. "Man, this kid's a trouper. He's amazing. Look at him! He's ready to get this show on the road. Do you folks have any questions for us?" she grinned.

Normally we'd have had a million questions for her. They never really described in full detail how the surgery would be performed. Nor did we really want to know every graphic and gruesome detail. They just said they'd open his head up, and cut what they could of the tumor out. They were hopeful they could get it out, but if they couldn't, they'd just "sew him back up." We really didn't want to know the actual specifics at that time; it would have only added to the terror we were facing.

"Nope, I guess we're all set." John tried to sound optimistic.

"Okay, we'll see you at 9:00 a.m. sharp," she chirped.

Dr. Jody was awesome. She never made the surgery sound like it was any big deal, which made us feel such relief and gave us confidence in the surgical team. I mean, these folks have done, and continue to do, dozens of brain surgeries every week. To them, it must be just another day at the office. Or so we convinced ourselves.

It was February 28, 2000. We'd been at the hospital for six days, but it seemed like a lifetime. Here it was, the morning of our son's surgery. Our minds were racing. Our stomachs were turning. Our hearts were bleeding. Slowly our family began to gather. I was growing more and more anxious, so I went downstairs to Au Bon Pain for some tea. I had no intention of drinking a sip; I just liked having it in my hand to hold. And I needed to remove myself from the situation, even if it was just for a moment in time. Coming back up on the elevator, I bumped into the curly-haired MRI technician from Friday.

We were alone and I was glad she spoke. "Hi," she said softly. "I can't imagine what you're going through right now. I want you to know I thought about you and your family all weekend long. I couldn't get Charlie off my mind. And I prayed like I've never prayed before...for Charlie," she said, as a tear filled her eye. "Good luck today," she said, touching my arm as she got off the elevator.

"Thank you," my voice trailed off. The doors shut and I froze. Her words were kind, and yet delivered a crushing blow. Here we were at one of the biggest, best pediatric hospitals in the world. And this person working in the MRI department at Boston's Children's Hospital, who saw hundreds of MRIs each week, thought enough of what she saw on Charlie's MRI to have it stick with her all weekend long.

I then realized that as serious and grave as we knew this surgery was, it was evident to the woman who actually saw the MRI develop that it was even more dire than we had ever comprehended it to be. I must have been in either complete shock or complete denial up until that point. We hadn't seen the scans. We were only told it was a "massive" and "impressive" tumor. I mean, how big could it be? How dangerous was its location? How much in denial was I? The elevator doors opened at 9 North and as I walked off, I lowered my head and vomited in my hands. I rushed to the bathroom, washed my hands and splashed cold water over my face, my body now trembling with fear.

I didn't mention the encounter to anyone when I reentered Charlie's room. By now, our entire family had arrived. It was so quiet you could hear a pin drop. John was leaning over Charlie, kissing him and telling him how much he loved him, and how brave he was, and how proud we were of him. I leaned over and rubbed John's back. It was so incredibly painful to witness this young father huddling over his infant son on his way into surgery that could take his precious life, or drastically change it forever. Everyone was leaning or holding on to whoever was standing next to them. You could hear sniffles, but other than that, it was dead silence.

"Okay, everyone, it feels like a wake in here," I said, cutting through the silence. "No more. It can't be this way. Please. We need to be positive for Charlie. We need to surround him with positive energy. He can tell we're scared. Please, start thinking positive thoughts." I heard mumbles, and then slowly everyone tried to perk up.

An unfamiliar nurse came in to say that the surgery was being pushed back. This sent John and me, whose nerves were already shot, completely

over the deep end. Because Charlie was having surgery that day, he had
not been allowed to eat anything. This was pure torture for a six-month-
old. Charlie was starving, it was 9:00 a.m., and he hadn't eaten since 8:00
p.m. the night before. He was now distraught and wailing in his hunger.
That poor nurse. Talk about shooting the messenger.

"No friggin' way! Forget it!" John said. "We're going to feed him.
He's starving!" He reached for a bottle on the nightstand.

"Don't!" the nurse yelled, grabbing the bottle. "Please, no, don't do
that. Mr. Capodanno, please don't feed him. They'll take him as soon
as they can. Please, I know this is so hard, but please don't feed him that
bottle," she pleaded. It was a silent standoff for a moment, and then John
surrendered and slowly placed the bottle back on the nightstand.

As Charlie screamed from hunger, John and I took turns rocking
him and pacing the floor. We sang to him, talked to him, kissed him,
and cuddled him. We had no idea what was ahead of us. We had no
idea what Charlie would be like, or what shape or form he'd be in when
he came out of surgery. Of course, in the back of our minds, there was
that horrific thought that he may not even survive the surgery. But we
didn't discuss it, and I didn't let myself think about it for more than a
split second.

At 10:30 a.m. the battered nurse came back in. "They're ready for
Charlie now," she said softly, lowering her head. We allowed each family
member a few minutes with Charlie to hug his precious little body and
to give him what we hoped would not be an everlasting kiss. This was
by far one of the most painful experiences I'd ever witnessed in my life.
Although it was not intentional, they appeared to be saying their final
goodbyes to him, as if they might never see him alive once he left the
room. You could see the absolute pain and despair on each individual
face. It was excruciating.

Eight Hours of Hell

As a family we all walked together, pushing Charlie's crib slowly down the hall to the elevator. When we reached the OR, we were directed to the waiting room. John and I were able to go into the pre-op holding room with Charlie. My entire body was trembling. The two of us were up inside the crib with him. He was wide awake and smiling and cooing at us. He had no idea what was ahead of him. A volunteer came over and introduced herself.

"We have a few gifts for little Charlie," she said, handing me a package covered in handmade wrapping paper with an Angel Teddy Bear Beanie Baby attached to it. Inside was a baby-sized hand-knit blanket. It was made by Project Linus, a group of women who knit blankets for children in the hospital. It was so beautiful and so touching; I felt an enormous lump growing in my throat.

Dr. Goumnerova arrived moments later. She was in her scrubs. As always, she had a gracious smile on her face. "How's our man today?" she asked cheerfully, reaching over and touching Charlie's arm. Without thinking, I immediately grabbed both her hands into my own.

"See these hands, Sweetie?" I said looking down at Charlie. "They're going to make you all better, Charlie. Please God, please bless these hands today," I said, stroking her fingers gently. I could feel tears welling up in my eyes, but I was determined not to cry in front of Charlie. I didn't want to scare him. The doctor squeezed my hands and I finally let her go.

The anesthesiologist came in and informed us of what they were going to use to sedate him, all of which went right over our heads. Next, Dr. Jody bounced over to see Charlie. "He's just amazing, this kid!" she said gleefully. "So, you understand what we're going to do, right?" she questioned, knowing full well we had no real concept of the complexity of the surgery they'd be performing on our son's brain. It was completely beyond our comprehension and we didn't need nor want to know the details of what kinds of drills, saws and other tools and machinery they'd be using to open his skull to get into his brain.

A very sweet, soft-spoken OR nurse came over. Her name was Jeannie. "Oh, he's gorgeous, look at those lashes!" she said. John asked her if they would need to shave his entire head.

"Sometimes they do, sometimes they don't. It all depends on the size of the area they'll need to work on."

"Any idea how big the incision will be?" John questioned.

"Usually it looks like a tiny horseshoe right around the ear." She outlined her ear with her finger. Her illustration looked like the size of a hearing aid. That didn't look so bad!

When it was time to take Charlie, Jeannie placed her hands on our shoulders.

"Time to go, kiddo," she whispered. We each leaned over and kissed him. We whispered in his ear to be brave. We said it was time to get that boo-boo out of his head, and that we'd both be right there for him the minute he woke up. And we told him we loved him more than life itself. We told him we were so proud to be his mommy and daddy and that he was our precious little gift from God. With that, the nurse stretched out her arms for me to release my son to her. This was the most excruciatingly painful and terrifying moment I had ever known. To release my precious child into the hands of a complete stranger, a stranger who was taking him to surgery to remove a massive tumor from his tiny head was unbearable. It felt as if my heart was bleeding. He was alive at that moment…would he be alive the next time I held him in my arms?

As we both turned away, John wrapped his arms around me from behind and kissed the top of my head. "Good, it's time to remove that thing from his head," he said. I buried my head in his chest for a moment, then, grabbing our new blanket, we headed hand-in-hand out to the waiting room as my teeth chattering with fear.

We had been informed that the surgery would take "a few" hours. So we were guessing it would be about three hours of waiting. Our family had taken over the entire back corner of the OR waiting room. They were all doing their best to stay upbeat. Someone pulled out a deck of cards. Others were chatting and flipping through magazines. Someone tried to crack a joke, but it was just too awkward. I found a chair in the far back corner, sat down, pulled my knees to my chest to contort my body into the fetal position as best I could, and buried my face in Charlie's blanket. By now it was lunchtime. The OR liaison had given us a beeper and said we were allowed to check in with her every hour. Beth suggested we all go to lunch at Longwoods, a restaurant directly across from the hospital.

"You guys all go. I'm not leaving," I said, shaking my head in protest. There was *no way* I was going to leave that waiting room or the hospital until I saw my son again.

"Come on, come on," everyone said, trying to coax me into joining them. "We all need to eat."

"Honey, please, please come," John pleaded. "We're going to be right across the street, and we have a beeper."

"I *don't* want to go, I really don't." I shook my head. It had been one hour since Charlie was taken into the OR.

"Come on," he replied, "let's go ask the liaison how long it will be before she thinks we'll hear anything. We have to eat, Honey, we need to be strong for Charlie when he comes out."

John asked the liaison if it was time for her to make her first call back to the OR. I couldn't believe they could actually call right in to the room where the surgery was under way. Jeannie answered, and told the liaison that they had finished prepping Charlie and she laughed, saying that he was giving them a hard time with the anesthesia. Typical Charlie! Never would my strong little man go down without a fight! So at that point the surgery hadn't even started.

With enormous hesitation, I regretfully joined my family at the restaurant. We had a huge, long table, and everyone was chatting and trying to act as if they were having a grand old time. My chin was about one inch from the table. If I couldn't be in the fetal position, I wasn't happy. John kept rubbing my shoulders. I was numb and yearned to get back to my son.

"Everything's fine, Honey, this is a good thing," he kept repeating. By this time, another half-hour had passed and our food had yet to arrive. I told John I needed to go back over to talk to the liaison again. I jumped from my seat, and ran as fast as I could back to the hospital, with John trailing behind me.

"They're in," she said, meaning they had opened his head. I winced. "It's going to be a while, go finish your lunch. I *will* page you if anything happens. I promise you." We sighed, and John dragged me back to the restaurant. How could I even consider eating, knowing they were "in" my baby boy's head? My salad went untouched. I never so much as picked up the fork. I watched as family members laughed and conversed with one another, but I don't think I heard a single word that was spoken. I watched their lips moving but couldn't hear any words. I was lost in my own mind, with my fears ricocheting inside my head. At one point, I found it so difficult to breathe that I thought my throat was beginning to close shut. Air. I needed air. I tried to inhale, but it felt like my windpipe was no wider than a straw, and my rib cage appeared to be caving in, crushing my lungs. I needed to get back to that hospital. I needed to be as close to Charlie as possible. After everyone finished their meal, and my father somehow unintentionally insulted the waiter, we headed back to the waiting room, walking shoulder to shoulder. Our corner of the waiting room had been taken over, so we all sort of scattered around the hallways. John and I paced and paced. And we prayed and prayed. And we negotiated whatever deals we could with God. And we watched the clock with every passing tick. 2:00, 2:12, 3:00, 3:20, 3:31, 3:50, 4:19, 4:30, 5:15. With each passing hour, we'd check in with the liaison. And with each passing minute, our fears grew deeper, and we became more tired, more anxious, more frightened and more silent.

"Still in there," the liaison informed us.

"Christ, what could be taking so long?" we'd wonder aloud. Was the fact that it was taking so long a good thing or a bad thing? None of us knew the answer. It was the longest, most agonizing day of all our lives.

Tears of Joy

John and I were slumped over in a chair, our bodies completely drained of every drop of emotion and energy, when John spotted Dr. G. We jumped to our feet, startling everyone around us. It had been close to eight hours since the start of the surgery. We searched her face frantically for any sign of information. "Come, come with me," she instructed us, letting out a sigh. She directed us into a consultation room and closed the door behind her.

"It went very well," she said, allowing herself to exhale and refill her lungs again. "Very well," she said with a smile engulfing her face. "We believe we got it all, in its entirety. Actually, it was the size of an oversized lemon. We were able to remove most of it in one big section; then we needed to suck the remaining part out. So, I'd say we got 99.999 percent of it. It had not spidered to other areas of his brain."

We were in absolute shock and overwhelmed as we tried to hear and absorb all her words. "Now, I need to tell you, from what we could biopsy in the OR, it is cancerous. But we'll need to send it out to a lab for further evaluation. But in my experience, he'll just need to be treated with some chemo, and he'll do just fine."

"What about brain damage?" John questioned.

"It's too early to tell, but no, I don't believe any damage was done. I think he'll develop normally. We'll have a better understanding once he's out of post-op." John and I began jumping up and down out of sheer elation. We both gave her a huge hug, almost crushing her tiny frame. Then John became suddenly still.

"Thank you, thank you for saving our son's life," I said as I sobbed tears of joy. I was overjoyed to hear that she was able to remove it all without any complications, but I think John could just hear "cancer" ringing through his head.

"But she said he'd do fine, Honey," I assured him. I think he was just in complete shock and his body could not react. We swung open the door and raced out into the hallway where most of our family was waiting. My dad, his girlfriend Bebe, and Mr. and Mrs. C were missing.

"She said she got it all, she got it! Well, 99.999 percent of it! She got it!" I screeched at the top of my lungs. And then at that moment, I became so overwhelmed I fell to my knees. We were all jumping up and down and screaming and hugging and crying. John was happy, of course, but it was apparent he was not bursting with excitement.

"People are jumping up and down, but Charlie still has cancer," he said, shaking his head.

The entire waiting room of complete strangers was crying too. I'm not sure if they even knew what we were all so elated about, but I guess they witnessed through our cheers of joy that something miraculous had happened in that operating room that day.

Just then, my dad and Mr. and Mrs. Capodanno came off the elevator and raced over toward the commotion. They could tell, without any of us saying anything, that we received joyous news. My dad burst into tears. "Thank you, God, thank you, Jesus," he yelled at the top of his lungs. My father-in-law swung his hands in the air. We all knew every one of our friends was holding their breath to hear the outcome of the surgery. Everyone grabbed cell phones and began dialing.

"They got it! It is cancer, but they got almost all of it out!" we all explained. Our friends were all in tears; some of them couldn't even speak because they were gasping out loud. It had been a long day for everyone who loved us, and to hear that it was removed without any major complications was astounding.

After about 15 minutes of phone calls placed across the entire country, we collapsed on the couch in exhaustion. "Oh no," my brother-in-law Matt said as he pushed himself up from the couch. "Now God's going to want me to cash in on all the bargains and promises I made to him." He was starting down the hall.

"Where are you going?" Jill questioned.

"I've got to make good on my first promise. I've got to go dance naked throughout the streets of Boston," he laughed.

"No kidding," my dad said. "Now I have to spend the rest of my life being a nice person to everyone I encounter!" We all sat there and laughed as we confessed what we swore we'd all do if Charlie could make it out of this surgery alive.

"Hey, you know what?" I said. "I'm hungry." Simultaneously every single person jumped to his or her feet. It was literally the first time in close to a week that I actually wanted to eat. Matt did the honors, sprinting down the hall to retrieve a huge bowl of Au Bon Pain clam chowder for me. It was just about the best thing I'd ever tasted!

Recovery

Once the surgeons finished "closing Charlie up," he was immediately moved into the post-operative Intensive Care Unit (PICU). Sadly, because there were so many dangerously ill children in the PICU that night, they had to set up an area for Charlie that was way in the back end of the unit.

Only John and I were permitted to see Charlie immediately following the surgery. As we rushed to be at his side, our hearts were pounding with anxiety and anticipation to see our baby boy, ALIVE, again. But when we arrived at his bedside, he was barely recognizable. Two nurses hovered over him. He was completely buried under bandages; the only noticeable body parts were his toes. His entire head was wrapped with turban-like gauze and net bandages, his tiny face was enormously swollen to the point of being unrecognizable, and he was hooked up to a hundred wires and machines. I just ached to touch his soft skin and kiss his face. But as I leaned over to kiss him, I realized there wasn't any skin visible or accessible to kiss! He looked like a victim of a horrific car accident or, as John put it trying to make light of the situation, "He looks like one of those crash test dummies after a crash." Charlie looked so lifeless lying there. I caught a glimpse of his chest rising and lowering as the machines helped him breathe, and I found comfort in just staring at his chest. Our eyes darted back and forth between Charlie's chest and the monitors for constant verification that he really was still alive under that bandaged and swollen bundle that lay on the bed.

I looked around to find a place where I could sit down next to Charlie and was immediately informed that it would be impossible to sleep with Charlie that night.

"I have to be here for him when he wakes up...he needs to see his mommy's face," I insisted. But it was a losing battle. I could tell they were completely jammed in the ICU as it was and my presence would only be a distraction and an annoyance for the doctors and nurses as they feverishly worked through the night on all of the children.

"Mr. and Mrs. Capodanno, someone will be at Charlie's side the entire night, but we just don't have room for you in here, we're so sorry."

"But," I started to say, as John took my hand. Knowing I could not be with him made me incredibly sad. I wanted to be there as he slept. And more important, I wanted to be there the minute he woke. The nurse reminded me it would be quite some time before they would allow him to wake from his sedated state.

We agreed John would go home to be with Jay and try to get a good night's sleep. We held each other silently for a long time before he left.

"Mrs. Capodanno, we'll show you to the parents' sleeping area," the nurse said as she handed me the room key code written on a piece of paper.

By now it was around 11:00 p.m. and there was absolutely no way I was going to be able to shut my eyes, let alone sleep! My heart was still bouncing around inside my chest. It was dark in the room I had been escorted to, so I just sat down on an empty cot for a moment and prayed, thanking Jesus for watching over Charlie's surgery that day and for allowing him to stay with us here on this earth for longer than six months. Suddenly, an overhead light in the room went on, and I could hear two women talking quietly.

"This is where I'll sleep tonight," the soft-spoken woman said. I could hear their voices getting closer. "Oh, I'm so sorry, did we wake you?" the woman asked politely as she approached my cot.

"No, no, I just got here, and I can't sleep."

"I'm Cathy Andrews*," she said as she extended her hand.

"Deirdre Capodanno, I'm new here," I said jokingly.

"Capodanno, are you Baby Charlie's mom?" she asked.

*Name changed to protect privacy.

67

"*Yes!*" I answered, surprised by her question, and wondering how she knew me.

"Oh, both our sons go to Dedham Medical. We have Dr. Fox. My son Bradley[*] was brought in for a cancerous brain tumor as well." For a moment, we just stared at each other silently and in shock.

It was eerie and unfathomable that two children from the same pediatric practice were in the hospital with cancerous brain tumors. I immediately asked how her son was doing, and she turned her eyes to the ground. "Not good, really, not good, they did emergency surgery last night to release the pressure, but the cancer had already spidered throughout his brain. He's in really bad shape. They're going to start chemo tomorrow morning."

"I'm so sorry," I said sincerely with my heart aching for this woman and her pain. I was hoping she didn't ask about Charlie, because I felt so terribly sad for her. But she immediately asked, and the excitement I felt about the success of Charlie's surgery escaped me at that moment. I instantly felt guilty. Of course I was still elated by Charlie's success, but my heart broke for this poor woman who did not get the same hopeful results that we did. Here I was, just an hour earlier hearing they were able to remove my son's cancerous tumor, and her child was in such grave condition with a brain tumor that they would immediately begin treating with chemo the very next day.

"He's doing amazingly well," I answered shyly.

"Thank God," she said, grabbing my hand as she sat down next to me on the cot. Here we sat, two complete strangers, not saying a word, just holding each other's hands as tightly as we could. Two mothers, brought together by unimaginable circumstance, while we waited to see how our sons' lives would unfold, and there was absolutely nothing we could do but watch and wait and pray.

---

[*]Name changed to protect privacy.

It was impossible to sleep. The words "we got it all" continued to race through my head. What about the cancer? How could he have gotten cancer? What would happen next? I didn't allow myself to focus too much on the cancer issue that night. I was just so overjoyed that he had actually survived the surgery, that he was in one piece, and the surgery was successful and my little boy was alive.

I got up a few times that night and crept into the ICU just to peek at my little baby until I was spotted by a nurse, and gently shooed away. I must have dozed off on the dilapidated cot around 3:00 a.m. I awoke around 6:00 a.m., still wearing the same clothes from the day before. I didn't even care. I sprinted back to ICU. There was my precious son, still covered in bandages, tubes, and surrounded by machinery, still lying motionless in the hospital crib. I sat staring at him for the next two hours. I just watched him breathe with the aid of a machine. I'd rub my finger gently across his tiny foot, the only skin I had access too. I must have told him over 1,000 times that I loved him and was so proud of him. What a little miracle he was! "Thank you, Jesus," I just kept repeating to myself over and over as tears streamed down my face and drenched his tiny toes.

Nurse Ratchet and the Determined Patient

John arrived at around 8:00 a.m. and they decided to move Charlie to a section of the ICU known as the "Outback." Basically, it was an ICU area that handled the overflow of ICU patients. We were happy with the move, because it was much quieter, and there was room for us to have one high-back chair for us to sit on right next to his crib. There was also a reclining chair, which got no use at all, since we hovered over Charlie every minute. We had no intention of leaving his side.

Charlie was assigned a new nurse whom I immediately named Nurse Ratchet because she was a bit rough around the edges, and she seemed to growl when she conversed with us. She seemed to have a real attitude problem toward her job, complaining that the ICU was overcrowded, that she had been working too many hours and that the hospital didn't have enough nurses…complain, complain, complain. Unlike the other nurses who had cared for Charlie, all of whom were very gentle with him, she was gruff, but extremely efficient. John and I asked her a million questions: "What's that tube for? What's that medication you're giving him? When will the swelling go down? When can we hold him?" She answered every one very firmly and with a grumble. It appeared we were an annoyance to her, and she made it seem as if we were constantly in her way. No softness with this one!

"Bitch," John said under his breath.

"Well, maybe she's just having a bad day. Who knows what she's got going on in her life?" I tried to be sympathetic, not wanting to cause any unnecessary angst.

At around 9:00 a.m. the phone next to Charlie's bed began ringing.

"Capodannos, you have visitors at the desk. Only one visitor at a time please; this is a busy area," Nurse Ratchet snapped. John's parents arrived, and we told them both to come back in, but that only one could stay at a time. Nurse Ratchet gave my in-laws the once over, and then shot John and me the furry eyebrow. It didn't faze us in the least. We just wanted them to take a peek at Charlie, to see that he was alive and breathing on his own. They had removed the breathing tube from his throat earlier that morning so we now had small areas around his lips and cheeks available for kisses. As we chatted with John's parents, Charlie started to wiggle and shift his tiny body around ever so slowly. His slight movements were exciting to us, but we knew he was still under heavy sedation. We weren't yet allowed to hold him, but we kissed him and stroked his body all over. With our touches, his body would react with wiggles. His eyes were swollen completely shut, but it was evident he was "awake." We knew he could hear us and he was responding to our voices and our touch. After a short period of time, Charlie was still again. He must have dozed off. Moments later, one of the ICU doctors appeared.

"Mr. and Mrs. Capodanno, at some point this morning we will need to wean Charlie off of some of his medications so we can see if he responds to certain tests," the barrel-chested doctor bellowed. "We want to see if there's been any paralysis, immobility, and those kinds of limitations. It will take a while for the medication to wear off, and we'll just test him by rubbing his feet, bending his limbs, and gentle, easy movements."

John and I glanced at each other, smiled and then turned back to the doctor. "Well, doctor, ah, you might not believe this, but just a few minutes ago he wiggled his toes and fingers when we were touching him. And when we leaned over and talked close to his ears, he bent his knees up a bit," John proclaimed with pride. The doctor gave us a strange look as if to say "That can't be right."

"He did what? Already, on his own?" he questioned us with a huge look of surprise on his face. "That's a terrific sign. Wow! That's amazing that he's responding so well, so quickly. What a strong kid!" John and I were beaming. "I'm serious," the doctor continued, "do you realize the strength of the medications he is on to keep him sedated? Holy cow!" What a good sign that Charlie was already showing us his strength and will to fight!

As the doctor checked his charts, Charlie stirred again, although his eyes were still swollen completely shut. We knew he was awake because of the subtle noises he would make and his slight movements. His head, even under the mountain of bandages, looked enormous. It appeared to be equal in size to the rest of his body. As I began to ask the doctor about my concern over the swelling, Charlie again tried to pull his arms and legs upright. He didn't seem in distress; it was clearly evident that he just did not want to stay lying down.

"Well folks, now we have a slight problem," the doctor stated with a grin. "Even though Charlie's determined to roll over and get the hell out of here, we can't have him do that just yet. He's got an entire head full of stitches, and with all the swelling, his head is way too heavy right now for him to hold upright. Plus, everything in his brain needs to relocate itself and shift back into position now that the tumor is gone, and that has to be done very slowly. So I'm afraid we're going to have to restrain him by tying his arms and legs down to the bed." I shot John a look, which the doctor read instantly. "Now, Mrs. Capodanno, he will still be under some sedation, but you have to realize we can't allow him to pull his stitches or injure himself in any way. This kid's a fighter, but this was major brain surgery."

"Oh boy, he's not going to like being tied down, I can tell you that," John chuckled. But we didn't want Charlie to cause any further injury, so they increased his sedation a bit and tied his tiny limbs to the bed for safety. He was six months and three days old, and he was a fighter. He was determined not to let this surgery or his disease slow him down. And he was letting John and me know he was "all there" beneath those bandages. I just wished I could see him smile. And I ached to hold him in my arms again.

We remained in the ICU for one more night. Dr. Goumnerova joined us the following morning.

"Wow, he looks great! But, um, why is he restrained?" she asked with a concerned look on her face.

"Oh, yesterday morning he wanted to climb right out of the crib!" we laughed.

"Amazing," she said, smiling. "He really is amazing! I'm very pleased."

I was still very concerned about how he looked—so swollen, bloated and pale—but according to Dr. G, there was no reason to keep him in ICU any longer. "Let's get him back down to 9 North," she instructed.

As she began to exit, I stopped her.

"Dr. Goumnerova, when will we know more about the type of cancer Charlie has?" I had tried not to focus on it, but the reality was we needed to know so we could prepare ourselves.

"Well, Dr. XXX and his team will meet you downstairs at some point today. They're the folks you really need to talk to about the cancer, all right?"

Nurse Ratchet returned to say Charlie needed another MRI before he was brought back to 9 North. Good. I'd had about enough of her and her crankiness. As she began preparing Charlie to go down to MRI, removing IV bags and loading our belongings under the bed, my friend Jane arrived. Her daughter Susie had been admitted to Children's due to her heart condition. She looked over at Charlie and said with a huge smile on her face, "He looks *great!* Oh, poor little Sweetie, but he looks so good, doesn't he?" I think she was trying to sound positive, because he actually looked frightening. I stepped out into the hallway to chat with Jane for a minute to inquire about how Susie was doing. As I went to re-enter the room, the automatic double doors flew open as Nurse Ratchet rushed Charlie in his crib past me.

"Where are you going?" I questioned, annoyed that I was not informed that Charlie was being moved right away.

"To MRI," she snipped. "Mom, you stay here," Ratchet demanded as she pointed her finger to the floor. She was rudely indicating where she wanted me to stay put. Right there, right then, as John put it, "I grew balls!" I could feel the anger brewing inside me and I thought that the blood that was boiling up in my face was going to spontaneously combust.

"Excuse me! He's *my* child," I said, pounding my chest with my fist. "Where he goes, I go. And YOU don't tell me where to stay!" And I shot her a look that could have cut her in half. John, who was standing behind Ratchet, had a smile a mile wide across his face, but didn't utter a word. He found the sudden fire in my eyes quite entertaining, in fact. I could feel the heat steaming from my beet-red face. Where did this witch get off telling me what to do? I no longer cared if she had had a bad night; it couldn't have been worse than the last few nights my entire family, let alone my youngest son, had suffered through. As we quickly pushed Charlie down the hall to the elevator, the nurse tried to make small talk, but I wasn't interested. I'd had enough of her and her attitude.

Back Home – To 9 North

Once the MRI was over, we made our way back up to our private room on 9 North. It was only the second day post-surgery when they decided we should try to hold Charlie at a 45-degree angle in our laps. As anxious as I was to cradle him in my arms once again, I was absolutely petrified. His head was still enormously swollen. Once he woke up from a long rest, two nurses picked him up and gently placed him in my waiting, but very hesitant, arms. I loved being close enough to him to smell his baby skin, but I was so afraid. He still seemed incredibly fragile. My hands were shaking out of control and I was terrified I'd drop him or injure him in some way. His head weighed a ton, and even though he should *not* have been capable of lifting it up at this point to a 90-degree angle, he tried with great determination, and he succeeded.

"Whoa. No!" said his nurse Lisa, smiling nervously. "Charlie, we can't have you doing that just yet, my friend. It takes time to get your blood flowing properly again, and for everything in your head to shift back so you have some balance back." Lisa reached down to take him from me to put him back in the crib. But at this point, I didn't want to let go. "No way, he's all mine," I said beaming.

One of the resident doctors entered the room. "Hey little guy, slow down," he said.

"I'm sorry; he keeps trying to sit upright." I was so nervous I was sweating.

"Well, as long as you are aware that his heavy head can flip backwards like a ton of bricks at any second, you should be okay. That's Charlie telling you that his body wants to recover quickly."

My mother-in-law arrived with her camera. It was the first time I had allowed anyone to take his picture. Prior to the surgery, I wouldn't let anyone photograph him in the hospital, because if he hadn't survived the surgery, I didn't want the last pictures of him to be lying in a hospital bed awaiting the removal of the tumor that cost him his life. I wanted the last pictures in his album to be of him and his brother playing at home, smiling and happy.

Just as his picture was about to be taken, Charlie popped open one of his eyes. How he managed it, I'll never know. They were black and blue, and so incredibly swollen. Moments later, Beth and Rob arrived with Jay. I wasn't aware they'd be bringing him in so soon after surgery, and was worried about how he would react to Charlie's appearance. At first, Jay bounced into the room, saw Charlie in my arms, and slowly shuffled over to his baby brother with a confused look on his face. Charlie did not look like himself at all. He looked like an alien who'd been in a bad crash.

"Hi, Charlie Bear," Jay said in his sweet voice as he leaned over to kiss him. He began touching his bandages and searched Charlie's face to confirm it was, in fact, his baby brother.

"Charlie's got lots of bandages from his boo-boo, doesn't he, Sweetie?" I asked Jay.

"Yup," he answered. And that was it. He seemed completely unfazed. He hung around the room for all of five minutes, checking out the latest toys people had sent in to Charlie, and then rushed off to find a willing grandparent or uncle to take him down to see the enormous fish tank in the lobby.

Dr. Goumnerova and her team returned the following afternoon. It was the third full day post surgery. "How's our little man?"

"Great!" We all answered in unison. At this point, he was still in my arms, and was actually taking a bottle from me.

"Terrific! I don't see any reason to keep him much longer than tomorrow," she informed us.

"*What?*" John and I yelled at the same time. Charlie's head was the size of a balloon. He was hooked up to an IV pole. He was on a ton of medications. Was she saying it was time for *us* to take him *home?* Alone?

"You're kidding me, right?" I said, looking at her as if she were insane.

"Really, we don't have any reason to keep him. Most of the children need about a week to 10 days to recover in the hospital from such extensive surgery, but Charlie's already done everything he needs to do to show us he's ready to go home," Dr. G said.

"Yeah, well he might be ready, but I'm not!" I chimed in. The thought of taking him home given his condition absolutely horrified me. But good old John said, "He'll probably feel much better at home." I looked at him as if to say, "Are you *nuts?*"

"Well, we don't want to release him until you are comfortable. The nurses will completely prepare you for Charlie's release. Let's plan on tomorrow afternoon." With that, she left the room. I looked over at

Charlie, who was comfortably snuggling up to Bebe. As much as I wanted to leave the hospital, I desperately feared leaving the safety of Room 919.

I could hear Dr. XXX's voice coming down the hall and it sent an instant chill right up the back of my neck. I felt intense fear and intimidation of this man. I looked over to John and frowned. "Here he comes," I warned him.

"Who? Who's coming?" John questioned.

"The Grim Reaper," I had cleverly nicknamed him. "He's heading our way," I said, shaking my head. On cue, Dr. XXX and his ducklings entered the room. It was the first time we'd seen them in days.

"Well, Mr. and Mrs. Capodanno, as you know, Charlie did test positive for malignancy," he said in his raspy, emotionless tone. "It will take a week or so to determine exactly what type of cancer it is. We will let you know when the results are in. Maybe while you're still in the hospital you can swing over to the Jimmy Fund Clinic. We'd like you to see the facility. It's not like what you might expect a children's cancer clinic to be. The kids are all running around, riding in Little Tikes cars up and down the halls. If you get a minute, stop over," he invited us thoughtfully. Well, I thought, this is the first time he's actually been semi-friendly to us.

"So right now, you can't tell us anything more about his cancer? We'll have to go home not knowing much for the next week?" I asked in disbelief.

"I'm afraid that's how long it will take. We have an idea that it is one of two forms of cancers, but we can't say for sure which one it is without further testing." He did not elaborate on or identify what two types of cancer they had narrowed it down to. I wanted to ask if it looked bad, was it rare, what his treatments would be like, what his survival rate was, but I didn't. I stood up from the rocking chair and walked over to him.

I felt my knees begin to shake, and I quickly adjusted my body to a full, upright position. "We're very hopeful, doctor, we are very optimistic," I said, firmly looking directly into his eyes.

I waited stoically for his response. He said nothing. His facial expression didn't change. He broke my stare, and looked past me at his colleagues. And with one solid movement of his head cocking to one side, he motioned the others to exit the room. "My office will call you to set up a time to come in to discuss the results within the next few days. You have my card."

I stood frozen in that spot with my feet pressed deeply into the flooring to hold me upright. I didn't answer him. I didn't reach out for his card, so he handed it to John. Was he just an extremely cold person, or did he know more than he was telling us and could not respond in a positive manner to my comment? I once again began to shake. John wandered over to me and placed a reassuring kiss on the top of my head. I turned around and once again buried my tearful face into the safety of his chest. And I wept openly once again.

Our New, Fragile Life Begins

It was March 4, 2000. We'd been in the hospital for ten straight days. The doctors and nurses were in agreement: it was time to release Charlie from the hospital and for us to go home. The swelling had started to go down around Charlie's eyes and head, he was able to open both his eyes successfully, and we actually got a smile out of him that morning. That gorgeous, precious, heart-stopping smile I begged God to let us see again was back, in full force, and beaming!

The only major concern the doctors had about Charlie's condition had shown itself that morning. When he tried to roll himself over, which rendered us all speechless and awestruck, he got his left arm caught underneath him. He was determined to master the skill again, and continued, with a head the size of a watermelon, to try to roll, and roll, and roll. But each time, he'd get stuck. "We'll need to keep a close eye on that," said the neurologist. But other than that, after undergoing eight hours of brain surgery, and having a tumor the size of a large lemon removed from his head, he seemed to have all his faculties about him. He was the same child, physically and mentally, that he was before his surgery.

Back in Charlie's room, one of the resident doctors entered and began filling out prescription after prescription—one to prevent seizures, one for pain, one to control the swelling, one for nausea, you name it, we had a prescription for it. Then the neurosurgery resident came down to remove the bandages. His entire head had been wrapped under a mountain of bandages for days and we were nervous about what we'd see underneath it all.

John and I were both curious to see how big the scar was. Dr. G had told us she had needed to shave his entire head, but she never mentioned how large the incision was or how big the scar would be. And in our mind, we kept thinking about what Jeannie the OR nurse had told us: "Probably a small horseshoe shape around his ear. Like the size of a hearing aid." We could deal with that.

John held Charlie tightly on his lap as the doctor began cutting away the turban bandage. Below that was another layer of bandage and netting. When he got to the third and final layer, I started staring at his ear looking for any sign of the incision. As he pulled away the final layer, I noticed there were no stitches anywhere in proximity to his left ear. Where the hell was it?

Just then, John let out a huge gasp. "Oh my GOD!" I followed his eyes to the very top of Charlie's now bald head.

"AHHHHHHHH. OH MY GOD, NO!" I yelled, finally noticing the enormous row of stitches and patches of dried blood. The stitches actually began at the top center of his forehead, ran directly back the entire length of his head, looped around, and made their way down the left side all the way to his ear. Virtually half his head was stitched together.

"*Oh…my…God!*" I screamed again. It was shaped like a horseshoe all right, but it was also the actual *size and length* of a horseshoe. "It's one whole side of his entire head," I screeched. The thought of how they had actually cut open the left side of his skull entered my mind and turned my stomach. We knew the tumor was enormous, we were told it was the size of a large lemon, but I guess we never realized how much was involved in the removal. There was still surgical tape over parts of the stitches, and tiny little hairs were growing through the tape. The incision was beet red, and there were patches of dried blood around certain areas.

"Poor little Sweetie," I said getting teary-eyed over the thought of what this tiny precious head had endured. It didn't matter to either of us that he was bald, and it didn't matter that he had the gigantic scar on his head, we just felt so bad for him. It must have been very painful, and uncomfortable, and we couldn't imagine that the stitches didn't bother him tremendously.

We warned every family member and friend as they entered the room that the scar was much bigger than we anticipated, and not to be alarmed. But still, even fully warned, everyone's eyes nearly popped out of their heads when they first caught a glimpse of Charlie's incision.

Our family members filled up two huge pushcarts with all of our belongings, luggage, cases of food, bags of magazines, piles of gifts, and bunches upon bunches of balloons and flowers. Since we'd made so many new friends inside the hospital, we decided to leave the food in the family kitchen area for those who would continue their stay longer than ours. We took most of the flowers home, but I had picked out one beautiful arrangement that I wanted to give a very special mom whose daughter had been in and out of Children's for the past 21 years with a horrible, debilitating neurological disorder.

"My husband and I would love for you to have these flowers. We hope they will brighten up the room for you." With that, she got up and without saying a word, gave me a huge hug that warmed me to the core.

"The flowers stopped coming for us long, long ago. Thank you. You are a kind family. I'll keep your little Charlie Bear in my prayers," she finally whispered in my ear. Once you've experienced having a child with a life-threatening illness or condition, you immediately bond with the other families who are going through similar circumstances. You feel for them. Your heart breaks for them. Only they can really understand your fears and frustrations. You share a common bond that now separates you from the rest of the outside world. It's like a club you never signed the membership application for, nor did you ever in your wildest dreams (or nightmares) think you'd be a member of.

Before we finally departed, I walked back down to ICU to see how the young boy from our pediatrician's office was doing. I could see a lot of commotion outside of his area; I waved to his mom, who looked very distraught. Things did not look good inside the confines of the glass walls. Again, I felt the pain and guilt that here we were leaving the hospital to go home with Charlie, and their son remained in critical condition. I raised my eyes to the ceiling and thanked God for His gift, and asked Him to please shine His healing powers down upon this family.

The nurses had put together an entire day-by-day chart for us to follow so that we could keep track of the dosage and times we administered Charlie's medication. "This is impossible to follow," I kept thinking. But by now, I just wanted to get out of there.

"Well, you should be all set. We'll call you later tonight to see how things are going. You have all our numbers?" the resident asked. I tapped the chest pocket of my overalls, which was overflowing with business cards and prescriptions. John was getting Charlie dressed and froze when it was time to put the shirt over his head.

"Ah, wait a minute, how are we supposed to do this?" he asked, not wanting to hurt Charlie or to touch his head.

"Just like this — he won't break." The doctor quickly yanked the shirt over his head, stitches and all. Our jaws dropped, but Charlie was completely fine. "You'll get used to it, don't worry. Just keep that bandage dry until we see you next week."

John finished getting the baby dressed, and we strapped him into the car seat. Six months earlier, we'd done the same thing as we were doing now at a different hospital a half-hour away. We were taking our little baby home. Only this time, he wasn't a newborn. But he seemed just as fragile. We walked at a snail's pace down the hall, stopping about 100 times to hug our nurses goodbye. This place, this hospital, with all its beeping IV machines and cold floors and squeaky cribs and slimy showers and endless supply of popsicles, saltine crackers and ginger ale, had become our home. Now we were leaving the safety of this place. And we were leaving this home to return to our real one, not knowing what was ahead of us.

I sat in the back seat with Charlie as John drove home at about 25 miles an hour down the highway. What should have been a 45-minute ride turned into one and a half hours. We pulled ever so slowly into our driveway and John put the car in park. By the time we pulled our own broken bodies out of the car, five neighbors came slowly out of their houses to see us. We pulled Charlie, who was still sleeping, out of the car, and placed his infant carrier on the driveway. With that he woke up and smiled. Tears filled everyone's eyes as we began to hug our neighbors.

We knew more than anything that everyone felt helpless and wanted to do something to rescue us from this nightmare. They wanted to take away our pain, to make everything all better. But this was completely out of our control. There wasn't anything anyone could do to fix the problem.

John grabbed the infant carrier and we proceeded to walk into the house. My body felt as if it were just a shell made of tiny slivers of glass. There was nothing inside of me; pieces of who I used to be were missing. We'd left the safety of the hospital, and now we were home to face our new life. We all needed to get some sleep. Although John and I thought we'd be checking on Charlie every 30 seconds during the night, we fell asleep instantly and slept soundly, for the first and last time.

Chapter 4
Searching for Answers

Charlie Shows His Strength

Over the next few days, Charlie's personality lifted everyone's spirits. He had a smile and a coo for everybody who came to the house to visit, and he'd show his excitement and energy by kicking his feet wildly and flapping his tiny arms. And to the amazement of all, by the third day he once again perfected rolling over. This was an enormous feat for someone who had just had brain surgery. But this was Charlie's way. Just as he was doing when they needed to restrain him in his hospital crib, he was showing us his inner strength, determination and willpower. He had every intention of continuing to grow and develop, and was not about to allow anything to slow him down or break his stride.

Visitors usually entered the house choked up with emotion and fearful to see the baby for the first time. But within minutes of seeing how great Charlie looked, and the energy he had, everyone immediately felt better. We literally had over 100 visitors that first week home, and the cards, gifts, food and flowers just kept pouring in. We had more homemade meals delivered than we could fit in our fridge, but with all the visitors, it was nice to always have enough food to feed everyone. My neighbor Anne and both my mother and John's made sure everyone had something to eat and drink, and they always handled the cleanup as well. For days, John and I just sat and chatted with our friends who came over to shower us with their love and support.

Though the days were easier, due to our steady stream of visitors, the nights were nothing short of torturous. Each night, after John and I would read Jay his ritualistic three bedtime stories, smother him with hugs and kisses and tuck him into bed, I'd bring Charlie into his room to rock him. And each night, the tears would stream down my face within seconds. I tried not to cry loudly so that Jay wouldn't hear me, but sometimes it was impossible. I would rock Charlie literally for hours on end, way past when he had finally fallen asleep. John would creep in, saying, "Honey, he's asleep. Why don't you put him down and get some rest?" I couldn't, because it was too difficult to release him from my arms. In the back of my mind I wondered, "How much longer will I have him and be able to rock him?" I just couldn't seem to let him go.

We still had no idea what form of cancer he had. And the uncertainty was beginning to take its toll on me. To me, nighttime meant the end of another day, which meant another day with our son had passed before us. How many more days and nights did we have left with him? As I rocked him, and sang to him "Amazing Grace" and "Edelweiss," my tears would drench his pajamas. And I would pray as hard as I could. "Please, dear God, save Charlie's life here on earth. Please, don't let it be a really bad form of cancer. Let it be curable. *Please* Jesus. *Please* let my son live. I promise Charlie will be a good person, and will do good things in this world. Please don't let him suffer. He is just a baby. Please," I'd beg and plead, "give his cancer to me, so that he can live a full life." I would only put him down gently in his crib when my arms literally could not support him anymore that night. I'd finally fall into bed completely exhausted, drained, and soaked by my own tears. Charlie's cancer was the last thing I thought of each night, it was what I dreamed about all night long, and was the first thing I thought of each morning upon opening my eyes. The fear of losing him was debilitating to me every single night.

But with each new day, I was greeted with the smiles of both my beautiful sons. And that was reason enough not to continue to be depressed all day long. John and I agreed, regardless of what we were going through, and regardless of our fears, our sons should not see how terrified we were. And, most important, we swore to each other that regardless of Charlie's disease and condition and what his life would entail, both our children still deserved a normal, happy childhood. We vowed we were not going to allow cancer to run or ruin our lives.

Our family and friends understood how important it was for us to keep Jay's life as normal as we could. Kristine volunteered to drive Jay to school every day so that his routine would not be disrupted. We were blessed with the incredible support of our family at the Barn Yard who made certain that his little friends surrounded Jay to help keep him happy. One day shortly after Charlie's surgery, the teachers put out some dolls, some bandages, and the "medical kit" to see if Jay or any of the other kids wanted to play doctor, and to see if any of them had any questions.

We had a steady flow of traffic through our home for an entire week as we anxiously awaited the pathology results. When people surrounded me, it kept my mind occupied and I was fine. I functioned pretty much like a normal human being. But the minute I was alone, even by myself in the bathroom or shower, my mind would wander. What had I done that resulted in Charlie getting cancer? I was convinced I had done something. What could it have been? Was it the Yankee candles I burned during pregnancy? Was it the one and only fried clam plate I ate on vacation while I was pregnant? I didn't smoke, I didn't drink, and I've never taken an illegal drug in my life. I wouldn't even help John paint the family room while I was pregnant because I was afraid to inhale the fumes. I had moved my office at work only four days after joining the company because someone there smoked near my office. *That's* how cautious I was about my pregnancy. But I knew...I just *knew*...I must have, in some way, caused this to happen. After all, he grew inside me. My blood had flowed through his veins. He ate what I ate, and he inhaled what I inhaled. I had caused this. I knew I had. I wasn't trying to blame myself. I just needed to admit it to myself that I had caused his cancer some way, somehow. But how?

One morning I shouted to John as I raced down the stairs, "It *must have* something to do with the Cape house!"

"What are you talking about?" he asked, looking up from the TV.

"Okay listen, we rent the same Cape house each year, with Jane and Paul, right?"

"Yeahhh," he answered sarcastically, wondering where I was going with this line of questioning.

"Well, Jane and I were pregnant at the same time last summer with Susie and Charlie!"

"Yup, you were," he replied, giving me a funny look.

"Don't you get it?" I said, grabbing hold of his shoulders. "We *both* were pregnant down there at the same time, and we *both* gave birth to babies who were born with life-threatening conditions!" I was actually proud of myself that I had come to this conclusion. I waited anxiously for him to agree with my wonderful revelation. He didn't.

"Honey, so what do you think?" John said, shaking his head at me with a smile, stroking my hair. "It was the water down at the Cape or something? Come on, Honey, you didn't do anything to cause Charlie's cancer." He stood up and wrapped his arms around me.

"How can you say that? He grew inside of me!" I was upset because in my own twisted little mind, I thought I'd found the answer.

"Sweetheart, you didn't do this. It just happened. Let's just wait and let the doctor tell us more about it when we meet with him." I agreed, but of course continued to question everything I'd done over the last 15 months. Hmm, could it have been that I allowed myself to pump my own gas? Or maybe it was the bags upon bags of Hershey's miniatures I consumed every day at my desk at work during my pregnancy.

"That's gotta be it, the chocolates!" I concluded pounding my fist on the kitchen table.

The Grim Reaper Comes Knocking

For almost a week we were very optimistic about our situation and Charlie's condition. Yes, we were crushed that our son had a form of cancer, but we were overjoyed that he had survived his brain surgery. And he appeared so healthy and happy; we all drew the same conclusion that his cancer must not have spread and we continued to remind ourselves that the doctor had removed all of it during surgery. We tried to put our fears on the back burner until the day the dreaded phone call came.

"Hi, this is Sally* from Dr. XXX's office. Could you and your husband come in tomorrow morning?" I told her we'd be there, and then scheduled an appointment for an hour after our appointment with Dr. XXX for Dr. G to remove Charlie's stitches. Then my heart sank once again.

That night, after rocking Charlie for nearly two straight hours, I climbed into bed next to John. "I'm so afraid. I'm *so* afraid of what he's going to tell us tomorrow," I cried.

---

*Name changed to protect privacy.

"I'm not," John answered. "I don't want to drag this out another minute. I just want to know now so we can get going on whatever we have to do to get Charlie better."

My sister agreed to come with us to help keep an eye on Charlie so that when we met with the doctor, we could concentrate on what he had to tell us. We were a bit early, so we walked around the lobby at the Dana-Farber Cancer Institute for a few minutes.

"I can *not* believe we are here with our six-month-old son," I mumbled, feeling my bottom lip start to tremble. I'd known a few people who were treated there, and everyone in the country associated with cancer knows the Dana-Farber. "It's one of the best in the country," everyone said reassuringly. Still, I just couldn't believe *why* we were there — to find out the results of our son's pathology biopsy — to find out what type of cancer was attacking our son's brain.

We entered the gift store, and Kel picked out two little hats for Charlie.

"Chemo hats," I said with great sadness.

"Oh, come on, they're cute and they'll keep his little head warm." She made her purchase and we exited the store. Just then a very old, fragile man approached us. He was dragging a respirator tank behind him.

He stopped directly in front of us, and gently positioned his tank in an upright position. He placed his shaking hand on Charlie's shoulder. "God bless him," he said. "How old is this little guy?" he asked in a frail voice.

"Six months," John mumbled.

"Cancer?" the gentleman questioned sheepishly. I could feel the tears filling my eyes. John grabbed a hold of my hand and squeezed it tightly. Neither John nor I could answer his question. We just couldn't say the words yet.

"Yup, but he's going to be fine," Kel chirped, trying to remain upbeat.

"You know it's these little ones that keep me fighting," he said as he slowly shuffled away. "They're amazing. God bless you all."

I could feel myself wanting to go back into the safety of my fetal position, but knew at this point it was impossible. I found myself walking in a circle around the lobby, looking for a way out. But there was no way to escape.

John directed me to the elevator doors. We pressed the button and got off at the Jimmy Fund Clinic. Kel checked us in and paraded around with Charlie, showing him the fish tank, the toys, the sunny windows.

"Don't let him touch anything, too many germs," I snapped, plucking a teething ring from the diaper bag. I was obsessed with germs. I wouldn't let anyone near him or hold him without washing their hands first.

I watched as the doctors and nurses scurried by. The clinic was so clean and bright, much cleaner than I ever expected. And as far as toys and games, they had *everything*. This place definitely had all the bells and whistles; it was evident that they had lots of money backing this institution. For a cancer center, it really was bursting with energy. Okay, so the Grim Reaper was right about that!

Suddenly, I spotted the Grim Reaper. In a split second my mood went from extremely nervous to absolutely terrified. I could feel my hands begin to tremble. John must have noticed too, since he immediately took my hand in his.

"I'll be with you in a minute," the doctor said, stone-faced. But he didn't return. Instead, the fellow from his training team escorted us to a treatment room. He had a smile on his face, and made small talk about the weather. He was really a very pleasant man, soft-spoken and kind. "Okay," I thought, starting to draw my own conclusions. He smiled at us. That's good. Would he have smiled if he knew Charlie was in major trouble? "Okay," I tried to convince myself, "this isn't going to be so bad after all."

The examination room door clicked as it opened, and it startled me. In walked the Grim Reaper, white lab coat and all. The fellow immediately stood up and excused himself. My heart sank. Oh God, why is he leaving? This can't be good.

"Hi, hi, doctor, how, how are you?" John stuttered out of nervousness.

"Well, I'm fine, thank you. But the news is not good," he started in immediately. And as he continued to deliver the diagnosis, his words were nailing our bodies like the spray of wild bullets. "We've confirmed that Charlie has choroid plexus carcinoma, known as CPC. It's a very rare and dangerous form of cancer that attacks the tissues lining the ventricles in the brain and in some cases, like with Charlie's, the CSF, his cerebrospinal fluid. We know with Charlie that even though we were fairly successful in removing the tumor, it has already leaked down into his CSF. We can see it on his scans. To us, it appears that he has a paintbrush of bad cells at the base of his spine." He didn't stop for our response or to acknowledge our shock, he just kept on going.

"Now, what's difficult about CPC is that fewer than 10 to 20 kids in the country are diagnosed with it each year." Still, there was no pause, no inflection, and no emotion from him at all. "So we have very little data on his disease to go by. We will need to be very aggressive with his treatments in hopes that he might have a chance to survive. But the success rate is not promising. If his cancer does not respond to the chemotherapy, he could very well die. It is evident that his cancer is very aggressive given the size of the tumor and his age. What's tricky is that the cancer in his spine is floating freely, which makes it extremely difficult to treat, and although the majority of the tumor was removed, there may be hundreds of malignant cells in the tumor bed that we cannot see," he continued. "As I said, the survival rate is not very promising at all."

I was completely frozen.

"Like, um, what, what are his chances?" John tried to form an audible sentence.

"Mr. and Mrs. Capodanno, given that Charlie is considered to be in Stage Four, there is a good chance Charlie could succumb to his disease." And with that, the room began to spin. I tried to concentrate on what he was saying, but I just couldn't. I tried focusing on his face, his lips, anything I could, but it was as if I wasn't hearing anything. My mind could not listen anymore. It was too unbearable. Survival rates not good…succumbing to his disease…malignant cells we can't see… I shook my head in disbelief and allowed my brain to shut down momentarily. Still, I had not moved a muscle since he began. I had not uttered a word. I had not taken a breath in minutes. He must have picked up on this because at that point he pulled a red pen from his pocket.

"It's like this," he said as he pulled a sheet of the examining room table paper down and began sketching on it. "This is Charlie's brain and spine, this is where the tumor was removed, and here is where we see a paint brush of bad cells at the base of his spine. The cells are floating all over the CSF." He made dots on the paper with his pen. "It's very difficult to treat cancers like this." I was still frozen, not saying a word. I wasn't crying. I wasn't screaming. I was completely speechless. My entire body and mind went numb. I was in a complete state of shock.

"But, I mean, maybe he can live though, right?" John asked, desperate to hear something positive.

"Well, I have no way of saying," the doctor continued. "This is what we are up against," he said, continuing to scribble, "and here are four treatment options that have been used in the past." And he began to rattle them off as he scribbled them in his own abbreviations on the exam paper. I remained frozen. John tried as best he could to comprehend what the doctor was telling us, but it was just too much to conceive. It was far beyond our worst fears and comprehension or any pain our bodies had ever endured.

The Reaper methodically went on to try to describe the treatment options; none of them made any sense whatsoever to either of us. The only things I heard were the statistics he tagged on: "Well, with this it's a 0-20% chance. With this, it's pretty much the same. This one would be 0%. This one we don't even use anymore." At one point I thought he mentioned the words 40%, but again, I was in a daze. He mentioned terminology, chemotherapy, radiation, bone marrow transplants, stem cell transplants, counts, and platelets, things we had never heard of and that we couldn't fully understand. He had already gone way over my head even with his illustrations.

"With this one, the chemo is so toxic; it literally brings the patient to the very edge of, well near death. This treatment option is no longer available, but was only 0-20% successful." I heard him mention the dangers of radiation, and how it could completely stunt Charlie's growth, because "you don't radiate a brain under the age of three without causing serious damage. Basically his torso would stop growing."

The only time the Reaper appeared to be the slightest bit encouraging was when he described what he called a Phase One study he was involved in. "Study 001" was a new protocol the doctor was spearheading with a group of doctors from across the country. Little did we know until later that afternoon that Phase One studies are only done on patients considered "terminal." They are done to test new medications and treatments to "see what happens" to the patient undergoing the treatment.

"We presently have an opening in Study 001 which I'm a part of. It's brand new. Only two children in the country are participating at this time. We'd drill a hole in Charlie's head and for six weeks straight, every day, we'd administer the chemo that way, intrathecally, to see how the tumor responds; to see what happens. Then we'd do spot radiation. Which could stunt the growth of his torso. Then we'd blast his entire body with intensive chemo; it can kill the malignant cells, as well as the healthy ones. Bone marrow transplantation can bring the body to the edge of death. It's a Phase One study and it's never been done before, but considering Charlie is Stage Four, it may be worth it."

"Stage Four? Stage Four? What does Stage Four mean?" I kept asking myself. Although I knew nothing about cancer, I was pretty certain there was no Stage Five.

"The outcome couldn't be any worse than if we went with any of these other protocols. We need to be very aggressive if we want to have a chance at survival. We should start treating him immediately," the doctor continued.

"How did he get it?" I finally uttered with absolutely no emotion.

"When Charlie was developing," he started.

"In utero?" I interrupted.

"Yes. As I was saying, when Charlie was developing, and his cells were dividing, one cell took a wrong turn and just kept going. It was nothing you did; nothing you could have done could have caused or prevented this. We do know the environment does not cause this form of cancer."

"If the chemo doesn't work," John interjected, "how...how long does he have?" I felt a wave of nausea overcome me and I closed my eyes trying not to hear the response.

"Well, I guess if the cancer continues to progress as quickly as it has, he may not be here to see Christmas..." I began to do the math in my head. That was in less than ten months.

"Think about which protocol you would want to pursue, discuss it with each other, and get back to me as soon as you've made your decision. You've got some tough ones to make," he said matter-of-factly.

There was no "I'm sorry" or "I know this must be difficult to hear, we believe in miracles" – not a single word of encouragement. He just stated the facts and that was it. He stood up, tore off the exam paper, and handed John the diagram he had scribbled. "Well, the good news is," he said, with a half smile, "the cancer we thought Charlie might have had was 100% incurable." It was the most bizarre, nauseating comment I'd ever heard. That was it. He opened the door and left.

John and I sat there in absolute silence for a solid five minutes, not moving an inch. Not making a sound.

"I…I…don't believe this," John said slowly. "Our son has less than a 0-20% chance to live."

"No, no, didn't he say 40% at one point?" I asked quietly.

"No," John answered, shaking his head. "He said on all the treatment options, he has a 0-20% chance…less than 20%…." His voice trailed off.

We didn't reach out for each other, and we weren't crying. We were unresponsive. I'm not sure if we were even breathing. We slowly stood up and shuffled to the door. John opened the door and we walked, in complete shock and in silence, down the hall. Again, no tears. Nothing. Just complete shock.

"Hey, that didn't take too long," I heard my sister say as I looked up. We had only been in the room with the doctor for about 20 minutes. That's all it took to destroy our entire lives. That's all the time it took to deliver the news that our son could die of brain cancer and that we had less then 10 months left with him on this earth. "How'd it go?" she asked, searching my face for an answer. I didn't as much as blink.

"Not good," John replied.

"What did he say, Dee?" she asked again nervously.

"Charlie's got, chor...how did he pronounce it?" I mumbled to John.

"I don't know," he answered.

"He's got a 0-20% chance to live," I said without any emotion.

"What?" Kel gulped.

"Less than 20%. That's it," I said matter-of-factly.

"We've got some decisions to make. Some pretty shitty decisions," John said.

We walked like zombies over to Children's Hospital, which was next to the Dana-Farber, to Dr. Goumnerova's office. I'd forgotten we'd made the appointment to have Charlie's stitches removed, and my sister needed to remind us. Tish, the nurse practitioner, greeted us with a smile. I was still in a daze and couldn't bring myself to hold Charlie to have his stitches removed. Kel and John took Charlie and disappeared with Tish, and I sank into the couch in the waiting room. My mind was blank, completely empty. I had no thoughts, nothing racing through my head. I couldn't think. To think hurt too much. I fixed my eyes on the fish in the fish tank and admired their beauty.

Charlie, John, and Kel returned after a few minutes. The stitch removal had taken no time at all. We left the office immediately.

"I gotta get the car," John said, racing ahead of us. "I'll meet you out front." And with that, he disappeared.

"Dee, Honey, say something. Can you tell me what the doctor said, please?" Kel asked, as she cradled Charlie over her shoulder and placed her arm around me. I couldn't speak. She leaned over and kissed the top of my head. "I love you so much," was all she could say as she squeezed me and Charlie as tight as she could. I felt her tears hitting my cheek. She basically carried both the baby and me down the stairs to the main lobby at Children's, where she strapped Charlie into his infant carrier and once again wrapped her arms around me. I stood emotionless, and motionless, as I leaned against a large cement beam.

"He's only six months old," I finally broke my silence. "That's just not old enough. You're not supposed to die when you're six months old. I can't let him go. I won't let him go. I'll have to go with him, I'm his mommy and he needs his mommy...if he goes..."

"Deirdre, don't...," my sister pleaded, covering her mouth with her hand. My words were too painful for her to hear.

"No," I went on in my numb state, "if he goes...I will have to go with him. I can't let him be alone. He's my baby and I love him." That was all I was able to say. My mind and my body were completely shut down. For the first time that morning, my eyes filled with silent tears. My six-month-old son had a rare form of cancer attacking his brain and spine. He hadn't yet learned to crawl or talk or walk. He hadn't yet learned to really live, and we were told he might die, very soon, of cancer.

Kel helped put Charlie in the car and kissed us all on the cheek. As she walked away, her head was turned up to the sky as she wiped the stream of tears from her face. Inside our car was dead silence. What we had just heard was inconceivable. We sat, completely stunned by what we had just been told. Charlie quickly fell asleep in the back seat.

"I don't believe this," John said, finally breaking the silence.

"This isn't real. It's not really happening," I said in denial.

"I couldn't even follow what he was saying, could you?" I said, turning my attention to John. "Once he said Charlie could die, I just completely tuned everything out."

"Twenty percent. Our baby boy has a 0-20% chance to live. 0-20%!" John shouted, startling the baby. "*Less* than 20%," he repeated over and over again.

"I know, I know, I can't understand this. What are we going to do? How are we supposed to decide on these treatments? I don't even know what a protocol is. I don't know anything about cancer." My voice crumbled.

"I love him so much," John said, with the voice of a broken heart. "He's such a good boy. He's my little boy," he added, peeking at Charlie through the rearview mirror.

"I can't let him go...I'll never be able to live without him; we can't let him go. Jay needs his brother too," my voice trailed off again. Warm tears streamed down my face as I once again turned my head toward the window.

Explaining the Unexplainable

We pulled into the Barn Yard parking lot. We never believed we'd receive news this grave, so we had planned to pick Jay up from day care ourselves.

"I can't … I just can't go in there right now, John," I said, knowing that our extended family at day care was also anxiously awaiting the news as well. I wasn't even sure I could stand up straight at that point.

John got out and disappeared into the school. Seconds later, Kristine emerged and raced over to the car. I rolled down the window, and she grabbed my hand with both of hers. Her voice was trembling.

"John looks upset. What happened? How did it go, what did they say?" she rambled in a panic.

"It's not good, Kristine," I said, my eyes looking forward through the windshield, not making any eye contact with her. "It's really bad. Charlie has less than a 20% chance to live, less than 20%, he even used the words 0% chance," I repeated as tears streamed down my face. Her body slumped over the open window and slid slightly down the side of the car. She tried to stand upright again, and buried her face in our clasped hands and all she could say was "Okay, okay," as she squeezed my hand as tightly as she could. That was all she could communicate at that moment. John came out of the school carrying a sleeping Jay on his shoulders.

"John, I..." Kristine searched for words but could only shake her head in shock.

"I know; can you believe this?" John replied. With that, he strapped Jay into the car seat and planted a loving and protective kiss on top of his forehead.

Back at the house, our family began to gather. As much as we needed their support, it was just too difficult to explain what the doctor had said because it was so inconceivable. John and I had turned into robots just spewing the information from our lips. "He's got a rare form of cancer; less than 20 kids across the country have it each year. He's got a less than 20% chance to live. We've got two choices, two treatment options that may or may not even work. One protocol is straight chemo that might destroy his bone marrow, the other is this experiment that's never been done before. They'd drill holes in his head, put him through radiation. It sounds like torture, but the doctor seems to think it's no worse than what the outcome could potentially be if we go with the conventional treatment."

We tried the best we could to provide answers to questions. We explained what we could comprehend ourselves. And then we watched in horror the impact the severity of Charlie's diagnosis had on everyone who loved us. Some people yelled out in anger, while others burst into tears in disbelief. Others were in complete shock and stood dead silent. We remained numb.

The phone rang off the hook; everyone was awaiting the news. By midday, my brain could no longer process what was going on. I literally could not speak. I made just one call, to Kristin, who was one of my closest friends. When Charlie was first diagnosed with the tumor,

Kristin and my sister became our family spokespeople to help field calls, answer questions and keep everyone informed the best they could.

"Krissy C," I said, lying on the floor of my family room in the fetal position. "Charlie's been given a 0-20% chance to live. I can't explain it, because I don't understand it myself. John and I need to make a decision as soon as possible on what treatment we will agree to let them perform on Charlie. Please, please apologize to everyone who has called us. I just can't talk any more right now. Just please, please ask everyone to pray for Charlie and to pray that John and I make the right decision." My voice was incredibly weak as I hung up the phone and began rocking back and forth.

Once again the phone rang and I covered my ears. "Dee, I think you should take this call, it is Dr. Cuozzo," my sister said.

John took the receiver first. "How'd it go?" she asked nervously.

"Not good," John said, handing me the phone.

"Dr. Cuozzo," I began sobbing. "It's not good, we got really bad news. It is worse than we ever imagined." I went on, choking on my tears, as I tried to explain what the Grim Reaper had told us. "We need to make a decision as soon as possible. How...how are we supposed to do this? What if we make the wrong decision? What if we choose a protocol, and he still...he still..," I couldn't even say the words as I sobbed.

"Okay, I'm going to make a few phone calls. I'll get back to you soon. Don't make any decisions until we talk again, okay? And don't give up hope," she added sweetly.

A Second Opinion

John and I were on the back deck when the phone rang again a few hours later. Kel answered it. She raced out onto the deck to get me. It was Dr. Cuozzo calling us back.

"Is John there too?" she asked.

"Yup," I replied.

"Please get him. Do you have a speaker phone?" She sounded upbeat. My heart jumped out of my chest.

"Yes!" I yelled. "Please, Jesus, let her have some good news," I prayed, searching the house for John.

"Okay guys, listen. I did my residency over at the Floating Hospital for Children in Boston," she began slowly. John and I looked at each other strangely. We had never heard of the Floating Hospital before and we'd both lived just outside of Boston our entire lives.

"I talked to a very well-known pediatric oncologist over there, Dr. Cynthia Kretschmar," she continued. "She's an expert in brain tumors. As a matter of fact, she was one of the founding members of the Brain Tumor Cancer Society. She said she knows of a protocol that she thinks you should try that Charlie could do very well on."

My face was beaming. I couldn't believe what I was hearing! We had not heard a single word of encouragement up until this very moment.

"She's seen kids with all sorts of brain tumors survive on this protocol. She was disturbed by what you were told over at the Farber. She'd love to meet with you as soon as possible," she said, excitedly. "When can you meet with her?"

John and I grabbed each other's hands and I jumped up and down in the air. I burst into tears. But for the first time in weeks, they weren't tears of pain and fear; they were tears of excitement.

"Give...give me her number, we'll call right now!" I yelled, scrambling for a pad of paper and a pen. This was the first glimmer of hope we were given. It was the first positive thing anyone had said to us. "Wait, wait, where the heck is the Floating?" I asked. "I've never heard of it."

"It is part of New England Medical Center," she answered.

"Oh, okay," I said. I was familiar with NEMC, but still had never heard of the Floating. We hung up the phone and raced out to the deck to let everyone know what she had said. Everyone in the house cheered at the news. We were finally given a glimmer of hope, a little nugget of optimism. Although the Dana-Farber was world-renowned, we were going to explore any option we could. That included calling the Mass General to schedule an appointment for a third opinion. If we were going to get a second opinion, we *surely* were going to get a third, as well!

In the meantime, John, my sister and I called a bunch of hospitals across the country, as well as the National Cancer Institute and the American Cancer Society, to see if we could find anyone who'd treated Charlie's cancer. Neither institute had any significant data or information on the disease, which was tough to hear. It was just as rare as the Grim Reaper said. John and I had decided immediately that for Charlie's treatments we'd go wherever we needed to go in the country or abroad; get on a plane in an instant and fly to wherever we could to get answers and to find a place that believed he could be cured. But after doing some research, surfing the web, and calling numerous hospitals across the country, we decided we really were in one of the best places in the world for Charlie to be treated, right here in Boston, Massachusetts.

Certain friends and family actually expressed concern when we told them we'd be getting opinions outside of the Dana-Farber. "You know, it's one of the finest cancer institutes in the world," they'd say, looking at us like we had three heads. I think some people really thought we'd lost our marbles and were just running from hospital to hospital in a desperate attempt to find someone who'd tell us Charlie would be fine.

"We know. We know," we responded each time. "The Farber has an outstanding and deserving reputation. We know people whose lives were saved there. But we're going to hear as many opinions as we can before we make this very difficult decision. We have to exhaust all areas. We have to feel confident in our choice."

A Family Meeting

We called the Grim Reaper's office to see if we could schedule a family meeting. Although we were going to look into other opinions, we wanted our entire family to hear, firsthand, from the doctor at the Dana-Farber. We also needed to re-listen to our options, since we could not conceivably comprehend what we were told during that initial meeting.

The Grim Reaper welcomed a second meeting and asked how many people would be coming.

"About five or so," we told him. Well, five turned into 13 family members that day. We didn't care; this was a life-altering decision. We were discussing Charlie's life, and we needed all the help we could get. We weren't experts in oncology. In fact, we knew absolutely nothing about it. We invited Dr. Cuozzo as well, and she accepted. My dad, Bebe, John's dad, Doug, my sister, her partner Laura, Jill, Matt, and even Beth and Rob came up from New Jersey to attend. My mother and John's mom stayed home to take care of Charlie.

When the Grim Reaper entered the room, sporting his white lab coat and carrying a huge file, and saw the number of people, he literally took a step backward. "Wow," he grinned, "now this is what I call a family meeting!" He laughed out loud, which totally caught me off guard.

The doctor was very cordial and spent the next one-and-a-half hours explaining Charlie's grave condition, as well as our two potential options, in infinite detail. Again he used illustrations, but this time he used colored markers on a huge presentation white board in the conference room. I gave him credit. With this large audience, he did his best to give us as much detail as possible; and he was extremely thorough. This time,

I tried as hard as I could to concentrate on what he was saying and took vigorous notes in my binder.

The doctor answered every question we threw at him. At the beginning of the meeting, everyone was upright in their chairs, methodically taking notes in their spiral notebooks, eager to hear what the doctor had to say. Every single person there was waiting, very anxiously, for this doctor to say one positive thing, just one nugget, to give us some hope to go on. But it never came. As the meeting went on, and the grim reality of Charlie's illness set in, everyone sunk deeper and deeper back into his or her chair. By the end of the meeting, everyone was pretty much slumped over in silence, looking beaten and distraught, as if they'd been defeated in a long, arduous battle. At one point, I heard a sniffle from behind me. I looked over and Doug had his head buried in his hands, leaning over on both knees, sobbing quietly. It was so difficult to hear what this doctor was saying, and even more painful to realize the severity of Charlie's condition and the agony of the decision John and I faced. We were talking about the life of a precious little boy; we were talking about our son, their grandson and nephew. They had spent the last hour listening to the grim, cruel, and shocking diagnosis that our precious baby, whom we all loved so much, now faced. Their minds were screaming and racing with information. Their hearts were, once more, heavy and breaking all over again.

As the doctor stood up to leave, my dad cleared his throat and looked up from the table. "Excuse me, Doctor, first of all, thank you for your time. You've been so very thorough with us, and we really appreciate it." The doctor nodded his head. "Um, Doctor," he again cleared his throat out of nervousness, and to prevent himself from choking up. "Well, um. Although things, ah-um, look pretty tough, you have to admit Charlie has shown amazing strength and determination considering what he's gone through already. I mean for a six-month-old, wouldn't you agree?"

My dad said all this with tremendous pride in his voice. His eyes at that moment glistened with tears he was fighting back as hard as he could.

"Oh, absolutely; you're right! Right now the only thing," he stumbled to correct his word choice, "yes, right now the best thing Charlie's got going for Charlie *is* Charlie, I agree. He's incredible," the doctor said, allowing a smile to support his words. To hear the Grim Reaper say something so profound was like music to our ears. It was as if my dad finally got him to admit how strong and courageous our Charlie was. We all believed this, too. Regardless of known survival rates, no matter how poorly the odds were stacked against us, it was *our Charlie* we were talking about; our child who never cried and continued to develop normally with the massive tumor attacking his brain, our child who needed to be tied down after eight hours of brain surgery, our child who left the hospital one week earlier than expected after surgery. We knew if anyone could survive this deadly disease, it would be our Charlie. The sense of pride we all had at that very moment was indescribable and yet very empowering to us.

As the Grim Reaper stood up and grabbed his file folder, I poked John in the side.

"Tell him," I whispered, tapping his elbow.

"Excuse me, Doctor," John interjected. "We just want you to know that we are going for a second opinion."

"Great, we encourage you to do so," he replied graciously. "Can I ask you with whom you're meeting?"

"Yes," I jumped in anxiously. "We're going to meet Dr. Cynthia Kretschmar over at the Floating. We..."

"Wait," the doctor interrupted before I had finished, and he lifted his hand into a "stop" position, shaking his head. "Cindy, ah, she, she's, well, she's a good doctor, but she's, well...no she's a fine doctor. Let me know how your conversation goes." With that, he grabbed his files, turned on his heels and left the room.

"What was *that* all about?" I questioned the group. "What's the deal? What's his problem with Dr. Kretschmar?" I was taken aback by the Grim Reaper's comment.

"Maybe he just doesn't want you to get another opinion," my sister suggested.

"I don't know, but now more than ever I can't wait to meet this woman!" I said, as my curiosity was getting the better of me.

We all decided while information was still fresh in our minds that we should go over to Children's, which is connected to the Dana-Farber, to discuss what was said and what our thoughts were. The Children's auditorium was empty at the time, so we all grabbed kiddie-sized chairs and sat in a circle. Everyone's eyes were red and swollen. Our hearts and minds were exhausted and completely drained. Our heads were hanging very low. We were all fighting back the tears. One by one each person quietly shared his or her thoughts, concerns and opinions with the group. Some folks were leaning toward the Phase One "experiment," because the outcome couldn't be "any worse" than the conventional protocol, which wasn't too promising either. Unfortunately, because it was new, there was no information to go on. So how could they say it couldn't be worse; they had no results. Some thought the conventional route was the safest because it would at least preserve Charlie's quality of life for as long as possible, with the least amount of pain.

"What are you two leaning toward at this time?" John's dad asked.

"I just, I just…" I once again was overcome with fear and burst into tears. "I just wonder if this is, I don't know, maybe it's God's way of having Charlie help find a cure for this cancer. I think He chose Charlie for a reason…maybe He wants us to do this experiment to help other kids…

but I don't want him to suffer. I can't let him suffer. What if we make the wrong decision?" I cried searching the group for their reactions.

"Deirdre, Sweetheart," Bebe said softly, "you'll never make the wrong decision. You'll do whatever you think is best for Charlie, and that's all you can do."

We talked for about a half hour more, and then, out of sheer exhaustion, we all decided it was time to go home. We didn't reach any decisions that afternoon. Our hearts were too heavy and our minds were completely drained from consuming all the information, the grim prognosis, the terrifying treatment options, the statistics, the damage that could be done, and the reality that we had the biggest uphill battle of our lives if, in fact, Charlie could survive. And although we all tried desperately to suppress these thoughts as long as we could, and without anyone admitting it openly, I think the majority of us were struggling with the reality that Charlie might not live.

Father Tom – It's in God's Hands

Later that afternoon, the pastor from our church, Father Tom Walsh, stopped over. I had called him and asked him if he could come down to talk to John and me as we agonized over the terrifying decision we were forced make. I was holding Charlie in my arms as I opened the front door to greet him.

"Oh, dear Lord, he's got the face of Jesus," Father Tom remarked, entering through our front door. This made me smile.

While family members distracted Jay and Charlie in the kitchen, we sat down with Father Tom in our living room.

"Thank you so much for coming," I began. "Father, we…we need to make a really tough decision," and with that, I lost it. John took over, bringing Father Tom up to speed with our conversation with the

Grim Reaper, how horrible the odds were for Charlie's survival, and he described, as he tried to control his emotions, the two treatment options we were left with. As John described the Phase One study, Father Tom closed his eyes and shook his head in disbelief. "Dear Lord," he whispered silently.

"They want to drill a hole in his little head, and do radiation, which they're not supposed to do," I said, trying helplessly to regain my composure. "We just can't do it to him." John wrapped his arm around my shoulder. "If...if he only has a few months left on this earth, I don't want him to suffer, to be in pain, to have a catheter implanted in his head to see 'what happens' when they give him deadly doses of chemotherapy! I want his life, whatever he may or may not have left here with us, to be happy. Just to be a baby boy. But...but...I also just want him to live," I sobbed. "I know he's a gift from God, but I don't want God to take him from us so soon."

"We love him so much," John choked on his words, but quickly cleared his throat.

"Father Tom," I continued, staring directly into his compassionate eyes, "I...well...I keep thinking that maybe God chose Charlie so that he could help find a cure. You know, that maybe He put Charlie on this earth so that doctors could do this experiment on him to help save the lives of other children and cancer patients down the road." I shook my head in confusion, because I was desperately searching for answers as to why this deadly disease had been given to my son.

"Sweetheart," Father Tom looked at me, shaking his head, "God doesn't work like that. He didn't put Charlie on this earth to suffer."

"Then why is this happening to our baby boy? And how do we make this life-or-death decision? *I don't want to play God,*" I shouted, startling Jay in the next room.

"I wish I had the answers to help make this decision for you," Father Tom began slowly. "But I agree with both of you. Charlie deserves happiness, regardless of how long he may remain with us here on earth. I think, like you do, that you're faced with a quality-of-life issue. You want and need to preserve Charlie's quality of life." He was exactly right. Of course, curing Charlie was the most important thing, but so was keeping his life happy.

"So how do we make this decision?" I asked weakly. "What if we make the wrong one and he...he dies?"

"Deirdre," Father Tom said gently, "what you need to understand, and this might be very difficult for you right now, is that whatever decision you make *is* the right one, because you are making it out of love for your son. I know it's hard, but try to keep that in perspective."

He stopped to search my face for a reaction. "And," he continued "you also have to realize that only God can make the final decision on when He will call his angels home to heaven."

I was contemplating his every word. I was listening with my ears, but even more so with my heart. I slowly edged my way back onto the couch, with John clutching my hand. At first I was scared by what I had just heard. Then I felt a true sense of understanding and resolve consume my entire body. As a mother, it was destroying me inside to come to terms with the fact that I couldn't fix my son's problem; I couldn't rescue him. I couldn't kiss the boo-boos away; I couldn't make it "all better." I believed in what Father Tom was saying. There are things in life that are out of our control. We needed to do all that we could out of our undying love for our son in order to make what we felt were the appropriate decisions to preserve his quality of life and ensure the best care possible.

We needed to put our trust and our child's life in God's hands. We would make our decision, and we'd pray that it would be the best one to keep Charlie's young life happy. Only God would decide his fate. And after a long and silent pause, I nodded my head in agreement with what he had just said.

"I understand exactly what you're saying, I honestly do. And I really needed to hear this; thank you, Father," I said, allowing a smile to creep across my face.

"I think you and John know in your hearts what is best for Charlie," he added. John squeezed my hand. Father Tom was right. We knew it in our hearts.

Chapter 5
The Decision

....

A Glimmer of Hope

Neither John nor I could sleep at all that night. Our meeting at the Floating was scheduled for the next morning at 11:00 a.m. We were to bring Charlie, as well as all of his medical records, MRIs and CT scans. We once again asked my sister to join us, too; we needed another set of ears to listen this time, in case we couldn't "hear" again.

The Floating Hospital is located on the edge of what used to be Boston's "red light district." Not the most attractive section of Boston, it has now been coined Chinatown. As we opened the door to the Pediatric Hematology/Oncology Clinic at the Floating, our jaws instantly dropped. Unlike the squeaky clean, light-and-bright bells and whistles of the Jimmy Fund Clinic, it looked dull, cramped and old. There was not a single window to shed natural light. Everything seemed worn and overused. And it was very, very crowded. I looked at John, and he rolled his eyes.

"Please, have a seat," the receptionist said sweetly.

"Seat? Uh...where are we supposed to sit?" John joked. We searched the room for a moment, and then the three of us planted and squeezed our adult-size behinds into three kiddie-size chairs around a small arts and crafts table. We watched the hustle and bustle as people went in and out of the clinic. And we sat, and we sat, and we sat. We couldn't help but wonder what was wrong with all these children. Did they *all* have cancer? "And what in the heck was hematology?" I wondered. Like the kids at the Jimmy Fund Clinic, most of them were extremely pale, with sunken eyes and bald. It was evident that their tiny bodies were in a major battle between the cancer that was attacking them and the horrible drugs racing through their fragile veins in an effort to combat the disease. And yet these brave little warriors all had energy and were racing around, climbing on things, smiling and playing. They looked sick, but they were happy kids.

We were getting very annoyed; we'd been there for 45 minutes, with no sign of the doctor.

"Forget this," John snapped. "Let's get out of here. This is a joke. We're not waiting all day for this doctor. We've got an appointment at Mass General in a half hour; it's going to take us that long to get across town."

"Honey, Dr. Cuozzo really wants us to meet with this woman," I reminded him.

"Five more minutes, and we're out of here, I swear," John insisted. This was such a switch. Normally, I'm the impatient one in the relationship, and John is forever telling me to calm down and relax. But his nerves were on edge, he was getting really annoyed, and he had every right to be.

"A lot different here than at the Farber, huh?" my sister asked, raising her eyebrows. It was sad. How could one hospital have so much more than another, when these kids are all battling the same diseases? Finally, the clinic door opened, and a woman who appeared to be a doctor walked in. The receptionist looked over and winked at me.

"That's gotta be her," I whispered to John, tugging on his sleeve.

"Yeah, well she's got five minutes," he snapped.

"Mr. and Mrs. Capodanno, Dr. Kretschmar will see Charlie in a minute. Come with me," a tall, thin nurse announced, ushering us down a small hallway to an examining room. As we walked, my heart once again began to bounce around uncontrollably inside my chest. I stopped for a moment to inhale a huge, deep breath. There was no way to prepare my heart and my mind to once again listen to Charlie's diagnosis and the less-than-promising treatments.

The door to the exam room squeaked opened, and Dr. Kretschmar appeared, welcoming us with a warm, heartfelt smile. I noticed immediately she was not wearing a lab coat – and I liked that! She looked to be in her mid-forties, with a really wild-looking hand-painted wooden necklace around her neck that was about 4 inches wide. She shook our hands.

"Oh, this must be Charlie. Isn't he beautiful!" she said, immediately going over to him and scooping him up out of my sister's arms. "Hello, handsome," she said, lifting him up in the air and handing him gently back to my sister. My jaw dropped. The Grim Reaper never, ever laid one single hand on Charlie in the two weeks he had been his doctor. Not once! He never made any physical contact with him whatsoever. He didn't even address Charlie by name; he referred to him as "the baby." Here was this woman, this complete stranger, going right over to him, *touching* him and engaging in eye contact with him; treating him as a living, breathing person — not a patient or a study candidate. As my eyes widened, a smile spread across my entire face. I liked this woman immediately.

She finally took a seat behind a small desk. John and I jumped up onto the examining table and Kel sat with Charlie on her lap in a chair.

"I've talked at length with Dr. Cuozzo, and she brought me up to speed with Charlie's situation. Why don't you folks fill me in on what's been going on with Charlie since his diagnosis," she asked politely. In as much detail as possible, we explained what had transpired with Charlie over the last three weeks. When we got to the meeting with the Grim Reaper, my eyes began to fill.

"He said Charlie's got less than a 20% chance to live," I still struggled to allow the words to exit my mouth. She immediately put her hand up as if to say "stop" and she shook her head.

"First of all, Mr. and Mrs. Capodanno, here at the Floating, we don't focus on statistics. We don't look at the numbers or percentages or any of that stuff. We treat the child, the individual, not as a number, but as a person. And here, the child's quality of life is *just* as important as curing the child. I know plenty of children who've done very, very well on conventional chemotherapy protocols, such as Baby POG. Here, look, I quickly printed out the only studies I could find on CPC. Look, look at this…this one was done in '93: out of 11 children, six of them were long-term survivors. And this one in '92: out of nine, four were also long-term survivors. Right there, that's more than 20%!" she said with an awkward laugh.

"But if numbers make you feel better, I say right off the bat I'd give him at least a 35% to 40% chance. But again, we don't go on statistics. Look, here we start with treatments we know *can* work and see how the child responds. If it works, hey, terrific! And if it doesn't, we try something else. But it makes sense to try something that we know has shown success first rather than put your child through something that there are no proven results on at all. Makes sense, doesn't it?" This made perfect sense to us!

"So what you're saying," I asked, slowly locking her in with eye contact, "is that you believe Charlie does have a chance of survival?"

"Of course I do! Absolutely!" she exclaimed with a huge smile across her face. I felt a wave of elation fill my entire body. This was what we desperately needed to hear. This was the ray of hope we were praying for. This woman was telling us our son could live!

For the first time in two weeks, I was excited. No, I was ecstatic! I was impressed and very grateful that given only a two-day notice, this woman took the time to look up what she could on CPC. And what I liked most of all was that she interacted with Charlie. She didn't speak at us. She chatted *with* us. She explained every detail in layman's terms. She was shocked to hear that the Grim Reaper mentioned radiation.

"Do you know what that could do? We'd *never* radiate under the age of three, never unless it was the absolute last possible option for survival."

"The Grim Reaper said we needed to make a decision as soon as possible," I informed her. She laughed out loud at our nickname for him. She knew him well; in fact, he had trained with her years before.

"Well, I agree, you need to make a decision soon. But allow yourself to take your time and make the right decision. Don't let him pressure you. Talk to whomever you need to talk to first," she said.

"Oh, no! Actually, we do have an appointment at Mass General right now," John suddenly remembered.

"Oh, I'm sorry. Let's get you out of here right away," she said.

We all stood up, John shook her hand in thanks, and I basically knocked her backwards with an unexpected bear hug!

"This is the most my wife has smiled in weeks," John said.

"Aw, well good. I'll call Mass General right now and tell them I made you late. Goodbye, Cutie-pie and good luck. Call me if I can answer any more questions," she said, touching Charlie's head.

We flew out of the clinic, ran down the hall, and climbed the seven flights of parking-garage stairs, which left us all breathless.

"Did you, did you hear what she said?" I gulped, as we jumped into the car. "Forty percent, I like the sound of that! No radiation, no experiments, and did you see how she interacted with Charlie?" I beamed.

"I know, I know! Can you believe those studies she pulled out?" Kel added.

"I really like her. I'll even let it slide that she was so late!" John said with a wink. We nodded our heads in agreement. "She's a ray of hope. The *only* hope anyone has given us. She believes in Charlie."

"So what do you think?" I screeched, bouncing up and down in the passenger's seat.

"Well, we still have a third opinion to get. Let's hear what they have to say."

"That clinic was sad though, wasn't it?" I said.

"It sure was. It's nothing like the Jimmy Fund Clinic, that's for sure. I guess we're just used to how things are at Children's. It's too bad, but who cares?" John said.

Massachusetts General Hospital is huge. I felt like I was in an airport trying to find the right terminal and our plane was about to take flight. We were already late and it took us 45 minutes to register, which made us that much later. The clinic there was the size of a shoebox. The doctor was very nice and gracious, but he was on the same team spearheading the Phase One study with the Grim Reaper. The conversation was all of five minutes long. He seemed surprised that we mentioned the Phase One study to him, and I think he was reluctant to break some pretty surprising news to us.

"I must tell you that the Phase One study is closed at this time, so it is not even an option for Charlie right now. You shouldn't be worrying about it, because it's not available." John and I shot each other a look of disbelief. We had agonized over this treatment option for days. We couldn't eat or sleep trying to make this painful decision on whether to allow Charlie to be used as a guinea pig for this study. Now here we were, finding out from a complete stranger that the study we were wavering on was not even an option after all! The study was closed, and the Grim Reaper never called to tell us. We were stunned.

As angry and shocked as we were to learn this, in our minds we had already made our decision. We were going to go with the only doctor who gave us hope, the only person who told us our child, not our patient, could survive! Someone believed, as we did, that miracles can happen. That's all we had on our side: our hope, our faith, and our Charlie.

The minute we walked into the house, we called Dr. Cuozzo. "We really liked her a lot!" I yelled into the phone.

"You sound so good," she said to me. She could hear the excitement in my voice.

"The only thing that bothers me is everything in that clinic was so worn and outdated. Even the scale resembled the same model my pediatrician's office had used 33 years ago, and the toys were so old. Nothing like the stuff at the Farber; you could eat off the floors there." I was babbling with excitement, but with a hint of concern.

"Mrs. Capodanno! *Don't* be concerned with the color of the paint and the carpeting on the floors when you're talking about saving your child's life," she said directly.

"Good point!" I replied. What she said really had a profound impact on me and it set me straight. It wasn't about appearance, or who had better, cleaner, newer machinery, equipment and toys; it was all about who wanted to preserve Charlie's quality of life, and about who wanted to cure him.

Following Our Hearts

That night, after I'd spent another two hours soaking Charlie's PJs with my tears, I joined John in our bedroom. Although we'd heard from the doctors at the Farber, Mass General and the Floating, after talking to his pediatrician, as well as doctors across the country, I was still scared to make that final decision on which hospital to choose to treat Charlie. I curled up in my comfortable fetal position, the only position I could seem to function in, and buried my face, once again, into my husband's brave and strong chest. One week had passed since the Grim Reaper delivered the news of Charlie's life-threatening diagnosis, and it was time for us to make our decision and move on.

"Well, what are we going to do tomorrow? Are we set on our decision?" I couldn't even look up at his face as I clung tightly to his body.

"You know what we're going to do," he said in a positive voice. "You and I both know how we feel. Like Father Tom said, it comes down to a quality-of-life issue and if our son only has a short time on this earth, we're going to make every day as happy as we can. The friggin' study doesn't even exist. And we sure as hell aren't going with the Grim Reaper. And he didn't even have the decency to call us and tell us? Screw him! Kretschmar gave us the hope. She believes in Charlie like we do. We're definitely going with her. Let's get going on this; let's just do it."

There were times my husband just amazed me. Wherever he rallied his strength from was beyond me. And he knew how to fuel my fire. Instead of being reduced to tears again, I looked up at him and smiled. We knew what we were up against. But we believed, as Dr. Kretschmar did, that it didn't matter what the stats were; we were talking about our son, our Charlie. We believed from the moment he was diagnosed that even if only one child in a million could survive, it would be Charlie!

I jumped out of bed the next morning, finally feeling as though we were going to accomplish something that day. My body didn't feel so fragile anymore. I didn't feel as if I was made of glass. There wasn't a hole in my heart or a lump in my throat that morning, and I felt as if I could straighten my back again to an upright position. I was excited to call Dr. Kretschmar to tell her our decision to go with her at the Floating. Yet I was still uncomfortable that I had to call the Grim Reaper to inform him of our decision, because I was so pathetically intimidated by him. The thought of having to have a conversation with him about our decision made my skin crawl. But it had to be done. We were going to move on!

It was early; I couldn't call the doctors until the clinics opened. But we wanted to share our decision with people. So we called anyone we knew was awake; our parents, siblings, neighbors, friends. We were ready to let people know we'd made our decision, and we wanted to get Charlie on the road to recovery.

Everyone was very supportive over the phone, but we knew for sure we made a lot of eyes roll and heads shake in disbelief that morning. People couldn't believe we would leave the world-renowned, highly profiled Dana-Farber Cancer Institute for a less known pediatric hospital on the other side of Boston. I really think people thought we'd lost our minds! Still, we made our decision very clear to everyone. We were going to the hospital with the doctor who gave us the only glimmer of hope. But we also knew that the Dana-Farber is incredibly deserving of its world-class reputation as one of the finest, most innovative cancer institutes in the world. It offers its patients incredible care and its cutting-edge research helps save many, many lives every day. Among those are people we know and love. We would never discredit this fine institution. Ours was an extremely difficult and painstaking decision, but in our hearts and in our minds, our Dana-Farber doctor appeared to be more focused on the clinical aspects of Charlie's disease, and not focused enough on Charlie as a person. It was because of one individual, and for no other reason, that we decided to leave. The Grim Reaper may be one of the finest doctors in the country, but he was not a fit for us.

We knew not everyone agreed with our decision to leave the Farber and go with the conventional chemotherapy option, but everyone expressed love, support and admiration for how we reached our decision.

I called the Floating right at 8:30 a.m. on the nose. "Dr. Kretschmar," I said excitedly, "we want you to oversee Charlie's care and treatment. Thank you for believing in Charlie, and for being so optimistic. We so needed a ray of hope, and you gave it to us," I said as my voice cracked and I bit my bottom lip.

"Hey! Terrific!" she cheered. "We will need to get started very soon. Why don't you come in tomorrow and we'll decide when to start the protocol."

"Okay, we'll be there tomorrow."

After my uplifting conversation with Dr. Kretschmar, I had to make the dreaded call to the Grim Reaper. I felt my stomach turn into a knot. Fortunately for me, the Grim Reaper was not available. I handed the phone to John, and he asked for the fellow on our case.

"Doctor," John began, "we're going to have Charlie treated at the Floating under the care of Dr. Kretschmar. She gives us more hope. She's so much more engaging with Charlie. There was just too much negativity with Dr. XXX," he explained truthfully from his heart. He thanked the fellow sincerely for all he'd done for us, but told him our decision was made and it was final. John and I were both glad we didn't have to actually have another conversation with the Grim Reaper, because his voice alone had made us cringe.

Knowing that Charlie would begin his treatment within the next week, we decided immediately to have his picture taken professionally. We had no way of knowing what was in store, how his body would react, or how sickly he might look on chemotherapy. We were so naïve. We had no idea, no comprehension whatsoever, of what lay ahead. We'd never known of anyone so young undergoing chemotherapy; we just had visions in our heads of sickly children with pale faces and bald heads. This became my mission. I had to have a picture of Charlie looking healthy immediately.

Like a crazy woman, I began calling neighbors and friends to get suggestions of good photographers in the area, and we went with a recommendation from our neighbor Leita. I called the photographer and explained our situation and the urgency in getting the pictures taken within the next few days. The photographer took us the very next day.

Charlie liked the photography studio, with all the lights and props. He sat up on cue, smiled for the camera, giggled, and laughed. "My God," said the photographer. "You'd never know anything was wrong with him. Well, except for the scar," he added. "But that's no problem; we can airbrush that out."

"No, no," John and I said simultaneously. "We won't do that. This is Charlie. The scar is a part of who Charlie is, and what he's going through at this stage. That scar is a very important part of our lives," I said proudly.

"Yup, and he's gorgeous just the way he is, scar and all," John grinned.

"You guys are amazingly strong. I don't know how you're dealing with this so well. I would be a basket case," the sweet photographer said as he snapped more photos.

"We get it from him!" I said, staring at Charlie, who had removed his sock and was chewing on it like a candy bar.

A Cruel and Crushing Blow

That afternoon, for the first time in a few days, John and I and the kids were alone in the house. No visitors; it seemed strange. It was quiet, but nice. Charlie was taking a nap and John was playing with Jay down in our playroom. I was putting away laundry when the phone rang.

"Hello," I answered, racing for the phone.

"Mrs. Capodanno?" I knew immediately by the raspy voice who it was. My stomach dropped. I was shocked to hear from him.

"Hello?" the voice said again.

"Yes, hello," I answered sheepishly.

"It's Dr. XXX from the Dana-Farber. I heard that you have made your decision to go with Cindy Kretschmar."

"Yes, we have," I said, trying to sound confident, though in the back of my mind, I was wondering why he was really calling.

The Grim Reaper continued, "Well, I just wanted to wish you well, and let you know if there is anything we can do for Charlie, please let us know." The Grim Reaper actually sounded sincere.

"Thank you," I replied. "We do appreciate your insight, doctor, but we just feel more comfortable with Dr. Kretschmar. She gave us more hope," I blurted out awkwardly, as if I was trying to defend our actions.

"Well," he said, clearing his throat, "let me ask you this: Does Cindy know anyone who has actually *survived* with CPC?" he questioned with intentional cockiness in his delivery. I felt a rush of fear race through my body. I was completely stunned by his question.

"Yes," I answered firmly. "Yes, yes she does. Goodbye." I clicked the off button on the phone and let it crash to the floor. My body began to tremble and my knees felt weak. I sank onto the carpeted staircase. I repeated his question over and over in my mind as I shook. Why did he ask that question? Why? Why would anyone be so cruel? Why did he want us to be in such pain? We'd finally gotten a glimmer of hope that our son could live, and this person, this cold-hearted, self-centered doctor took every ounce of wind out of my sail in a split second. I felt saliva building up under my tongue, which has always been my body's way of warning me I was on the verge of vomiting. I turned on my hands and knees and started crawling up the stairs to my bedroom. I looked like an animal that had been badly beaten, cowering for safety. I could hear John approaching from around the corner.

"Who was that on the phone?" he asked. I couldn't answer him. Once he reached me on the stairs, the sight of my crumbled position frightened him.

"Honey, what's wrong?" He sat down next to me on the stairs, leaned over and tried to lift my head into an upright position.

"It was him," I said quietly as I continued to shake.

"Who?" John began to look worried.

"Him. The Grim Reaper," I said, my eyes still fixated up the stairs.

"What's wrong? Sweetheart, Deirdre, what did he say?" John's voice grew alarming. He knew this man had said something very malicious to make me so distraught.

"He...he...he asked me if Dr. Kretschmar knew anyone who has survived with Charlie's disease." I grabbed onto John's shoulder. "And he said it with a snicker in his voice, like we were *crazy fools* to believe anyone could survive this." I continued shaking, searching for answers in John's eyes. I rambled on like a child, "Why would he do that? Why would he be so mean? What's his gripe with us? What did we do to this man?"

"He's a jackass," John yelled furiously. "He's mad that we're taking Charlie somewhere else. I'm sure it makes him look bad."

John tried to explain why the doctor would be upset with us. But it wasn't working. I was destroyed. Both my father and John's dad had tried to cut the Grim Reaper some slack in the days leading up to our decision. They thought John and I didn't like him because he was the one who broke the horrible news to us regarding Charlie's condition. And we just didn't approve of his bedside manner. At first, I questioned whether they were right. But this confirmed to me how heartless, cruel, and inconsiderate he was to the core. In a split second, he had shattered the only hope I had. The only hope I was clinging to, the only hope that kept me going.

I slowly got into my bed, and stayed there, alone, for five hours straight. John came up constantly to check on me. I wasn't sleeping, I wasn't crying. I was just sitting there, staring off into space, recounting his question over and over in my head. Were we crazy? Did Dr. Kretschmar give us false hope? Did she just tell us this stuff to make us feel better? Were there really no known survivors? Why did this man hate us? Did he find pleasure in our pain? I couldn't get out of that bed. I couldn't function. This man had taken every bit of positive energy and hope I had and shattered it in a three-minute phone conversation.

After I sat in my frozen state for what seemed to be an eternity, John decided it was time to rescue me. "Come on, we've got company," he said in a cheerful voice, scooping me out of bed and spinning me around like a bride. But I didn't want to talk to anyone, and I didn't want to leave the security of my bed. "Hey," he said, pressing his forehead against mine, "you're going to let that dope keep you down? The guy's a jerk, Honey. Don't let him take away how psyched we are about the decision we made. Don't, Honey. Don't let *him* of all people get the best of you. He obviously doesn't know how to treat people. We'll show him. Once Charlie's cured, we'll bring him marching back to the Grim Reaper's office and show him our *son* is a survivor of CPC, so then he'll know one! Come on, that's it, you're coming with me. Take a shower, get dressed, and come downstairs. We all miss you," he said, handing me a towel. "I miss you."

John was right. I shouldn't give in to this evil man. I couldn't let him destroy me. Who did he think he was? Now, more than ever, I *knew* we'd made the right decision. This guy wanted Charlie because he wanted to use him for his experiment, not to cure our son. I'll never regret, from that day on, that we left him. He may have been a brilliant doctor, but in my opinion, he should be in a lab finding a cure for cancer, not working with patients, especially children!

New Members of the Cancer Club

The next morning, we ventured back into the Floating to discuss Charlie's protocol, when he would begin, and what preparations needed to be made. Dr. Kretschmar explained everything as best she could in layman's terms, reiterating that we would need to be very aggressive with Charlie's treatment in order to win the battle. John and I agreed to the protocol Dr. K recommended, known as Baby POG.

We listened intently, trying to comprehend and absorb every detail. She was bombarding us with a tremendous amount of information all at once, and it was overwhelming. At certain points during her dissertation her words just starting swirling around in my head, and I'd need to adjust my eyes and posture to regain my focus. "Charlie will have a Broviac central line placed in his chest where we'll administer the chemo, and it runs through his heart...normally this protocol calls for treatments every four weeks, but we need to be aggressive...so he'll receive chemo every three weeks...you'll come in for overnights, sometimes for two or three nights, plus every Monday...he'll receive three different chemotherapies... Cytoxan, Cysplatin, VP16...wonderful new anti-nausea meds will help him with nausea and vomiting...he'll be hooked up to a pump for 72 hours..." She went on and on. "And on the weeks he isn't admitted to the hospital for chemo, you'll still need to come to the clinic every Monday to have his blood tests, and to receive a fourth type of chemo known as Vincristine." At one point she pulled out two pages of paper from her notebook.

"These are the side effects for each chemo," she explained. "Sorry, not fun stuff to read, but you'll need to, and sign them both."

"Oooh, lovely," I said, rolling my eyes at John as I skimmed the paperwork. Each drug had at least three paragraphs worth of side effects: "Diarrhea, nausea, vomiting, suppressed immune system, deafness, kidney failure, loss of muscle control, seizures, damage to the peripheral nerves, severe mouth sores, low blood counts, increased risk of infection, jaw pain, loss of reflexes," you name the side effect, it was listed on the paper.

"I need you to sign here, acknowledging that you've read the side effects and understand them, and that you still consent to the treatments," she said. John and I made eye contact with each other, and then grabbed the pen off the table. We didn't have a choice. We signed the forms.

"It's better than what we signed off on over at Children's before the surgery!" John reminded me.

"I want you to know that I've been in contact with Dr. Goumnerova at Children's; she seems lovely," Dr. K informed us. We had already informed her that even though we were switching our oncology care to the Floating, we had every intention of keeping his neurosurgeon at Children's. Without any doubt, we credit Dr. G with saving Charlie's life and miraculously performing eight hours of brain surgery without doing any harm to him physically or mentally. I was pleased to hear Dr. Kretschmar made the effort to contact Dr. Goumnerova. I thought it was going to be difficult to coordinate Charlie's care between two different hospitals, and I was glad they both planned to cooperate with each other.

"She's faxed me some notes from the surgery, and wants to be kept in the loop with Charlie's case," she continued.

"Did she say anything at all about our leaving the Farber?" I asked curiously.

"Not really. She was very professional. Just wants to keep Charlie's best interests at the forefront of our minds. But I was curious too, so I questioned her as to why Dr. XXX would even consider putting Charlie on a Phase One study."

"What did she say?" I asked, as my eyes widened.

Dr. K let out a nervous giggle and said, "Well, actually, she said it was because Charlie was, I guess, the perfect candidate for the study."

My jaw dropped. And I stared blankly at John, who was having the same reaction.

"You're kidding me. *That's* why they wanted Charlie? To them, he was a perfect candidate; a guinea pig for his science experiment. He was just what they needed for their study. Not our son, a person, a child. A candidate. That's unbelievable," I said, feeling a large lump growing in my throat. It was so disheartening to hear. I turned to John and shook my head in disbelief. "That confirms even more my belief that, regardless of what happens; we made the right decision leaving Dr. XXX. The perfect candidate," I repeated. At first I was upset that Dr. G would consider Charlie as a candidate, but I realized those weren't her words. She sits on many teams, including ones spearheaded by the Grim Reaper.

Nursing 101

After our meeting with Dr. K, we were introduced to two nurses. One of them carried a small medical kit and had a small Raggedy Ann doll tucked under her arm. We sat at a table in the kitchenette with kiddie-size chairs. The nurse took the doll and placed it on the table.

The doll had a large white tube about 9 inches long dangling out of her chest.

"Let me guess, is this doll supposed to be Charlie?" I asked.

"Yup, this is what the Broviac central line looks like. We are going to teach you how to care for the line, how to flush it, keep it clean and dry." She took a bunch of medical supplies out of her kit. She filled a syringe with saline, prepped the tip of the line with rubbing alcohol, screwed the tip of the syringe to the line, and pushed the saline slowly up into the line, a procedure known as "flushing" the line. She went on to show us how to change the dressing around the "central" site location, where the line exited his chest. It involved a kit and a ton of other medical supplies, sterile gloves, masks, Betadine, alcohol, tape, bandages, syringes, and more. They demonstrated the procedure once and then asked us both to give it a try. Keeping the area sterile was crucial. Each time we started, they quickly stopped us. "No, no, not like that, like this," they'd correct us. Flushing the line was scary even on the doll. How could I do this to my baby! We were also instructed how to scrub Charlie's mouth to prevent mouth sores, which were caused by the chemo. Once we "passed" the dressing changes, flushes and mouth care on the doll, we thought we were done.

"Oh no," Beth, one of the nurses said, laughing. "There's one more thing. Did the doctor mention you'll be giving Charlie shots at home?"

"Are you kidding me? I'm *not* giving my baby shots! Nope. No way! I'm done. I quit. This is where I draw the line," I protested, and I was serious. John bravely volunteered for the job. The nurses showed us the proper technique by demonstrating on an orange. Beth even volunteered to let John stick her in the arm with the needle.

"I'm never doing that!" I yelled.

So in a half-hour period, we had our first class on how to be nurses. We were to flush Charlie's line twice a day, change his dressing three times a week, scrub his mouth three times a day, and give him a shot once a day, every day, for six days after each course of his chemo treatments. We were also supposed to keep the site and line dry, as well as prevent our little one from pulling on this line that dangled out of his chest! All we could do was laugh and shake our heads in disbelief.

"Do you believe this?" John snickered.

"Ahh…noooope. Never wanted to be a nurse, an EMT maybe… they get to see more action, but never a nurse," I said jokingly, resigning myself to our new responsibilities.

We weren't given a choice. My husband and I were going to be our son's home nurses. What a frightening thought.

Acts of Kindness

We went home and tried our best to forget what was going to happen in the next four days. Our day care established a "meals on wheels" program for us. Kristine hung a sign-up sheet for those families who were interested in making a meal. In a matter of days, the sign-up sheet was filled for four straight months, seven days a week. The meals were extraordinary – delivered in baskets, on platters, including everything from soup to nuts. Most were accompanied by the most heartfelt cards we'd ever received. You see, these families were just like us — young parents, working moms and dads, with toddlers and preschool kids. And it was so incredibly difficult for them to see a family, just like their own, going through something so unbelievably shocking and painful. The dinners were a tremendous help since I didn't have the time or energy to focus on cooking.

One evening my sister-in-law Suzanne called. She worked for the advertising agency I had worked at seven years before, the agency that Jack Connors still owned.

"Okay, listen, just hear me out before you say anything," she warned me. "Here goes: a mini task force has been put in place here at Hill, Holliday. We've come up with a few ideas and we want to run them by you. We don't care what you say; we're going to do this, whether you accept it or not, so just listen. It's all been approved by Jack so you can't say no."

Whatever she had up her sleeve, I had no idea. "Okay, we're setting you up with Streamline, so you can food shop on-line, saving you from having to take time to go to the grocery store. And, of course, the agency will pick up the tab. Also, we're sending a house cleaner over twice a month, we're sending you a driver to take you to and from chemo treatments, and we're going to have someone come and service your lawn. This is all to help you guys just spend time with the kids, and to focus on taking care of Charlie. So, how's that sound?" She sounded out of breath. I just burst into tears.

"We can't accept that. No way. It's too generous. No, we can't!" I cried. To have people offer things like this was just so humbling. I didn't want to appear as if our family was a charity case.

"Like I said, you don't have a choice. It's all in the works. It's been signed off by the big guy...it's a done deal," Suzanne continued. We graciously but humbly accepted the grocery delivery service and the house cleaning. But that was where we drew the line.

And the generosity continued the very next day when I went to pick Jay up at school. I loved to steal moments of time alone with him, even if it was only the half-hour car ride home from day care. My friend Maria, who owned the day care, called me into her office; I was worried she was going to tell me Jay was having some sort of trouble.

"Listen, I want to tell you something, and I know you well, Deirdre, so I know how you're going to respond," she said softly. "We have a family here, who wishes to remain anonymous, that has paid Jay's day care tuition for the next three months," she explained.

"What?" I screeched as my eyes welled. "No, I can't, we can't...It's too hard to accept this, really, no...But thank the family anyway."

"Dee, Deirdre, it's done. You can't say no. They've already written the check. They want to do this, and what's so special is, no one knows except them and me," she said, rubbing my back as I sobbed. Maria began to cry as well.

"No, I have to know so I can say thank you to them," I pleaded.

"Nope. I made a promise to them, and honestly, I think it's awesome that they want to remain anonymous. They don't want you to thank them. They're doing this out of the goodness of their hearts because they so want to help you in any way they can," Maria said, struggling to regain her composure.

The outpouring of generosity was completely overwhelming.

We were constantly told that this was the only way people felt they could do something to help us, because they otherwise felt helpless. Family, friends and even complete strangers wanted to lessen our financial strain so we could focus on curing Charlie of his disease and maintaining as best we could a happy, uninterrupted life for Jay.

Cracking Under Stress

The Sunday before our first inpatient treatment was the first time John and I had an argument over Charlie's situation. I insisted on taking Charlie to a healing service at Mission Church in Roxbury, Mass. It's the church my dad grew up attending, and the healing priest there, Father McDonaugh, was well-known across the country for healing people. He had an actual following of devoted people, some of whom came from pretty far away on busses to have him pray over them. There is a shrine at the Mission Church where people whom Father McDonaugh has prayed over and healed have left their canes, crutches, and walkers. I had heard about him many, many times. He's a frail man, in his 80s. I understood that the service was a few hours long, much longer than a six-month-old could tolerate. But I wanted desperately to take Charlie, especially since he was just about to begin his journey on chemotherapy.

"I really want us to take Charlie to this service today," I informed John that morning.

"You can go. I'm not up for it," John replied quickly.

"What? Why not?" I asked, annoyed.

"Honey, I just don't want to. That's all. I don't. I'm not into that stuff," he answered seriously.

"Not into what?" I snapped.

"I don't go to healing services. I go to church. I pray. But I'm not into watching people fall backwards, and that kind of stuff."

"Honey, not everyone falls backwards!" I said, shaking my head in annoyance. "I really, really want us to take Charlie, and I want us to go together. My dad and Bebe want to go too," I added.

"Fine, you go. I *really* don't want to." He was adamant about it. I could feel the tears welling in my eyes. I turned on my heels and started walking out of the room.

"Fine, I'll take him myself," I fumed.

"What, so now you're mad because I don't want to go?" he snarled.

"No. Yes. Yes, I'm mad because I would do whatever it takes, and I mean *whatever* it takes, to cure Charlie of this disease. And if it means four hours out of our day to take him to a Mass, to have someone pray over him, I'll do it! I'd lie down and die if it would cure Charlie. I'd walk on glass, run through a fire, jump from a building; I'd do anything, *anything* that would help Charlie live! *That's* why I'm mad!" I said, glaring into his face.

My dad and Bebe were there, and were pretending not to hear anything. My sister had come over with her three kids to watch Jay. John stormed off upstairs as I raced around the house packing the diaper bag. As I snapped Charlie into his car seat and climbed into the back of my father's car, John raced out the door, jumped in the back seat, slammed the door, and didn't utter another word. He wasn't happy, but he was there. I knew that, beyond any shadow of a doubt, he too would do anything to save his child. I reached for his hand and whispered in his ear, "Thanks…and I'm sorry for freaking out."

The service was very engaging and highly emotional. The beauty of the church and the singing overwhelmed me. I had tears rolling down my face as I listened to Father McDonaugh address the congregation. I swayed back and forth to the music as I cradled Charlie in my arms. As I went to wipe a tear, I felt John's arm wrap around my shoulder. He didn't say a word, but leaned over and kissed my head. I was so glad he was at my side. After Mass, we waited close to a half hour in line to have Father McDonough pray over Charlie. Only we'd actually gotten into the wrong line! We never made it to Father McDonough. Instead, we were in line for the pastor of the church. It was too late and we couldn't get back in line. Charlie had had enough. As we approached the pastor he asked what our intentions were. With John's hand on my shoulder, I uttered through my tears, "Our baby has cancer. We want God to cure our baby of his disease. We want him to live," I cried. The pastor placed his hand on Charlie's head and began to pray. It only took a few seconds and we were done, but it felt good to know that we were doing whatever we could to cure Charlie of his disease.

Chapter 6
Treatment Begins

....

The First Day of Spring and Chemotherapy

The night before our first inpatient chemo treatment, I was a wreck. They had told me to pack "lots of onesies in case he throws up a lot" and a few "transitional toys" to make him feel comfortable being away from home. I ran around like a maniac packing just about every article of clothing I could find for both Charlie and myself. I also packed one entire LL Bean canvas bag full of stuffed animals, toys, a cassette player, and tapes, basically everything Charlie would enjoy and that would keep him occupied. I was avoiding going to bed that night at all costs, because I did not want the next day to arrive. I agonized over what was ahead of us. I didn't want my precious baby to get violently ill. I didn't want chemotherapy running through his six-month-old veins. I didn't want him to suffer. I didn't want his development to stop. He had all the energy of a normal six-month-old. He was trying to wiggle himself into an upright position. He laughed and giggled and smiled all day long.

His smile could melt anyone's heart. It was quite evident that this child loved life.

But it was inevitable; the next morning we'd be bringing Charlie into the hospital to have another operation so that a tube could be placed in his chest. And that afternoon, his tiny little body, weighing all of 20 pounds, would absorb toxic chemicals that we prayed would destroy the malignant cells in his body.

It was March 20, 2000, the first day of spring, and the first day of chemotherapy. We got up very early to get Jay ready for school. We had explained to him that Charlie was going to have to sleep at the hospital for a few nights to get some special medicines to help fix the boo-boo in his head.

"Why?" he asked quietly in his sweet three-year-old voice. "Why does he have to go to the hops-it-al?"

"Because the medicine he needs is real strong, and only the doctors and nurses can give it to him. But he'll be home in three days, and you'll have a special night with just Daddy tonight. Then you and I will have a special night tomorrow, and Choochie will be home the next day, after you get out of school." I explained it as best I could without trying to alarm him in any way.

"But I'll miss Chooch," Jay said, with tears welling up in his eyes. He loved his little brother so much. And even at his young age, he was very protective of him.

"He'll miss you, too, Sweetie, so much. But he really needs this special medicine." I felt a huge tug at my heart, and tried to stifle the lump growing in my throat.

Jay walked over to Charlie, knelt down next to his baby brother, kissed his cheek, and rubbed his bald little head.

"Wish Charlie good luck," I said, swallowing hard and quickly brushing a tear from my cheek.

"Good luck, C-Bear. I love you," he said. He then bent over one last time and placed a very gentle and loving kiss on the top of Charlie's head.

John and I made an agreement that one of us would always try to sleep at home with Jay whenever possible. We'd do our best to have him sleep in his own bed so that his routine was not disrupted and to let him know how special and important he was to us too.

Kristine picked Jay up and they were on their way. John loaded the car with four duffle bags, strapped Charlie in the car seat, and headed down the Massachusetts Turnpike to Boston. For most of the trip, we were silent. We were scared, very scared. The fear of the unknown was eating us up inside.

We met the general surgeon in the waiting room.

"I'm doctor so and so. I'll be implanting the Broviac central line. Now, I do have some papers for you to sign; please look these over," he grumbled. John rolled his eyes. Cripes, not another one. It was quite clear that this guy was lacking in the personality department.

The doctor explained in a matter of seconds the procedure for implanting the line. "We thread the line under his collar bone, and it runs right into his heart and exits right above his nipple," he explained. "Now, rarely, maybe once a year, we can't run it through the appropriate vein under the collar, and we have to cut into the jugular vein. But that's very rare," he continued.

"Yeah, well you're looking at Mister Rare," John chimed in. The doctor didn't even acknowledge the comment. I gave John a slight kick under the table.

"Well, we're all set here; he should be in the operating room in less than one hour."

The surgery seemed to fly by, lasting little more than an hour. The gruff doctor emerged from the OR scratching his head.

"Capodanno?" he yelled to the crowd in the waiting room. We jumped up. "Everything is fine. But for some reason, we couldn't run the line the way we wanted, so we did in fact have to make an incision in his neck. That's very rare," he said. I winked at John.

"Everything about Charlie is rare, believe me!" John replied.

After Charlie spent a few hours in the recovery room, he was moved to a room on 7 Medical, the wing of the hospital for pediatric inpatients. The rooms horrified me; they were very dark, very dreary, and everything seemed old.

"Ugh. This is gross. Nothing like at Children's. Look at that crib!" I was upset. The crib looked like it was about eighty years old; it was made of cold metal bars, like jail, and the sides were draped with thick plastic and covered with old, half-peeled-off stickers. Of course, the cribs at Children's were brand spanking new, and resembled a bassinet more than a jail cell. At that moment, I really missed the comforts and familiarity of Children's.

"You're a Children's snob," John joked. I didn't think it was funny. But he was right.

Suddenly, the door to the room flew open.

"Hi!" A perky young woman bounced in and said, "I'm Chris Wood, Charlie's primary nurse." She smiled and immediately rushed over to Charlie. Talking in baby talk, she said sweetly, "Look at you, handsome boy. Oh gosh, he's so cute. I love the babies. No one ever wants the babies, so I always sign up for them!" Charlie liked her right away. He gave her a big smile and started kicking his legs wildly. "We're going to start his chemo in about three hours. First we'll need to do his stats, then he'll get about one hour of pre-meds, then the chemo will run over eight hours."

She was rambling on as if we knew what the heck she was talking about. But she was great. Very friendly, very upbeat and you could tell that she loved children. "I'll go get his pre-meds going," she said.

When she returned, I bombarded her with questions.

"What are the pre-meds for? How sick will he get from the chemo? What can you give him when he gets sick? How bad will it be? Will he be in pain? What does chemo look like? Can he feel it in his veins? I'm planning to sleep with him in that crib. Do you see many brain tumors? Do kids with brain tumors...live?"

"Ah," she laughed. "New Hem/Onc parents; gotta love them!" I guess she had heard all my questions a hundred times before. She did her best to answer all of them and was very calm and reassuring.

John needed to leave by seven o'clock so that he'd be home for Jay. I was terrified to see him go, because I was so afraid of how sick Charlie might get once they administered the chemotherapy.

"You'll do great, Mommy," he said, kissing my head. "Be good, little man. You're a strong boy, and take care of Mommy." He held Charlie tight. And then he left.

Chris came in carrying a glass bottle with a black "danger" symbol marking the clear liquid inside.

"Chemo?" I asked nervously as I felt the blood drain from my face.

"Yup, sure is!" she said cheerfully. She was wearing gloves and a mask and her body was covered in a yellow smock.

"Gloves and a mask. That can't be good," I commented. I was scared.

"Of course I have to wear gloves; this stuff is baaad," she laughed. But realizing I was getting anxious, she tried to make light of the situation.

"Ah, no, come on, this is the stuff that's going to make him all better. He needs it; it's good stuff, really. Gotta kill those bad cells, right?" She tried to sound comforting in her Boston accent. But I still was reacting to the fact that the bottle had a black "dangerous" symbol on it. My heart sank.

"This is going to be bad, isn't it?" I asked, my eyes filling with tears.

"No, no, don't be sad. It won't be that bad, I promise. It's not like you see in the movies, I swear. Really, it's not that bad. And if he does get sick, we'll give him something to make him feel better," she said, smiling. She hung the bottle, pressed the numbers on the IV pump, and waited for a minute to make sure it was going. Then she was paged to another room. "Oh God," I thought, "don't leave me in this room alone." I thought once the chemo hit Charlie's body, he'd become violently ill.

"I'll be back. You're fine." She promised. By now it was about 9 p.m. I sat rocking Charlie back and forth in the rocking chair, just slowly watching the toxic chemicals drip from the bottle into the IV line that was implanted in his heart. I watched and I waited. And I prayed. My heart was pounding as I stared at the clear liquid dripping. I watched. I waited. And I cried.

"*Blah!*" Charlie gurgled as I felt the vomit hit my chest and chin. It was pitch black in the room; the only light was spilling in from under the closed door. "*Blah!*" He swung his head back. This time, the vomit splattered down my thighs, landing all over my feet.

We must have dozed off at some point during the night. The nurses had been in and out of the room every hour to check on us, but at this point, there was no one there but me and my baby boy.

"Cripes!" I yelled. "Where's that nurses' bell?" I struggled to keep Charlie upright as I slid on the puddle of puke on the floor and reached for the crib to catch my balance.

This violent vomiting episode lasted a solid 15 minutes. I managed to change his clothes in the dark as I sobbed tears of despair and disbelief for what my child's tiny body had to endure. Somehow Charlie fell back to sleep. The overnight nurse increased the anti-nausea medication.

142

This same scene happened twice more that night. At first I tried to sleep with him in the jail crib, then finally gave up and brought him into the parent bed with me, which was really not allowed.

"God, please," I begged. "Let him feel better. Please. Please Jesus. Let him live, please. He's just a baby," I said, crying myself to sleep. The agony of witnessing my child's violent and painful reaction to the poison that was racing through his precious veins drained me to sheer exhaustion.

John was in bright and early the next morning. He could tell the second he walked into the room what kind of night we had had. But Charlie woke with a huge smile on his face, gobbled down his bottle and a jar of pears for breakfast, and greeted every new doctor and nurse with a glorious smile.

Fortunately, Charlie had a better night with his daddy. It was my turn to stay at home, but I didn't sleep a wink. I just couldn't get my mind off of what was going on at the hospital. I checked on Jay more than twenty times that night, and finally just crawled right into bed with him so I could feel his little body next to mine. I spent the night watching his chest rise and fall; I just wanted to see him breathe.

I dropped Jay off at school the next morning, arming him with a box of munchkins to share with his little friends. "Choochie will be home today!" we cheered, as we walked into school. I raced down the Expressway to the hospital. Charlie would still be getting chemo today, but if all went well, we'd be out of there by early afternoon. He was holding up amazingly well, continually smiling and cooing at every person he met on our many, many walks through the halls to kill time. He *loved* to be carried around. John held him high on his shoulder, and I pushed that damn pole that held bottles of chemotherapy and much needed fluids. I came to refer to it playfully as "Our third child."

Finally, at around three o'clock, we were released. Chris made up an entire weekly chart for us so we would know when to give Charlie the various medications.

"This is nuts," I protested. We would be administering six different medications to him, ten times a day!

"And don't forget his GCSF shots, every day, at the exact same time, and his dressing changes, and his flushes, and his mouth care," she drilled us. "And this is the anti-nausea prescription, and don't forget the seizure medication from Children's, and this is Bactrim to prevent pneumonia... he needs that every Monday, Tuesday, and Wednesday," and she went on and on.

"I'll never remember all this!" I shook my head. This was not only a lot to remember, it was a big responsibility. "We're stopping at Staples on the way home," I informed John.

"Why?" he questioned.

"We've got to get organized," I replied. So we stopped and purchased a wall-sized "write on/wipe off" board, which took up one entire wall in our home. We used it to track his medications, dressing changes, mouth-care cleanings, what days he needed shots, what days he needed certain drugs, what days we had doctors' appointments, and what weeks we had chemo. This "wall" became our bible. We lived by it, referencing it numerous times throughout the day and night. And if you happened to forget to mark down a dosage or dressing change, you were in trouble with the head nurse – me!

Mommy Puts Her Foot Down into a Puddle of Blood

Charlie's next inpatient chemo was, regretfully, even more eventful and taxing on our emotions than the first round. We'd waited six hours just to be admitted to a room. Needless to say, my nerves were shot by that point. I was by myself with Charlie. He was hooked up to his pole, just getting fluids until the chemo was ready. A new nurse, whom we'd never worked with before, entered the room. As we conversed, Charlie dozed off in my arms. The young nurse leaned over to switch the tubing (line) of the IV bag, turned around and left the room. I sat back onto a rocking chair, cradling my little boy in my arms. The frustration from the waiting overtook me, and I closed my eyes for what seemed to be about 20 minutes for a quick rest. I was awakened by a noise in the hallway that startled me. I tried to adjust my position in the rocking chair, pushing back against my feet. Instantly I slipped backwards, almost missing the seat of the rocker.

"What the..." I said under my breath. I felt wetness at my ankle. I looked down and saw that my entire right sneaker was completely covered in a pool of blood. *Charlie's* blood! "HELP!" I yelled, and my scream woke Charlie from his sound sleep.

The new nurse came running into the room.

"Oops," she said softly as she bent over to retrieve the end of the IV line that had landed on the dirty floor. It had unscrewed from another part of the line causing it to "back up," drawing blood right out of Charlie's chest.

"Is this bad, is this dangerous?" I questioned frantically.

"No, ah, well...wait a minute," she said, looking back and forth at the two ends of IV line. It was evident by the look of confusion on her face that she was definitely unsure of what she should do. She grabbed the end of the tubing that was still attached to Charlie's chest and tugged the two ends closer as she tried to screw them back together.

"*Wait!* What are you *doing? That was just on the floor!* It's *dirty!*" I yelled. Mary Beth, one of our favorite nurses, heard the commotion and raced into the room. "Mary Beth, that was on the floor; should he be hooked back up to that?" I asked, horrified.

"No!" she answered, shooting a dagger-laden look at the young nurse who lowered her head and scurried out the door.

"She...she was going to reattach that to the line in his chest!" I was furious. Mary Beth assured me that the pool of blood on the floor looked worse than it was, and that he had not lost all that much blood or anything dangerous like that. "He's fine," she reassured me, squeezing my shoulder. I wasn't so sure the young nurse would be fine, though. I had really lit into her. I am an understanding woman, I really am. And I know everyone makes mistakes. But to pick the IV line off the dirty hospital floor and actually consider reattaching it to a patient was inexcusable. I wasn't even a nurse and I knew that! Pam, the nurse supervisor, poked her head in.

"Mrs. Capodanno, I apologize. That should never have happened. It must have been very scary for you. Please know that it will not happen again." She tried to calm my nerves. "Is there anything I can do for you to make you more comfortable?" she offered.

"Pam, I'm sorry. I know we all make mistakes. But I don't want that nurse on Charlie's team anymore. She may be a nice girl, and she may be a good nurse, but I don't want her to work with my son again," I said adamantly. And I meant it. My defenses were up. And I didn't care if I was offending people or not. I wasn't in this to win the favorite mother competition. My job was to protect my child.

During our following Monday visit, I had mentioned to the nurse that Charlie was still rubbing the side of his head, which was completely freaking me out, since to me, this was his way of letting me know he had a massive tumor waiting to hemorrhage in there. They called down the head of otolaryngology, who was the sweetest guy.

"Yup, just what I suspected," he said seriously as he peeked inside Charlie's ear. My heart sank. What could he see? Another tumor, I thought.

"Wax. And major fluid building up!" he smiled. "I suggest we place tubes in there. We can do it real soon, get it out of the way, real fast," he offered.

"Ugh." John and I looked at each other.

"It's really not a big deal," the doctor said.

"Yeah, we know, it's not a big deal after eight hours of brain surgery, but it's the third one in two months," John replied.

Surgery Number Three

We scheduled the surgery for the next Monday when he'd be admitted for chemo.

"I'll have him in and out of here in no time," Dr. Volk, the otolaryngologist, informed us.

"Well, don't feel you have to rush, we're here for the next four days," I joked.

"This will be a walk in the park for you folks. Make yourselves comfortable, and I'll meet you in the waiting room very soon." With that, he scooped Charlie up and disappeared. John suggested we grab something to eat.

"I'm not leaving," I said to John.

"Honey," John said, "he's getting tubes dropped in his ears. Nothing is going to happen. We've gone through worse."

"Yeah, we have, and look what happened the last time you needed a snack. Remember Newton-Wellesley?" I smirked, reminding him how we left for seven minutes and Charlie stopped breathing.

"Come on, I'm starving," John said, grabbing my elbow and directing me down the hall.

We took the elevator down to the first floor and grabbed milk, two muffins and a cup of tea at Au Bon Pain. We sat down, and I had just lifted the cover off my teacup when I heard the tail end of a page over the load speaker. "Capodanno, please report back to Day Surgery." I literally jumped out of my chair, spilling John's drink.

"Did you hear that?" I yelled with a mouth full of muffin.

"What?" John looked at me as if I had three heads.

"I just heard our name over the load speaker!" I grabbed my purse and ran as fast as I could toward the elevator. John, still wanting to eat, grabbed our food and chased me. Then we heard it again. "Would the parents of Charlie Capodanno please report back to surgery," the voice instructed. I grabbed my mouth in my hands.

"What could have happened?" I panicked. Now I had John worried. Our hearts were pounding. We couldn't have been gone more than fifteen minutes in total from when we handed him over in the pre-op. I practically slammed my body down on the nurse's station.

"What happened? Where's Charlie, my son?" I was shaking. Just then, Dr. Volk came out of the OR.

"Hey guys!" he chirped, with a huge smile on his face. "We're all set, piece of cake, takes no time," he smiled. When he saw the look of horror on our faces, his facial expression changed.

"What's wrong?" he asked sincerely.

"Oh…it's just…did you need to call us over the PA system? We thought it was an emergency," I said, rolling my head back.

"She's a real drama queen," John added.

"I wasn't *always* this way," I defended myself. "It's just the cancer thing. It kind of makes a mother a little nuts!"

A Terrifying Scare

After taking off two months through the Family Leave Act, it was time for John to return to work, which he dreaded. But since he carried our health benefits, and since we needed an income, he really had no choice.

It was a Thursday morning. John had gotten up early for his first day back, and he thought it would be a nice idea for him to drop Jay off at school. I got up about a half hour after John left. Charlie normally was like clockwork, never sleeping past 6:00 a.m., even after his major surgery.

I looked up at the clock. It was almost 7:00 a.m. I was surprised that Charlie was not awake but thought that after the last round of chemo, perhaps he needed more rest. I walked up to his crib about ten times within a half hour to check on him. Finally, at 8:00 a.m., out of sheer concern, I scooped him up into my arms. He didn't wake instantly, which terrified me. His eyelids did not move at all.

"Charlie." I began gently shaking him. "Charlie!" My voice rose and my bottom lip began to quiver. I could see he was breathing, but he was not waking. After a solid minute, he slowly opened one eye, and then the other, and then shut them both. He was extremely lethargic, as if he was drugged. I carried him downstairs and propped him on my shoulder. "Maybe he needs some fluids. Don't panic," I told myself. I quickly heated up a bottle and tried to feed him. He managed to take a few effortless sips, but he continued to lay limp and seemingly lifeless in my arms. The clinic wasn't due to open for another ten minutes, so we sat down on the couch to wait and I prayed. Charlie instantly threw up all over me.

"Please, please, God, let this just be the chemo catching up to him," I begged. I kept thinking back to when Charlie would always throw up that morning bottle, which we later found out might have been an indication that he had something wrong with him. I dialed the clinic at 8:30 a.m. on the dot.

"Mary Jo," I said, fighting to keep my composure. "It's Charlie. He's very, very lethargic. He finally opened his eyes after about 10 minutes of my rubbing his back and trying to feed him. He just threw up...he's very droopy...he, um, he can't seem to hold up his head...but he is breathing..." My voice trailed off.

"Is he alert enough for you to bring him in? Or should you call an ambulance?" she questioned. At this point, he was still limp, but his eyes were open and he was making eye contact with me. He looked incredibly pale and fragile.

"No, I don't think I need an ambulance," I answered. But the thought of driving him in there alone without being with him in the back seat terrified me.

"Where's John?" she asked.

"Oh my God, today is his first day back to work!" I gasped. I didn't want to alarm him just yet until I knew what was wrong. I decided I wasn't going to contact him until I had gotten Charlie to the hospital to be seen.

Without changing him from his feetsie-PJs, I fled down the Pike doing about 90 miles an hour. By the time I reached the clinic, Charlie had once again dozed off, and it was difficult to arouse him. The minute he finally mustered up the strength to open his eyes, a horrific vomiting episode began. Instead of trying to work so hard to keep that vomit from getting all over us, I just draped myself with towels and allowed him to throw up as he needed. At first I tried to convince myself it was a delayed reaction to the chemo.

When the oncologist on clinic duty arrived, she looked extremely concerned.

"Could this just be an accumulation of the chemo he had last week?" I asked, with my knees shaking.

"Well, it could be. Actually it could be a few things. One, he could have a stomach bug. But it doesn't look like any stomach bug I've ever seen. Or two, it could be the chemo, but it's very rare that he would have such a delayed reaction. Usually they get sick right away. Or three, well, the tumor could have grown back." I felt a terrifying chill rush up my spine as I shook my head in disbelief. I *never* expected to hear her say that.

Once again, my world stopped spinning and I was frozen in my own body. Sure, I thought he was sick with something, but never in a million years would I have thought a tumor could have grown back so quickly. Here it was, less than two months after the eight-hour surgery to remove the original tumor. I was absolutely crushed by her words. In sheer panic, I rocked Charlie uncontrollably in a rocker, stroking and kissing his head frantically.

"I need...I need to get in touch with my husband right now," I sniffled.

John arrived a half hour later.

"What the hell's going on?" he asked with deep concern in his voice. He knew something must have been really wrong because the receptionist had to page him to tell him to come to the clinic immediately. He was scared. I was pertified.

Once again, I was faced with delivering terrifying news to my husband.

"Well, it could be a bunch of things, the chemo, a bug, or, she said maybe it could be the tumor again," I gulped, with my eyes immediately welling up with tears.

"Nooo...it couldn't be...it just couldn't be." He shook his head back and forth. The doctor walked by the room. "Dr. Pelidis, what do you think this is?" John asked, frantically.

"As I told your wife, we can't be certain. But we need to run some tests immediately. The nurse is scheduling an MRI right now," she said. Hearing that they were preparing to do an MRI immediately clearly indicated something could be gravely wrong. He actually had an MRI scheduled for the following Monday. "We just can't wait until Monday," the doctor said.

"Oh my God, they must think the tumor could be back. Why else would they do an MRI immediately?" I whispered to John through my tears.

It was 6:00 p.m. and we were still waiting in the clinic. The plan was to have Charlie admitted overnight for round-the-clock observation, and then we'd have the MRI first thing in the morning. Friday morning.

Both John and I stayed in the hospital that night. Once again afraid of the unknown, we desperately needed to be together. Our bodies and our minds were completely numb just as they had been before. We'd felt this intense fear and pain only a few short weeks earlier, and never thought we'd feel this way again, at least not so soon. How could this be happening? Did they not remove the entire tumor even though they thought they did? Could the tumor grow back so soon? Was the chemo not working at all? We knew if that were the case, there'd be no hope at all for survival. The Grim Reaper had convinced us of that fact. "If the tumor doesn't respond to the chemo, there's nothing else to do," we had been told.

"This just can't be happening, it just can't be," I repeated over and over as the emotional roller coaster that controlled our life once again took a terrifying downward spiral.

Good Friday

As exhausted as we were, we couldn't sleep. We sat there, just staring at Charlie as he slept. We didn't talk much. The only noise to be heard was the sound of the IV pump quietly ticking through the night. I spent every minute praying as hard as I could, begging God to not let it be the tumor again. "Please, Jesus, don't take him from us, please. Don't let it be the tumor. Please. I promise he'll make a difference on this earth if You let him live. I promise."

We saw the sunrise from outside the hospital window. Our scan was scheduled for 10 a.m. that morning. John and I barely spoke because neither one of us wanted to engage in a "what if" conversation. Nor did either of us have the strength to comfort or console the other.

Charlie seemed more alert, but still looked very weak and pale. They allowed him a few sips of water before the scan, but that was it. At 9:00 a.m. I climbed up into the crib with him just to hold his beautiful, tiny, frail body next to mine. Since I hadn't slept the night before, I was exhausted. I was sitting upright in the crib with my back against the metal jail bars at the head of the crib. Charlie had fallen asleep on my thighs. Again, I began praying, asking God to let the MRI show nothing but good results. Usually saying my prayers calmed my nerves, but I was too much of a wreck at this moment to allow for any calmness.

"Please," I pleaded. "Please let the chemo be working. Please don't take Charlie from us," I begged as I blinked a few tears from my eyes, and finally allowed them to close. I could hear the subtle noises of the activity going on in the hallway, but my brain and my body had succumbed to the exhaustion.

I was in a state of semi-consciousness, when a vision crept into my mind. What I saw was a figure of a hand wearing a gray glove reaching downward. As I fell deeper into sleep, my head fell forward sharply, and I woke up. Startled, I looked over, and John was asleep on the bed. Charlie was still asleep in my lap, resting his head on my thigh.

"What was that glove?" I muttered to myself through my grogginess. I again closed my eyes, and continued to pray, "Please Jesus, don't take him, please, let him stay..." I again fell into a deep sleep. In my dream, an elderly woman appeared to me wearing a gray suit. I couldn't see her face — only her back. She had a thick mop of gray hair, and she appeared to be stomping her feet.

"He's coming to Jesus," a female voice whispered softly but swiftly.

"No!" another female voice, this one deeper, quickly responded. "Not yet." A cold chill ran up my neck, and I instantly woke up and shot straight up in the crib. I had drool coming down my cheek. My body was drenched in sweat and I was shaking uncontrollably. I looked around the room. Although I had startled Charlie when I jumped, he repositioned himself and returned to sleep. Everything in the room appeared to be in order, and I could hear the hustle and bustle of the hallway activity outside the door.

"What's going on?" I wondered to myself, searching the room for clues, answers, anything. Who was that woman? I wasn't sure. I wanted the woman to come back, because I had more questions. I closed my eyes and tried to envision her again. But she was gone and didn't reappear. What did the voice mean, "Not yet"? And whose voices were they? I was afraid. My heart was pounding and I had to remind myself to breathe. How should I interpret the message? And who sent it to me?

John had dozed off, but woke when the nurse entered the room to prepare Charlie for his MRI.

"Why are you shaking like this," he asked. I just shrugged my shoulders and walked out of the room. I was too shaken at that point to mention it to John. I knew what had happened was real, and I was terrified.

The MRI took about an hour and a half. The three of us hung around the room for about five hours after the scan, anxiously awaiting the results. We paced back and forth trying not to show our fear to Charlie. John flicked through the remote control, changing channels about 50 times a minute. By then, Charlie's vomiting had subsided, and they were thinking about letting us go home. John and I stood firm: we did not want to leave the hospital without results of the MRI.

There was a knock at the door. It was Dr. Grodman, another one of the oncologists from the clinic who specialized in bone marrow transplants and leukemia.

"Hey folks, I just sat down with the radiologist," he began. John had Charlie in his arms, and we both slowly sat back down on the edge of the parent bed.

"Well, what's the news?" I asked anxiously, rubbing my hands nervously across my face and neck. He could see the fear burning in our eyes.

"Oh, oh, it's good news, great news actually. Well, most of it. No, but its great news! Anyway, the spots that Charlie still has on his brain, the two spots that we can still see, well, they're definitely shrinking...we can see it on the scan. They're shrinking quite impressively, I might add. This is terrific news!"

We were still completely stone-faced as he looked at us. As he delivered this extraordinary news, we did not so much as blink an eyelash in response.

"Hello? Well, are you guys psyched or what?" he asked, looking at us strangely, awaiting some kind of reaction.

"Yeah, that's great, it really is," John replied softly with no inflection in his voice. We were just too numb to react. Since the day the Grim

Reaper gave us the grave news of Charlie's chances for survival, we had begun building our "wall of defense." We needed to protect our feelings, our hearts, our baby, and ourselves. Our emotions had been completely drained; we had hardly any reserves left. And once the sky falls down on you, no matter how optimistic you want to be, in the far corners of your mind, your guard is always up to protect yourself in case, just in case, the sky begins to fall again.

"What's the other news?" I muttered, not sure if I wanted to know.

"Oh yeah, right. Well, his temporal horn is backing up, causing his spinal fluid to pool in his left ventricle. He may need to have a shunt put in," Dr. Grodman said bluntly.

Again, dead silence.

"Guys?" Dr. Grodman said.

"What's a shunt?" I asked, staring blankly into his eyes.

"Oh, it's like plumbing for the brain, to help drain the fluid," he described playfully. "I've paged Dr. Heilman, our neurosurgeon, to come down and talk to you about it. We know Charlie's neurosurgeon is at Children's, but at least Dr. Heilman can give you more information on what we believe needs to be done."

Dr. Heilman was a handsome young man with very gentle mannerisms. He stopped by the room to explain to us the situation with Charlie's spinal fluid. "He's got a trapped temporal horn in the lateral ventricle," he began. I looked at him with a very confused look on my face.

"Ah, his spinal fluid is backing up and getting trapped in his brain. It is more than likely being caused by scarring from the surgery. I would recommend a VP shunt placement. If the fluid continues pooling, the pressure will cause a great deal of pain, and it can be dangerous," he explained. I fixed my eyes on Charlie's little head. "Oh, he's not in any danger right now, but I would take care of this as soon as possible," he said. We informed him that we appreciated his insight, but we'd more than likely have his surgery done over at Children's. We felt strongly we wanted Dr. Goumnerova to continue to handle his brain surgeries.

"Please take no offense," I said, slightly embarrassed. I never wanted to hurt anyone's feelings. And I certainly didn't want this man to think we didn't feel he was a competent surgeon.

"None taken. Don't worry about it," Dr. Heilman said. "Let me know if I can help out in any way," he added, extending his hand.

Both doctors exited the room, and John and I were left alone with Charlie.

"So that's awesome news," John said quietly, running his fingers through his jet-black hair.

"Ya, definitely, it definitely is. I know. It's weird that we aren't jumping for joy. Because it is the best news," I replied in my zombie-like state.

"It's all way too much, you know, after the day from hell we just had yesterday," John added.

I was still sitting on the parent bed, just staring at Charlie, when I felt an immediate desire to break through the numbness and thank God for once again answering our prayers. I felt a smile come across my face.

"He is a miracle, you know that? He survived his surgery, and now we know the chemo is working, and the tumor is shrinking. Our prayers are being heard and answered," I continued. I grabbed John's hand, realizing something very magical had happened.

"Oh my God, do you know what today is?" I gasped.

"Friday?" John guessed.

"Not just any Friday, Honey. Today is Good Friday. And we just got the most miraculous news on one of the holiest days of the year. Unbelievable." I could feel tears welling in my eyes. "Thank you, Jesus, thank you," I said, raising my eyes and hands to the ceiling.

Chapter 7
Our Not-So-Normal Life

Go, Auntie, Go

My sister Kel ran in the Boston Marathon in honor of Charlie. She didn't have time to do a great deal of training in less than two short months, but she was bound and determined to run. She's a runner anyway, and has been for years. But this was more than a marathon for her. This was a mission of love. And as she trained during the months and days leading up to the event, while she ran in the rain and the cold, and when her bum knee began to ache, she'd immediately think of Charlie, and it would give her the strength and the desire to keep going.

"I swear," she confessed, "I run for hours and I cry the minute I leave the driveway until the minute I finish. I think about him with every stride I take. He's my inspiration."

The morning of the Marathon, we went to cheer her on in her hometown of Hopkinton where the 26-mile race to Boston begins. But we missed her in the massive crowd of runners. We were so disappointed not to be able to cheer her on. So we dashed home, and for hours, continued to flip through every single news channel to see if we could catch a glimpse of her during the broadcast footage. Although the chances were slim, we kept watching. Right before the news was about to end, from the corner of the screen, we could see her coming up a hill, approaching Kenmore Square.

"There she is," I screamed, jumping off the couch. "Look, it's Auntie!" Kel ran right up to the camera and pulled the front of her shirt right into the camera's lens. She had a beautiful color photo of Charlie on her shirt, with big, bold letters across her chest. "Go Charlie," it said. "I love you, Chooch," she said into the camera, and without breaking her stride, she kept going. "People cheered 'Go Charlie' the entire 26 miles," Kel later informed us. For my birthday, which was two weeks later, she had her Marathon shirt with her official Marathon number and her medal framed in a custom-made box frame and engraved with the inscription, "For Charlie, the most courageous little boy to crawl the earth. You are truly a miracle and have taught me so much. Love, Auntie Kel."

Paging Dr. Mommy and Dr. Daddy!

Once treatments started, our house was overloaded with medical supplies. We stashed them everywhere. Everything was stored neatly in Rubbermaid containers and labeled. Our diaper bags were overflowing with gauze, surgical tape, syringes, medicine droppers, bottles of medication, and a pair of plastic clamps, just in case Charlie's central line ever broke. The worst-hit room was definitely our dining room, which resembled the OR on the hit television show *MASH*.

By this time, we had gotten into a groove of sorts, flushing his line with ease in the morning and evening, and although I protested doing the dressing changes in the beginning, I finally decided it was my time to do it. Of course, both John and I had to be there, one to do the actual dressing change, the other to hold Charlie's hands and arms so that he wouldn't contaminate the site. He was exceptionally patient while sitting through the dressing changes. John and I watched every step the other person took to administer the change.

"Oh, no, you forgot the Betadine," I'd inform him.

"Oh, crap, you forgot to swipe with the alcohol wipes before I connected the syringe!" He'd yell. Mistakes in the early days were terrifying. The nurses put the fear of God in us. "Never get the site wet, never get it dirty, and always swipe that line three times before screwing in the syringe." I hated that central line. *Hated* it! The fact that it was attached to his heart and just dangled from his chest freaked me out. And I was petrified it would get pulled out. I warned everyone who picked him up to hug him, "Watch the line. Make sure it doesn't pull!"

One night, early on, I was flushing the line by myself and it wouldn't flush. "Don't panic," I thought. I tried again, pushing with a bit more force on the syringe. No luck. *"John!"* I yelled frantically. He came rushing to my side. "It won't flush. Does this mean there's a clog? Does it mean it's not working? Should we call the nurse?" I was a wreck.

"Calm down, let me try it," which he did, to no avail.

We had no idea what could be wrong with the line. All we knew was that if it didn't flush, it was a problem, potentially a very big problem.

"All right, Honey, relax. Let's call the VNA (Visiting Nurses Association) hotline to see what they say," John said calmly. I was scared that something like a blood clot in his heart could be causing it not to flush properly. I dialed the number, and quickly tossed John the phone. I didn't want to hear what could potentially be wrong. I paced up and down until I heard John talking. He held the phone to his ear with his chin, and followed the instructions the nurse was providing to him over the phone.

"Yup, the syringe is screwed on right. Nope, the tubing isn't twisted at all." He answered all her questions, and waited for further directions. I sat in a dining room chair, holding Charlie down by the arms, kissing his forehead. "All right," John said, trying again. "Nope, damn, it still won't flush. Okay, I'll do that, hold on," and placing one hand to hold the syringe securely, he used the other hand to pull back on the clear syringe, rather than trying to push it forward with the heparin. When he pulled back, the syringe immediately filled with blood.

"*Oh my God!*" I screamed. I thought for sure we'd just about killed our baby. To see his blood swirling down the entire length of the central line and pooling into the syringe was enough to make me almost pass out! Not that I had a fear of blood, but I thought we must have done something terribly wrong to be drawing blood from his heart!

"What did you just do?" I yelled, with a look of horror across my face.

"Shhh." John waved his hand at me to be quiet as he waited to hear further instructions. "Yup, it worked," John said, nodding his head in response to whatever the nurse was saying. "Honey, it was supposed to do that; it means its working." I heard him laugh, "No, she's fine, she just thought I had drained his entire body of blood." He smiled, shaking his head at me. "Thanks for your help. We'll have the line looked at tomorrow." He continued to shake his head.

"What?" I pouted. "Oh, I'm supposed to know that drawing blood from his heart is a good thing? Sorry. I'm not an expert in nursing." I was being totally defensive and sounding like a brat. But hey, it's not every day you think you've just about killed your child on your dining room table!

Our Precious Jay Bird

John and I talked at length about how it was so important for us to keep Jay's life as normal and happy as we possibly could. We both were in agreement that we were not going to allow cancer to destroy a joyful childhood for either of our children. We didn't want Charlie's disease to dictate our lives.

Although Jay was very young, not even three, he was very bright and very curious about everything.

"Mommy, what's this?" he'd ask about every single, solitary piece of medical supply equipment we had in the house.

"A syringe, heparin, dressing changes, gauze," I'd answer. Of course, just naming the product didn't do it for him. And we wanted to be honest with him, without scaring him and without giving him too much information. The questions never stopped: "Why does Charlie have that tube? Why can he only get the special medicine in the hospital? Can I help with the dressing changes? Can I flush the line? Does that hurt him? Do I need shots? When can he take a bath with me again?"

Jay's feelings were always a priority for all of us. As much as we wanted his daily life to remain normal and happy, we also wanted to make certain that he never felt slighted, left out, or any less important or loved. Most people always remembered to send Jay a gift when sending one for Charlie. But it was hard when we bumped into people at church, or the grocery store, or at school, because the first question anyone asked, even when Jay was with us, was, "So, how's Charlie doing?" It was natural for people to ask about Charlie, but I always felt bad for Jay. I'd answer by saying, "He's fine. He's doing well. And Jay's doing great too!" I overcompensated to the point where it was obnoxious. But I was very sensitive to Jay's feelings, and I often wondered how he felt when people only asked about his brother. Jay knew Charlie had boo-boos but that was it. I actually used to call certain people who would be coming to visit and ask them to please make a big deal of Jay before asking about Charlie. Jay never ever gave any sign that his feelings were hurt, that he was ever left out, or that he was ever feeling sad about anything. I think it was honestly more me, that I worried too much about his feelings.

The only time I ever saw him behave as if he had felt jilted was once when we were at Mass and our favorite usher named Irish began walking over to us as we were filing into our pew. Jay was very fond of Irish, because he was very friendly and always shook the boys' hands. Jay was sitting closest to the aisle, with a huge smile on his face. He wanted to say hi to his friend Irish. But not knowing he was doing it, Irish looked right past Jay, reaching out his hand to touch Charlie. "Hey, big boy! How's my Charlie Bear doing?" Irish grinned, shaking the baby's hand. I could see Jay's smile slowly turn into a frown, and he sunk into the pew, lowering his head. My heart sank and I scooped Jay up into my arms.

"Oh, Irish," I immediately reacted. "Did you see how big Jay is getting? He's mommy's big, big boy!" Irish realized what had just transpired.

"Hey, hey, Jay. How's my buddy doing?" he said, rubbing Jay's head with his hand. And with that, Jay's smile returned as he gave Irish a big high-five.

Jay always kept us laughing, especially when showing us the world through his three-year-old eyes. One afternoon, John decided to surprise Charlie and me at the clinic during one of our outpatient treatments by bringing Jay in after school. The hospital garage stairwell absolutely reeked of urine. It made me sick every time I entered it. I would try to hold my breath and run down the seven flights of stairs to avoid inhaling the stench. (God forbid the elevator in the garage should work!) Anyhow, the maintenance crew forever tried to mask the foul odor with a repulsive combination of a sweet-smelling deodorizer and bleach. It was bogus. The day John carried Jay down the stairs, Jay announced,

"Mmm, daddy, it smells like candy in here! Like Sweet Tarts! Daddy, can you buy me some Sweet Tarts?"

John was laughing so hard that he almost dropped Jay.

Even when his brother had pushed him to the limit, Jay always kept his composure. "Mom," he asked politely after Charlie had ripped a toy right out of his hands, "is Charlie ever going to turn into a sister?" When I answered him with a "No, Honey," he replied, "Well, where can I buy one then?"

Jay was a constant reminder for us to see the good in every single day. His innocence kept us grounded and he was such a ray of sunshine even on the darkest days.

The Chemo Spill

Our May inpatient chemotherapy was another one for the record books. We were in for four straight days and three nights. Jay came in for a visit on day three. He thought the hospital was the best – tons of toys in the playroom, endless long hallways to run through, and free Popsicles 24/7. My mother-in-law had come in for a visit, and although we'd never done it before, we left Charlie alone with her for an hour as he slept so that John and I could spend some time together with just Jay. We went for a walk in the Boston Public Garden, showed him the Swan Boats, fed the ducks and had a little picnic. Breathing the fresh spring air outside the hospital was heavenly. And just watching Jay run around was so peaceful. He too was such a gift from God. Having to drag ourselves back into the hospital after feeling "free" for a few hours was a total bummer.

"I feel like a prisoner heading back to jail after a day release pass," John joked.

By the fourth day, we were exhausted and cranky, and we just wanted to get the hell out of the confines of that hospital. On day four of treatments, Charlie received a chemo known as VP 16, which can cause hypotension. This meant the nurses needed to check his blood pressure every 15 minutes as the chemo was administered. It meant we couldn't go for walks; couldn't escape to the playroom. We were trapped in his room with a blood pressure cuff wrapped around his ankle, which was attached to another machine. Needless to say, this didn't make for a happy Charlie, Mom or Dad.

"Cool, only 16 more cc's and we can bust out of this joint," I said, as I scurried around the room, packing up. John was standing in the doorway with Charlie, watching all the people walking by. He leaned over the parent bed to pass Charlie to me so he could run our bags to the car, when suddenly the IV line pulled out at one of the connector locations.

We both looked down and saw clear fluid creating a small puddle on the floor.

"Oh crap, that's the chemo!" I leaned over to retrieve the line.

We yelled out to the first nurse who walked by.

"Um, the line pulled out at the connector, and that's chemo," John said, pointing calmly to the floor. The nurse's eyes showed her alarm. She clamped off the line closest to Charlie's heart, grabbed a mask and gloves, and yelled loudly for back-up. We were immediately ordered out of the room, and heard a loud page for the maintenance department to come to our floor *stat*. Baffled, John and I remained in the hallway watching the commotion inside our room. Suddenly a man appeared wearing head-to-toe protection, consisting of a rubber suit, boots, mask and gloves. It reminded me of the outfit Homer Simpson wears at the Springfield nuclear power plant! The man cleaned the entire room from one corner to the other, removing all the furniture, bedding, luggage, tables, telephones - everything.

My jaw was on the floor. John was equally horrified. The entire staff was in a panic because a few drops of chemo leaked out, and *this* is the same liquid poison that was flowing through our little baby's veins. It was an incredibly eerie feeling.

"That's some toxic stuff!" John said. My stomach turned.

The Saints and Rosary Beads Come Marching In

Our late May MRI was particularly nerve-racking. John and I both went down to the MRI room with Charlie. I sometimes drove the anesthesiologists crazy. I would question everything they did, everything they gave him. I told them a hundred times in six minutes that during his first spinal he had stopped breathing. You name it; I drilled it into their heads. Also, I insisted that I go into the MRI room with Charlie. The anesthesiologist protested.

"Nothing will happen, Mrs. Capodanno, and it can actually be dangerous for you to be in there," he insisted.

"I need to be in there with him. I've always gone in with him. I promise you, if an emergency arises, you have my word I will stay out of your way."

"This is against my better judgment, but okay," the doctor said, rolling his eyes. Once again, I watched as they prepared his tiny body for the procedure. As instructed, I put the earplugs in my ears. I cuddled up in the chair with a blanket, and as the procedure began, I clutched my rosary beads and began to cry quietly. It was so heart-wrenching to see Charlie sedated, covered in tubes and strapped to a table.

Once the doctors left the room, I would begin praying out loud. I prayed to my favorite patron saints, St. Theresa, St. Jude and St. Anthony.

I prayed and pleaded to all of them to cure Charlie 100% of his disease, and once he was cured to never let cancer or any other form of life-threatening disease return to his precious body again. I had chosen my saints wisely. I'd been praying to St. Theresa since I was pregnant with Jay. Her prayer is about a "little flower (a gift) from heaven." I consider both my sons to be my flowers from her heavenly garden. St. Jude is the saint of "hopeless cases and things despaired of." Given his odds, Charlie was a hopeless and desperate case. Then there was St. Anthony, the saint of miracles. And boy, did we need him! But I also gave him some additional responsibilities, not just to cure Charlie of his cancer, but to watch out for Charlie to make sure he didn't have any mishaps along the way, like seizures, or fevers, or anything dangerous that would land us longer stays in the hospital. All three saints had their hands full with me and my prayers, that is for sure! After saying my prayers, I'd say the Rosary – my own version of the Rosary, that is, because I really didn't know how to say it correctly. Then, out loud, I would plead to God.

It was inevitable; I'd become overwhelmed with emotion during these MRIs, and this day was to be no different. About 20 minutes into the scan, I had tears streaming down my face, and I was rocking uncontrollably back and forth in the chair, which wasn't a rocking chair. Basically, I looked like Sybil banging back and forth in a trance.

"Jesus, please," I begged through the sobbing, "please, give me a sign, any sign that this MRI will be good, that Charlie will survive." I buried my face in my hands and wept loudly. But moments later, the tears suddenly stopped along with the sobbing. I slowly lifted my head as I cleared my throat with a sniffle. I looked up from my hands, and even if I tried, I couldn't cry. I honestly couldn't cry at that moment if my life had depended on it. I took a deep breath and exhaled. "Is this the sign, God?" I asked, looking up to the ceiling. A smile came across my face. I felt calm. "Thank You," I whispered.

The Waiting Game

Of course, waiting for the MRI and spinal tap results made me insane. I couldn't eat, couldn't sleep, and basically couldn't function as a normal human being. Remember in high school when you'd be waiting for your boyfriend to call, and you'd check the phone 100 times to make sure it still had a dial tone? Well, that was how I was waiting for the results of an MRI. Of course, we had caller ID, call answering, and call waiting. Yet I continued to act like a freak, checking the phone, carrying it with me from room to room, and not leaving the house. This time, we waited two and a half days, and I was fit to be tied. I called the clinic five times over the two-day period, at first pretending I was asking them some random question, and finally letting them know that I was near hyperventilation awaiting the results. Obviously, I annoyed someone.

The phone finally rang. It was Dr. Wolfe, the head of pediatric oncology. He politely informed me that the results of the MRI were good. There was no shrinkage, but there was no growth either. My heart sank. I was disappointed with this information because I wanted him to say there was shrinkage! He could sense my discouragement.

"No growth is very good news, Mrs. Capodanno. It means the chemo is working because it is not allowing the tumor to spread."

I kept Dr. Wolfe on the phone for 45 minutes. After my barrage of questions, he gently tried to explain to me that I shouldn't panic every time they do an MRI and that it usually takes two days for the results. I, in my own gentle manner, explained to him that I'm just a mom of a very sick child and that I'm not an expert in the field of brain tumors, nor can I control my heart and head from freaking out while I wait to know the results. We live day by day, and these results keep us going. I didn't really care if I was annoying people; I'm not running for the most-popular-parent-at-the-clinic contest! He also told me that from his vantage point, Charlie was doing very well. "Right now, the arrow is pointing in the right direction for Charlie, and this is very positive. However," he continued, "the arrow could turn the other way at any time." I knew that; he didn't need to remind me.

"You're at a crossroads right now, Mrs. Capodanno," he said. "You and your family can choose to take the positive route, and try to lead a normal life as best you can, or you can take the other route, where you live in fear of losing your child."

"Oh, Dr. Wolfe, please understand, we've always taken the positive route. Even when everyone else was telling us there was no way Charlie could survive, we believed in him. But *you've* got to understand that just because we're anxious for test results does not mean we believe in doom and gloom. We're just as anxious to hear that it's positive news!" I proceeded to give him my speech about the sky falling and that, even though it wasn't done consciously, our guard was up and we felt we needed to protect ourselves. And that I had decided that it was okay to act like a freak every now and again. I think we were entitled to it!

"Dr. Wolfe," I said, "I'm sure you can understand that MRI results to parents like us can only have one of two outcomes. They can be joyous or disastrous; there's no in-between."

"Understood," the doctor replied gently.

Saint Mary's

God had truly surrounded us with family and friends to help us navigate through this tumultuous journey. We were also blessed with love and support from our church. Our parish at St. Mary's had been praying for Charlie since the day he was diagnosed with the brain tumor. St. Mary's offers a 9:00 a.m. children's Mass every Sunday. The children are all invited to gather on the altar after the Gospel reading, and the priest tailors the homily so that it is more kid friendly. Now, after the homily was finished, and before the kids ventured back to their seats, Father Tom would yell into his microphone, "Who are we praying for?" And all the children would yell back "Charlie!" At one Mass, as the kids raced back to their seats, they chanted "Go, Charlie, Go!" This was very heartwarming to us.

In early June, Father Tom had asked us to bring Charlie up to the altar so the children could be introduced to the child they'd all been praying for. As the little ones gathered at his feet, he cheered, "Who are we praying for?" and the kids yelled "Charlie!" "Well," Father Tom said quietly, "guess what? I have a surprise for you all — Charlie is right here on the altar with all of you, right now!" He motioned for me to stand up with Charlie. I did, and the entire congregation stood up and applauded. I just about melted in my shoes. I could feel my face beaming with pride. As we walked back to our seats, people remained standing, I saw people wiping tears from their eyes, and a few people reached out and patted my back. To feel the love and support of people we don't even know, but who knew us, was overwhelming.

After Mass, we strapped the boys in their car seats, started the car and turned on the radio. At that moment, the DJ was reporting, "Eighty-six percent of all Americans believe in miracles." John and I just looked at each other and smiled. We believe!

Development Continues

Although our two-week intervals at home between chemo treatments were precious to us, they were also very hectic. I was constantly on the phone questioning the doctors, harassing the clinic, scheduling the visiting nurses and making early intervention appointments.

Every person who had interaction with Charlie was just in awe of how he was developing, given what his body had endured at such a young, fragile age in the developmental cycle. "You'd never know anything was wrong with this child," people would say.

We had our first visit with the early intervention "team" at nine months. The team consisted of a nurse, a speech therapist, a physical therapist, and an occupational therapist. I didn't realize there would be so many people, and I was ill prepared with the amount of cookies I had baked! Regardless, this first meeting was very entertaining. The team huddled around Charlie like he was on display, and each scribbled notes into their binders.

But as the evaluation progressed, I felt this odd sense that they were actually trying to find something wrong with him! They had Charlie do a bunch of different "activities" to show how his motor skills were developing. The nurse placed Charlie on the top of our carpeted staircase, to see how he would come down. Mimicking what he'd witnessed his brother do, he came down on his tiny bum-bum, in an upright position.

"Nope, that's not good," the nurse chimed in.

"What's not good?" I asked. The nurse flipped through a booklet she held in her hand.

"It states here in this chart that at age nine months, he should be crawling down stairs backwards on his knees," she proclaimed.

"If that is the only problem we can find with his motor skills, I'm very, very happy," I laughed. "I think we'll pass on physical therapy right now," I said with a wink.

I established a wonderful relationship with Lisa, Charlie's speech therapist, and anxiously awaited her arrival every other week. She was a welcome visitor to our closed-off world and Charlie was very fond of her. She'd work with Charlie for about half-an-hour and then she and I would sit and chat up a storm at my kitchen table, sharing tea and some tasty treat that I would bake for her. She was very fond of my homemade biscotti. "Hey, how about peanut butter cookies with Hershey kisses next week?" I'd yell from the front door as she pulled out of the driveway.

Marriage Mania

John and I were informed at only our second clinic visit, by a very boisterous and over-sharing clinic mom, that "right around 86 percent of the parents in our clinic are divorced!" The other two mothers sitting around the table nodded their heads in agreement. This was unsolicited; she just came right out and said it. Precisely NOT what we newcomers to this "club" (which we didn't want to join in the first place) wanted to hear. John let out a good laugh. "Cool," he responded jokingly. I just kind of looked at her strangely, not sure why she felt compelled to tell us this. It was like, "Hey, a month ago you were told your son might die; now I'm letting you know that your marriage will fall apart too!"

I didn't know how to respond to her. I had no comeback. Was what she said true?

Little did I know, others were wondering the same thing. For instance, a college friend called me about two months after Charlie was diagnosed to check in to see how things were going. She asked about the baby, how Jay was doing, how I was handling things. Then she asked politely how John and I were doing — as a couple. "Fine," I replied pleasantly. Her tone changed. "No, come on, how are you guys really getting along?" she drilled. "No, really, we're doing fine. Actually, I think we're doing incredibly well considering," I said proudly. "Well," she said bluntly, "it was the first thing I thought of when Charlie was diagnosed – Boy, how is their marriage going to survive something like this?"

I was completely caught off guard by her comment. It blew me away! Although I considered her a friend, she really didn't know much about my marriage because she lived far away. But still, it wasn't as if she was under the impression we had a bad marriage and that this would just be the final straw in crushing it. "Well, believe it or not," I said defensively, "we really are doing well. We have a very strong balance between the two of us." I kind of felt like I was on trial to defend my marriage. "I'm insane, he's sane. I guess that's what keeps us going," I added, trying to make light of the awkward conversation.

If they're honest, most married couples would agree: marriage can be stressful. When you add children to the mix, the marriage becomes a tad more stressful. Now try mixing this combination together, and see what boils over: being married, having two children, and one of them has a disease that you've been told could end his life. See what I'm getting at? I think it's safe to say this type of situation brings new meaning to the phrase "stressful marriage." In our case, we were stressed – a lot! But it was more than stress. It was fear, terror, exhaustion and frustration all rolled into one. Every morning, for the first months after Charlie was diagnosed, Charlie's disease was the first thing on our minds as we woke, and every night it was the last thing on our minds as we fell asleep. This was every night. And, of course, every waking minute was consumed by this fear too. And fear can eat away at your mind. So I think it's safe to say that Charlie's disease could very well have weighed heavily on our marriage.

Like Charlie's condition, which had its ups and downs, there were times when our marriage did too, but never for long. Most of that time, our relationship grew even stronger. We were committed to each other and to the beautiful family we created. But at certain periods, for no apparent reason, it seemed we just "existed" together. These "existing" episodes usually lasted only a few days. We rarely talked, because we were so drained. We never really showed each other any affection – it took too much effort. We'd snap at each other or sling a dig at the other out of pure frustration and exhaustion. After the one-hour ordeal of getting Charlie to bed, John would assume his position in front of "the other woman" in his life, his large-screen TV, and I would log on to the computer in an attempt to connect to the world outside via emailing my friends.

We'd occasionally argue about really stupid things, as most couples do. I'd complain that I didn't get enough help around the house and that I felt I had *three* children to pick up after. John's usual gripe with me was the same, age-old complaint, "We don't fool around enough." Of course it's pretty hard to have fun between the sheets when your youngest child sleeps in between those same sheets with you! Plus, I think it's pretty safe to say it's rather tough to "get yourself in the mood" and "perform" well when your mind is consumed with thoughts of your son's cancer. This is not to say John wasn't compassionate about Charlie's situation, because he always was. But he is also a guy. Need I say more?

So for those of us in the "cancer club," any normal marital issues or arguments are compounded with the lingering fear in the back of our minds that we could lose our child. And exhaustion and anxiety never help the situation either! When you get, oh, three or four hours of sleep a night, max, interrupted by a child's toenail in your eye, it makes things just that much harder! It means conversations can become disagreements, and disagreements are much more likely to become arguments.

Financial Frustrations

Aside from Charlie's condition, the other major issue that made our lives more stressful was our financial situation. John busted his butt at UPS and made a very good salary. But the minute I walked out the door of my office to pick Charlie up with a fever that fateful day in February of 2000, I also walked away from a very handsome salary that was a significant contribution to our dual-income family. It became a very scary time for us financially, and it put a lot of pressure and added stress on both of us.

I could not stand having to watch every purchase. I hated that we'd have to put off painting the bathroom "until next year." This, I can honestly say, was what really got under my skin. Cancer robbed us of a normal way of living, doing what we wanted to do when we wanted. It put our lives on hold. I had never had to question whether or not I wanted to cook shrimp scampi or some other family favorite. Now, here we were, buying mac and cheese at BJ's because it was cheaper. We watched as our friends put additions on their homes, or in some cases were buying summer homes. We never felt jealousy, just envy that there lives were moving forward, as they should be.

I hated telling John we couldn't afford something, especially something he wanted. He worked so hard, and to tell him we couldn't have something or do something because of our financial situation was very difficult. He'd say, "I need to get a pair of sneakers this weekend," and I'd say, "Oh, can you wait until you get paid next week?" Granted, we weren't poor. We just had to cut some corners and cut back on spending. But the guilt of going to the Gap Outlet and breaking into a sweat because I wanted to buy a sweater that was half off really bummed me out.

One afternoon during an inpatient treatment, I was taking a snooze with Charlie on the parent bed. We both awoke to the sound of the hospital room phone ringing off the hook. In my daze, I grabbed the phone and shook my head to regain consciousness.

"Hel…Hello?" I said clearing my voice.

"DC!" The voice boomed with cheer. I recognized it immediately. It was Terry Carleton, a former boss from my days at Hill, Holliday whom I remained very close to over the years.

"Hey!" I said. Hearing his voice perked me up. "How are you?"

"Forget about me, how are you?" His tone changed from playful to concern. I felt a lump growing in my throat.

"Hanging in there," I said, looking down at my child who was hooked up to his IV pole that was pumping chemo into his tiny body.

"Dee, I'm so sorry for what you're going through. But I'm a betting man, you know I am. And my money is on Charlie...he's a fighter, that kid," he said, trying to sound reassuring.

"I know he is," I said softly. "You're sweet to call."

"Well, listen, what can I do to help you out? No request is too big with me, you know that," he said thoughtfully. He has always been an extremely generous person. I remembered when I worked for him during my early days at Hill, Holliday I was given a 1% raise one year, not much of an increase on an $18,000 annual salary. He was so upset with the raise, or lack thereof, that he reached into the top drawer of his desk and pulled out his personal check book. "Here, let me give you something..." I refused to take the money, but was so impressed that he offered, and I never forgot it.

"I, we, we're good," I said, trying to suppress the tears welling in my eyes.

"Hey, I've been very lucky in business. Let me give you a loan," he offered.

"I can't, no, we'll be fine," I said, letting out a soft cry.

"If you don't tell me what you need, I'm just going to start sending you checks. Here's my thought: I'm going to guess your mortgage is the biggest of all your current expenses. Expect a check from me each month. No big deal."

"NO! Terry, no. I can't accept that. I can't, and I'd probably never be able to pay you back."

"Consider it done. I'm not giving you a choice. And I never will expect a dime back from you. It's non-negotiable," he said in his business executive voice. "Now go take care of that baby, my money's on Charlie!" and with that, he hung up the phone. And each month, FedEx would deliver his check to our door.

Although many people went out of their way to help us out financially, we still had to be cautious with our money, because we didn't know how long we'd be in this financial situation.

But, other than being sleep-deprived, sexually deprived, occasionally crazed and a bit financially deprived, all in all, we seemed to always manage to keep it together.

The Capodanno family at Charlie's Christening.

Charlie one week before being diagnosed with a "lemon-size" brain tumor.

Charlie and his grandmother, Bebe, three days post brain surgery.

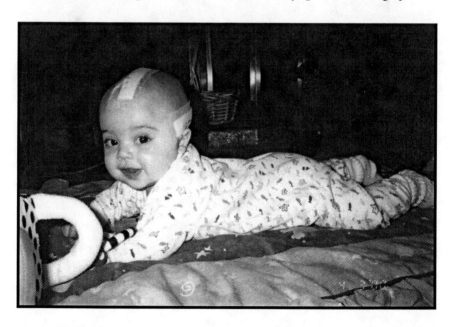

Charlie ten days post brain surgery and gorgeous as ever!

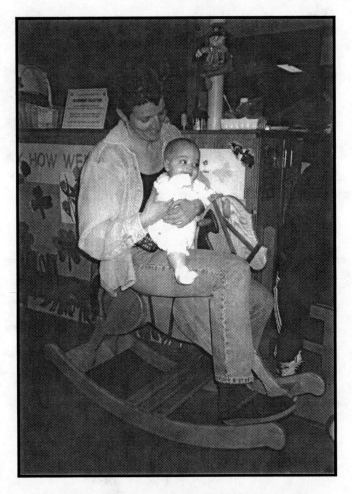

Auntie Kel & Charlie wait to meet Dr. Kretschmar for the first time at the Floating Hospital for Children in Boston.

Charlie at seven months old, one month post surgery, and one week before his chemotherapy treatments begin.

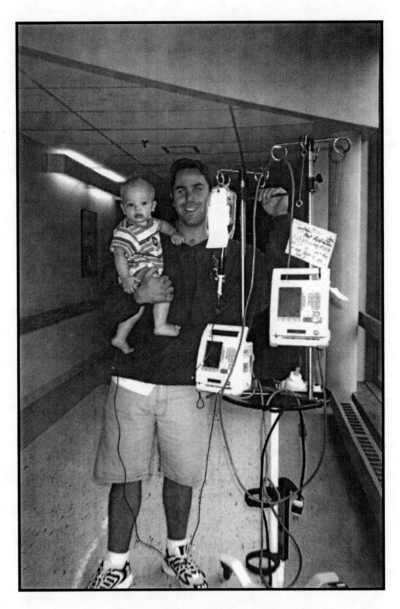

Charlie, Daddy and "The Pole" during a
four hour blood transfusion.

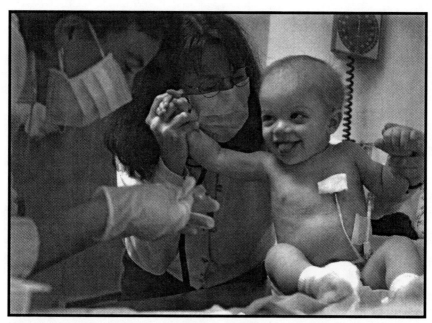

Mommy & Nurse Mary Jo tackle a central line dressing change at the clinic.

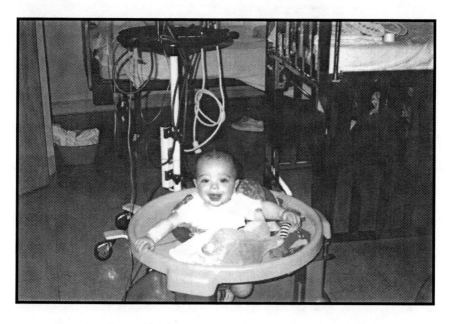

Trying to keep Charlie entertained during an inpatient chemo treatment. Have Exersaucer, will travel!

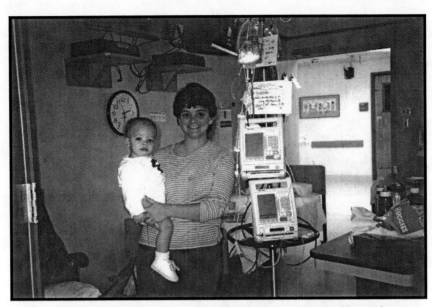

Mommy & Charlie during an overnight stay at the hospital.
As you can see, Mommy has eaten way too much
Au Bon Pain clam chowder!

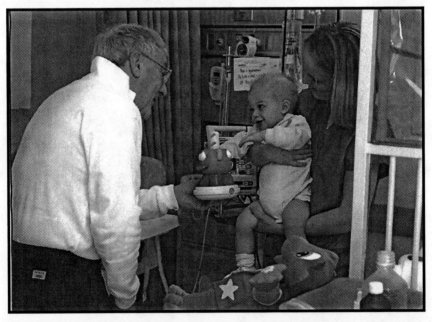

Neither Grampy nor Mr. Potato Head ever
missed an inpatient visit.

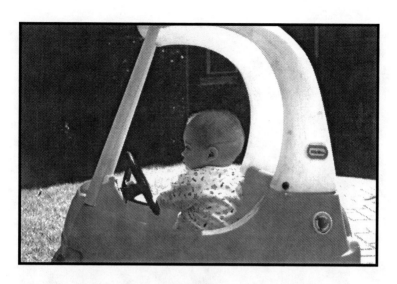

Charlie takes his Cozy Coupe for a spin around the driveway.

*Eleven month old Charlie at the First Annual
Charlie Bear Fund Fest.*

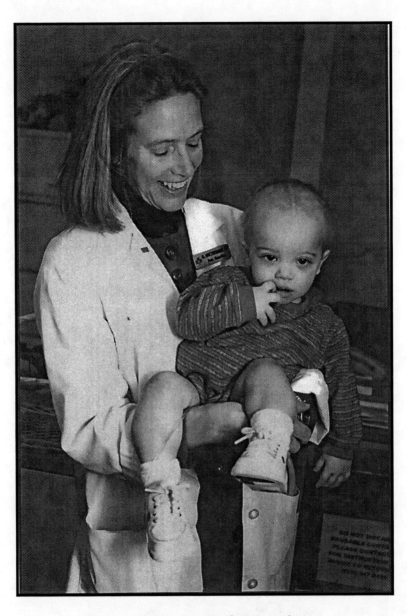

Our oncologist, Dr. Cynthia Kretschmar,
and a very tired and sickly Charlie.

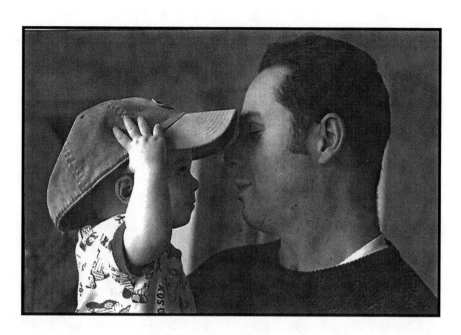

Daddy's little hero.

Mommy steals a kiss from her very brave little boy.

Big brother Jay sits close by his little buddy after Charlie returns home from a four day stay in the hospital. Mommy said she'd look sad, too, if she had to wear that outfit! But after chemo, we only put Charlie in clothes that we didn't worry about him vomiting all over.

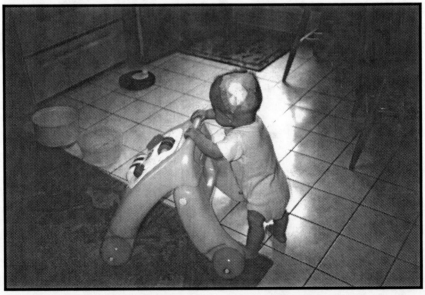

Choochie learns to walk just days after his VP Shunt placement. Nothing slowed this baby boy down!

Chalrie stops in front of our "Windows to the World" to devour a cupcake his Nana brought in for him.

The Capodanno family's year 2000 Christmas card photo.

Charlie and Jay pose for a holiday picture with their adoring cousins Shaun, Julia and Patrick.

Charlie pointing to the lights on the hospital's Christmas tree.

Deirdre, John, Charlie and Jay on Easter Sunday 2001.

Two handsome boys visit their grandparents,
Money & Papa, in Naples, FL.

Charlie shows his silly personality during a photo shoot with Jay.

To infinity and beyond! Jay & Charlie prepare to meet their idol,
Buzz Lightyear, on a Make-A-Wish vacation to Disney World.

Charlie & Jay participate in the Cycle for Life bike ride to benefit the Floating Hospital for Children's Cancer Center.

Santa's little helpers prepare for Christmas 2002.

Charlie & Jay enjoy some fun-in-the-sun at our favorite beach on Cape Cod during the summer of 2003.

*Charlie's kindergarten photograph. Look how
handsome and healthy he looks!*

The boys and Mommy sail the high seas during a 2005 vacation.

Jay (age 9) and Charlie (age 7) aboard a Royal Caribbean family cruise in December of 2006.

Chapter 8
The Roller Coaster Continues

....

"Will He Ever Be the Same?"

In June, Charlie turned 10 months old. Continuing to hit every milestone, he learned to push his baby walker across the kitchen floor in an effort to learn to walk. Of course, every now and again, he'd slip backwards and the thing would roll right over him. But he just laughed and laughed. He'd chase our two dogs around the first floor like a maniac! And we'd bring the walker into the hospital with us, which created the added challenge of trying to chase him as he pushed it along, dragging his IV pole behind him.

That month's inpatient treatment was one of the most terrifying for us. It started out okay, and on the first night, things were pretty uneventful. But Tuesday afternoon, things got ugly. Charlie had given a good yank to his central line while doing his normal combat crawl across the hospital floor that I had lined with sheets. It would require a few stitches, which undoubtedly would be very painful and traumatic for him. He wasn't feeling very good that evening and had vomited a few times and just seemed nauseous. The doctor on duty decided we'd try a new anti-nausea medication known as Compazine. "It might make him feel a bit better," the doctor informed us. By now it was 6:30 and I needed to get home to Jay. My heart ached leaving Charlie feeling so lousy, but I knew he was in perfectly safe hands with his daddy. By the time I walked in the front door at home, the phone was ringing. Jay was a step behind me. I dropped my overnight bag and grabbed the phone. It was 8:00 p.m.

"Um, Honey?" a nervous John said from the other end of the phone line.

"What's wrong? What happened?" I could tell by the tone and urgency in his voice something was very wrong.

"They're prepping Charlie for a CT scan," he began.

"*What?*" I screamed, startling Jay. I pulled Jay onto my lap and began stroking his hair, trying to remain calm so I wouldn't scare him. "A CT scan? *Why?*" I cried.

"Well, they're not really sure. One minute I was holding Charlie, and he seemed perfectly fine, and the next minute, he was arching his back way far back, almost falling out of my arms, and he was just staring off into space for quite a while," he explained, trying to be calm.

"What would cause that? Was it a seizure or something? What was he doing when it started?" I drilled him as I shook.

"I don't know. Like I said, I was holding him, he arched over backwards, and he wouldn't respond. He was breathing and everything, but he was unresponsive to us. Dr. Pelidis was clapping in his face and flashing a light in his eyes, and he didn't even blink. No response, nothing," he continued.

"What's the doctor thinking? I've got to come back in. What's he doing right now?" I asked in a panic.

"He's just lying in my arms. He's not in pain or anything; he's just out of it. It's like he's in a trance," John explained. "I don't know, but it was scary as hell. And it lasted about 35 minutes!" John added.

"*What?* Are you kidding me? Oh my God, let me call someone; let me call Matt and Jill. I need to be there!"

"Honey, please don't. Really. He honestly seems better now, and I don't want you driving in here, obviously shaken up. Let's just get the scan done and I'll call you. Please, stay with Jay. He's gotta be excited you're home." John tried to calm me down.

My brother-in-law Matt came over to be with me. About an hour went by, and the ringing of the phone broke the silence in the room.

"Hey, Honey, he's doing better, much better. He seems to know who I am now, at least. The scan looks good, no growth, or tumor or anything," John said with a sigh of relief in his voice.

"So what was it, a seizure?"

"No, well, they still don't know, but they think it was a dystonic reaction to the Compazine, that new anti-nausea medicine they gave him. They don't know if it was an actual seizure, they're not calling it that. It's a bad reaction, that's all. They've seen it happen before. They're going to do an EEG tomorrow on his brain to see if it was an actual seizure or not, but he seems okay now, just kinda out of it still. So there is *no* reason for you to come in here. We'll be fine and we'll see you in the morning. Okay?"

"If anything and I mean *anything*, happens tonight, you'd better call me," I pleaded with John.

I dropped Jay off at school the next morning and was in the hospital by 9:00 — a record for getting there. I pressed the elevator button 100 times as if it would make the elevator arrive faster. I got off at the 7th floor and ran toward Charlie's room. He and John were actually hanging out by the chalkboard near the nurse's station. From the back, Charlie appeared fine, hanging onto John's shoulder. But as I came around to his front, I was shocked to see the condition he was in. He looked like a different child. It appeared as if he had some kind of brain damage. He was totally unresponsive to me, not even acknowledging I was there.

"Oh my God John, what's wrong with him?" I gasped. Charlie's eyes were only open at half-mast. His eyes were fixated toward the floor, and his tongue was literally dangling over his bottom lip. "What is wrong with him....ohhhh?" I could feel the panic taking over.

"He's fine. Well, he should be fine. It was that reaction; they think he's still coming out of it." I grabbed Charlie from John's arms and began pacing back and forth with him.

Carol, one of our most knowledgeable nurses, came over.

"Carol!" I already had tears in my eyes. "Carol, what's wrong with him? Does he, does he have brain damage from that reaction?" I asked, terrified to hear the answer. John was rubbing my shoulders.

"Oh gosh, no, no, no. I don't think so. That was a pretty bad reaction he had, it's gonna take a while for it to wear off. And we gave him some Benadryl too, so he's just feeling pretty yucky right now." She tried to sound reassuring.

"How long is a while? Days?" I wanted him to look and feel better now!

"I'm not sure, but hopefully by later today he'll be feeling more like himself," Carol smiled.

"Charlie, Charlie, I love you so much. Mommy's here, Sweetie. Can you see me, Mommy, Sweetie...." I tried to get some sort of reaction, but there wasn't one. I was very frightened at that moment. Charlie sort of grunted at one point, and that was about it. He remained in that state for about two hours, until he slowly came around. Finally, after about six hours, he was back to his normal, chipper self. I can honestly say that scare took a good ten years off my life.

The Miserable Mass Pike

It was inevitable. There was no escaping it. It happened every single time. Our overnight bags would be packed and placed neatly in the trunk. I'd vacuum the family room rug one last time. I'd write Jay a little note to leave on his pillow. Then I'd let out a big sigh, snap Charlie into the car seat, and away we'd go. Off to another dreaded series of chemotherapy treatments. I'd be able to maintain my composure for the 20-minute drive up Route 495, but the minute I hit the Massachusetts Turnpike, I'd be in tears. It never failed. Who would have ever thought a stretch of roadway could wreak such havoc on a person's mental well-being.

The drive into the hospital was at a minimum an hour. If there was so much as a drop of rain or snow, it could take no less than two hours. That was a tremendously long time for me to be alone with my thoughts and fears, without any distractions. The ride on the Pike was very lonely, scary, and emotionally draining. It wasn't just that it meant another ride to the hospital, another clinic visit, or another week of chemo treatments. It meant another hour to be reminded of what happened to us, what happened to our son. I relived the horror over and over as the entire ordeal replayed in my head. My deepest, darkest fears and memories came out to haunt me on those grueling rides.

It was a miracle that I managed to keep from getting into an accident, because my eyes were literally blinded by my tears. I would just cry and pray, and cry and pray, begging and pleading with God to please save Charlie's life. I'd relive watching John fall to pieces when I told him about Charlie's tumor, replay how the Grim Reaper coldly delivered the horrific diagnosis, rethink all the "what-ifs" – all of it would come crashing down on me during those car rides. "What if he loses his hearing? What if he has seizures? What if the MRI comes back with signs of growth? What if this chemo isn't working? What if he gets leukemia from the chemo? What if this disease is genetic? What about Jay? Would Jay end up being an only child? Should we consider having another child? What if he needs radiation or a bone marrow transplant? And the thought that made me shudder the most: What if he doesn't make it? I tried not to think about the worst but again, the Pike and my own fearful mind had a hold on me. I couldn't escape. There was no way to distract myself. Even the radio was my enemy. I could bet my life, every time I'd get on the Pike, that at one point during the torturous ride, I'd hear, from start to finish, REM's song, "Hold On." It killed me to listen to it, but I could never change it. I'd hear that song, singing it as loud as I could, even with Charlie snoozing in the back seat, and I'd be drowning in my own tears.

I could see people looking over at me in traffic stops, witnessing my breakdown. I had no control. I was in such agony during those rides. And every time I arrived at the hospital, my makeup would be all smeared all over my face; I'd look drained and exhausted.

One Sunday night before a treatment week, I remember pleading with John, "I can't get on the Pike tomorrow! Please, I can't…don't make me get on the Pike again tomorrow!"

"What? Why?" John questioned.

"Please, call in sick, please, I'm not joking. I can't drive the Pike again alone. I fall apart every time. I'm scared to be alone in the car. Everything comes rushing back to me, Honey. Please, I'm serious, I can't do it," I begged, as I stared at him with a frightened and desperate look in my eyes.

"Maybe you should take the Expressway tomorrow, just for a change of scenery. Maybe that would help," he suggested thoughtfully.

"I don't believe it's the specific road or the foliage or the scenery that I have issues with, Honey, it's being alone in the car that sends me over the edge, every time!" I began to weep.

I knew it was impossible for John to take a day off, and I knew in some way the idea of him calling in sick because of his wife's fear of being alone with her thoughts on the Mass Pike wouldn't fly with UPS. But I just needed a break from that hellish ride. John managed to get out of work early, and without taking a rest, he drove to the hospital to be with me.

Surgery Number Four

A visit to Children's in mid-June confirmed that Charlie would definitely need another surgery to relieve the pooling in his brain. The pooling caused a swelling that was actually visible to the naked eye. Dr. Goumnerova would again need to perform surgery. Her goal was to go in and see how serious the scarring was that was causing the backing up of his spinal fluid. She was hoping not to have to implant a shunt in his head. "I really don't want to do the shunt right now," I told her frankly. "It's just, he's got enough foreign objects in his body already with the central line and everything, and I'm just afraid it would be another thing we'd have to worry about."

"Another brain surgery?" John asked, when we returned home.

"Yeah, and it's not just another surgery, it's the fourth one in four months!" I complained. But we didn't have a choice; there was no battle to fight here; it needed to be done.

"Ultimately, the pooling can cause a great deal of pain for Charlie and can also cause significant damage," Dr. Goumnerova explained.

"Let's get it done then," John replied.

We scheduled the surgery for June 26 at 9:00 a.m. Although we expected to be hanging out in the waiting room for the day, Dr. Goumnerova exited the OR in little under an hour. It was a scary flashback seeing her in her scrubs again, exiting the room.

"What, what are you doing here already?" I gasped. She smiled. She must deal with nut-case moms like me every day.

"Glad to see me, huh?" she laughed.

"No, yes, I mean, are you done? How'd it go?" I was all over her.

"Very well," she grinned. I loved it when she'd say that after being inside my son's brain! "Actually, in true Charlie style, the most difficult part was sedating him," she laughed.

"Typical Charlie," John beamed, "he never goes down without a fight." It's so true; all the anesthesiologists we've dealt with can't believe what a fight he gives them. He's just so incredibly strong and determined. And he'd had them all charmed and wrapped around his fingers in a heartbeat. He had that effect on everyone.

Dr. Goumnerova continued to explain that she was able to drain most of the fluid, and decided that rather than putting a shunt in, she opted for a catheter. When the word "catheter" came out of her mouth, both John's and my jaws dropped. The only "catheters" we knew about dangled outside the body.

"Excuse me...a catheter?" I asked. "Like, what kind? Is there something sticking out of his head?"

"No, no." She shook her head at me. "It's completely under his skin. You can't see it, but you can feel it by touching it. He'll be fine," she told us. Initially, she thought she'd be able to cut through his existing scar to drain the fluid, but she wasn't able to. "The only thing is, I did need to make another incision."

In the scheme of things, this was no big deal. Cripes, with the mega-scar that took up his entire head, what was one more?

"Oooh, poor little Head-wound Harry! When can we see him?" I asked. John and I were just happy that things went well and that Charlie didn't need the shunt. We'd finally reached the point where we knew when to panic and when to let things roll; when to get upset, and when to just deal.

The nurses in the OR fell in love with Charlie immediately. A few of them came out to personally tell us how beautiful he was. "I want to see where he gets those eyelashes from," one of them said.

"Not from me. I can't even get those out of a bottle!" I laughed. As they wheeled his gurney from the OR to the post-op, we noticed a heart-shaped bandage on his head covering his new incision that his nurse made.

A Memorable Slow Dance

I didn't realize being back at Children's would be quite so overwhelming. I was actually looking forward to being there, since I'd spent so much time over at the Floating. It was like a homecoming of sorts. How pathetic was my life? I was looking forward to the change of hospital scenery! Plus, we knew Children's like the back of our hands and we had lots of old friends there. If truth be told, Children's had a much better food selection with all the restaurants surrounding the hospital. What the heck; this time I'd actually be able to eat! But the minute we walked into that lobby, I froze. I cried at every corner. Walking by the MRI room made me shake, strolling through the theater where Sunday Mass was held when we all prayed for the success of Charlie's surgery made me shudder, sitting in the same waiting room that we paced for eight hours waiting for the results of the initial brain surgery brought me to tears – it was just too much for my mind to handle at once. Even going back up to 9 North felt eerie, but not for long. Some of our favorite nurses, who graciously treated us like family four months before, were still there, and that was very comforting.

"Can we have the VIP suite again?" I asked, only half jokingly.

"Nope. No such luck this time! You should be thrilled you're not in here for an emergency again," our nurse Christine laughed.

The morning after surgery, Charlie decided we'd start the day at around 5:00 a.m. After all, he must've figured, there's certainly no need to lie in bed! So, we were up and strolling the halls, greeting all the cleaning people and nurses we came across.

"Hey!" I heard a loud, friendly voice call. "It's the amazing Charlie!"

It was Dr. Jody Smith, the neurosurgeon who had assisted during Charlie's surgery. She was surrounded by a group of residents and med students.

"Folks," she said, extending her arm to introduce Charlie, "this is little Charlie Capodanno. He was about six months old when I assisted in the removal of his tumor. It was the *biggest* one I'd ever assisted in removing in my entire career, not to mention on the youngest patient," she said proudly. Her comment stunned me. She'd never shared that rather disturbing news with us before! I don't think I necessarily needed to hear it, but, oh well; at least she's using it as a success story! I smiled a half smile, as if we were famous, and I felt like Charlie should have taken a bow or something. I kind of curtsied as a joke.

By 6:30 a.m. we'd already done about 40 laps around 9 North, so I thought we'd venture downstairs. The children's theater was empty. By this point, my arms were throbbing from carrying Charlie. I had begged the nurse to unhook him from the IV pole earlier because he didn't need it. There's a jukebox in the corner of the theater, and as the music began to play, I slowly began to dance with my baby boy. There I was, in my pajamas, with my hair matted to my head and fur on my teeth. And there was precious Charlie, head to toe in bandages, wearing his onesie, and we were dancing. And we danced for about a half hour. I didn't care how goofy I looked as all the people raced by to get to work or to their appointments. I was holding on to his little body as tight as I could, and I was singing in his ear, and tears were streaming down my face. I whispered into his ear that we had a lifetime of dances ahead of us, and that I'd be the proudest mommy in the world when I danced with him on his wedding day. I wasn't sure if I was feeling fear or joy or pride at that bittersweet moment. But I had a tremendous smile across my face and it was a moment I'll treasure for the rest of my life. The love I have for this child is worth every minute of the pain and anguish and fear my family and I were suffering. It was this child's love that gave us the strength to persevere. At that moment I realized, although I was cradling Charlie in my arms, it was he who was holding me up!

After a while, Charlie began to wiggle around in my arms. He'd had enough of this mushy stuff and wanted to explore. At first I didn't want to let him out of my arms, but he was determined. So I placed him gently on the floor next to me. And with his one leg bandaged and boarded up from his IV line, and his chest bandaged with his central line, and his heart-shaped bandage on his head from his surgery, he crawled slowly, dragging his little body across the floor to a chair next to the jukebox. There he guardedly pulled himself up to a standing position, and with Neil Diamond's *Sweet Caroline* blaring in the background, he turned, smiled at me, and turned back around. Then he started swaying his tiny, delicate body back and forth like he was dancing on his own. Right then, right there, I realized I was crying happy tears, because my baby was telling me that he was just fine and that nothing would stop him from dancing or living — *nothing!*

We headed back upstairs at around 7:30 a.m. and bumped into Dr. Goumnerova outside our room.

"I'm going to let you go home today," she said with a big smile on her face.

"Are you kidding?" I asked. She had told John and me we'd probably stay two or three days for Charlie to recover.

"Look at him! I can't find a reason to keep him," she added.

"But he had surgery on his brain less than 24 hours ago!"

Dr. Goumnerova said she'd check back with me in an hour, but for me to plan on being released before lunch. John showed up around 9:00. I greeted him with a quick "We're outta here!" The resident who came down to discharge us after lunch told us to try to limit Charlie's activity the first few days. He needed to rest, and he might feel a bit "wobbly."

So off we went. We were home by 2:00 p.m. and by 4:00 Charlie was crawling around trying to catch Jay, when he lost his balance and clipped his head on the corner of the wooden staircase banister. John and I held our breath for a few seconds, waiting to hear a wail, but it never came.

"The kid's a rock," proclaimed John as he grinned proudly.

Father Ainello

The following Wednesday, I planned to take Charlie to a healing service being held in the basement of the church. It started at about 8:00 p.m., which was actually Charlie's bedtime. But it was important to me, and I really wanted to go. I firmly believed in "healings." It had been months since we'd taken him to the first healing service, and I wanted to have someone pray over him again. Charlie was dressed in his PJs. I knew he'd be noisy, so I immediately sat down in the very back of the church. There were about 25 people there. The priest, Father Ainello, was just beginning to explain how the service would take place. I liked him immediately. He had a thick Italian accent, but he wasn't a "Holy Roller." He just seemed like a very kind and gentle man.

"A bolt of lightning isn't going to strike down on us tonight," he joked. "The earth isn't going to shake. Look, I have a gift, a gift from God, and it is to help heal people. That's it. That's why I am here to try to help heal people through God."

Charlie was entertaining himself by crawling up and down the carpeted stairs we were sitting on. Father Ainello continued slowly, with his eyes closed, "I feel at least two people, a male and a female, will be healed tonight. I don't know who they are or what they're here for, I just feel it, and…" He paused with his eyes still closed. "And, yes," he continued, "I also see a small face too." I sat straight up and felt my face flush. He was a visiting priest. We didn't know him and he didn't know us. Did he mean Charlie's small face? I could have been the one who was being prayed over. The Mass continued for about 20 minutes and Charlie had a great time climbing through the pews and up the stairs. He managed to poop twice in an hour, and he finally made himself comfortable in a laundry basket that was used to hold all the prayer books.

Finally it was time to walk him up to the altar. I found myself to be particularly calm until the moment I had to speak.

"I…he…," I tried to explain to the priest as he laid one hand on Charlie and the other on me. "The baby…cancer…his brain and spine…please…"

And that was it, that's all I could get out through my sobs. I closed my eyes and wept, clutching Charlie as tight as I could, stroking his head. I could hear Father Ainello whispering his prayers and I felt him stroke my cheek. I opened my eyes.

"We'll pray for you too. Never give up, never," he said, looking straight into my eyes and placing his finger against my chin to hold our stare.

"Oh no, we never will," I answered quietly. As I turned to leave the altar, I could hear people sniffling, and a few were outwardly crying. Let's face it, I must have looked pretty pathetic and frail up there clinging to my baby, whose skin was pasty white, and aside from a few feather-like hairs, the only thing visible on his head were two beet-red scars. I had to sit down before I could go back to the stairs. A tiny woman came over to me. She didn't say a word, but instead placed one of her arms over my shoulder and handed me a tissue. She had the sweetest, warmest smile on her face.

"We're glad you're here; we'll keep praying for both of you," she whispered softly into my ear. Her name was Donna.

The whole way home I contemplated whether or not to tell John about what the priest said about "the little face." Not that he's a cynic, but I wasn't sure how big he was into healing services.

"How'd it go?" he asked.

"Nice. It was really nice. The priest felt that he was going to be able to heal two people, as well as a 'little face.' Charlie was the only little face there," I said, watching for his response.

"Wow. That's weird, huh? Well great," was all he said. End of discussion.

A Mystery Woman

On July 1 I got stuck in a grueling two-hour traffic jam on the Mass Pike. We were heading in for a three-night stay, so my nerves were already completely shot by the time I exited the parking garage and raced to the elevators, clutching tightly a giggling Charlie and two enormous LL Bean duffle bags overflowing with toys, stuffed animals, our clothes, and pillows. "Out of Order" read the sign taped to the elevator door. This only infuriated me more. We darted down the seven flights of stairs, and I lost my balance while trying to negotiate the last step. Miraculously, I didn't fall. "Christ!" I yelled out loud, feeling tears of frustration welling in my eye.

Charlie found the near fall quite amusing and he let out a "wooo!"

"I wish I could see the humor you see in this, Chooch," I said with a pant.

I stopped to adjust the bags and the baby I was transporting. As I turned my back to head down the hall, I noticed a strikingly beautiful African American woman standing next to me. She was wearing a long-sleeved, tight-knit sweater and a black and gold ankle-length skirt. Her hair was pulled back tightly into a French twist. I was taken aback by this woman for some reason and caught myself staring at her. She took a few steps in front of me, and turned and looked directly into my eyes.

"It's going to be okay," she said calmly.

"I sure hope so," I said, swinging the Bean bag over my shoulder.

"No," she continued, redirecting my eyes into hers, "it really is going to be okay." She smiled, turned on her heals, and without breaking her stride, continued to walk down the hall in front of me until she disappeared into a sea of people.

Who was this woman?

I never saw her again.

Busting Out of the Joint!

We spent three days in the hospital for chemo over the Fourth of July holiday. It was a gorgeous week, and we were totally bummed to be trapped inside the hospital while the sun was beaming outside. "It's the Fourth of July; let's do something to celebrate!" John suggested. "Let's order pizza."

"Sure," I agreed. Jay was with us, and he loves pizza, so a pizza party would entertain him too.

"No, I mean, for everyone. Let's just do it. For the whole floor!" Mister Generosity said. So we did. It was a great way to brighten up the floor.

"It's just so nice out, I wish we could go outside," John said.

"You know what? I'm gonna ask," I replied. "I'm gonna see if they'll unhook Charlie, just for one hour, so we can go outside for just a little break."

I flagged down Dr. Grodman. "Dr. Grodman, it's the Fourth of July. It's gorgeous out, and right now, the only thing Charlie's getting is hydration. His chemo doesn't start again until tonight. Any chance we can sneak out, just for one hour? We won't go far, I promise. Just over to the Boston Common to sit on the grass. Please? I know, it's illegal, it's wrong, it's breaking the rules, but we won't tell!" I winked at him.

"Sure, why not. But only for an hour. Promise? I could get in trouble for this! Hey, actually, the Shriners Parade starts in about 20 minutes. Maybe you can catch that. But come right back. Deal?"

"Definitely!" I jumped up, and off we went. Jay and Charlie watched some of the parade, rolled around together in the grass, had an Italian slush and we all sat under a tree just enjoying the freedom of being out of the hospital. It was these stolen moments, these little escapes that made our lives feel like our own again. It's what made everything bearable for us.

A Bloody Mess and a Screaming Match

Chemo went well that night for the most part. But the next afternoon was a different story. As usual, we found out that Charlie would need a blood transfusion before we could leave. I hated that. It was just the longest procedure, usually taking at least four to six hours. "Nothing we can do about it," John said. Because it was a holiday week, John had taken the day off, and had once again brought in Jay. Charlie wasn't feeling great, and understandably so after three straight days of chemo. I was pushing Jay around the hallway in circles in our umbrella stroller, doing lap after lap to keep him entertained. John was doing his best to keep Charlie distracted as well. He was standing right outside the nurse's station, talking to another parent, when he heard a snap, and immediately felt his shirt become wet. "Oh, CRAP!" he yelled. Two seconds later, I came wheeling Jay around the corner on one wheel. John instantly shot me a look as if to say, "Don't come over here."

Charlie's central line had burst, and blood was everywhere. Cathy, one of the nurses, calmly strolled over and clamped off the line so that it was not drawing any more blood from his heart, and to prevent infection. Another nurse came over and swooshed Jay away. There was John, holding Charlie at arm's length, the two of them covered in splattered blood.

"I'll page surgery," one nurse said calmly as she dialed the phone.

"Why?" I said, but I knew the answer. They'd have to see if the line needed to be replaced. We were bummed. We were exhausted. We were supposed to have been out of there hours ago. It was about 6:00 p.m., we'd been there for three days, and now he might have to have the line replaced or repaired.

It took a few hours before the surgeon on call came down to the floor. He was a small, stocky, bald guy who was no taller than I was. He was less than thrilled to see us. The feeling was mutual. He had the personality of a pebble, miserable the minute he opened his mouth. We brought Charlie into the treatment room. "Let's look," he grumbled as he lifted up Charlie's onesie. "Well, it needs to be fixed," he sighed in an irritated tone.

"Fixed? Fixed like replaced or fixed as in repaired?" John asked, hoping to God it could be repaired without requiring another surgery.

"Repaired," he answered quickly. "But," he said, walking toward the door, "I don't have a repair kit available. Sometimes we don't have them in stock. It will have to wait until tomorrow," he mumbled, never making eye contact with either of us.

It was 8:30 p.m. and we were spent and in dire need to get home. And the only way that was going to happen was if this doctor could repair the line right then.

"Wait, I think we already have a kit. Someone brought one down right when it broke," I said. A nurse had already located a kit, and had put it in Charlie's room.

"Couldn't have; we don't keep them in stock all the time," he said, as he continued to walk away from us.

"*Wait!*" I yelled, dashing into Charlie's room. The kit was gone. The doctor never broke his stride as he tried to escape. With my eyes ablaze, I felt a deep-rooted anger overpowering my semi-normal sense of composure. I chased the doctor and caught up to him right in front of the nurses' station, cutting him off at the path. I stepped right in front of his face. Now, this move might not have been as effective if the guy wasn't at my same eye level! At that moment, I wanted to rip his face off! My teeth were clenched as tightly as they could be.

"Listen!" I growled. "We've been trapped in this friggin' hospital for four days and three nights now! We're not staying another one!" I was yelling very loudly and everything went quiet around us. "And just because you don't feel like dealing with this right now, tough! My child didn't volunteer to have cancer! I didn't sign up to be the mother of a child with cancer! God made those decisions for us – that's why *we're* here *tonight*! *You* chose this career! *You* chose to be here tonight! That's why *you're* here!"

My eyes were bulging out of my head at this point. For a minute, there was dead silence. Everyone around pretended to act busy, but they were all anxiously waiting to witness what would happen next. He still wouldn't look me in the eye.

"Well," he said, shuffling off, "if I can find a kit, we can do it; if not, it will have to wait until the morning." John walked up and placed the kit on the nurse's station desk with a bang. Again, silence. With a snap, the doctor grabbed the kit and walked off mumbling to himself.

"Way to show him, home girl," John chuckled. Surprisingly, Dr. I-Don't-Feel-Like-Working-Tonight returned in ten minutes ready, but not eager, to repair the line.

John bravely volunteered to go through the procedure with Charlie since my nerves were shot. According to John, it was a very stressful, tedious procedure. Fully conscious, Charlie was strapped to a board while screaming bloody murder. The surgeon delicately repaired the tiny tubing that is as thin as spaghetti, with more tubing and glue. I could hear Charlie scream from five doors away, and that was very painful for me.

When they finally exited the procedure room, John was sweating and he looked visibly shaken. "The guy might be a jerk, but he's got a steady hand. Man, that's a lot of pressure!" Charlie looked traumatized as John tried to console him by stroking his back.

It had been a long day for all of us. Fortunately, we were released to go home that night. We had driven separate cars, so I packed my car with the boys and our belongings and headed home.

An Anger Brews from Deep Within

By the time John left the hospital that night, his brain was fried. His head was spinning, reliving the ordeal that Charlie had endured throughout the day. It's wildly difficult and disheartening to watch your child suffer through grueling treatments and painful procedures. Although he was emotionally drained and exhausted, he decided to stop for Chinese take-out. While waiting to place his order, he noticed an obnoxious male customer harassing the female cashier behind the counter.

"You people always try to cheat my mother. You people always do this!" The man was relentless.

"Hey buddy, give her break, would you? She's not trying to cheat you; you're just not understanding her," John said.

"Mind your own business; I've had a bad day!" the guy hollered into John's face.

"Oh, you think you've had a bad day, do you? You have no idea what a bad day is," John said, with fire in his eyes.

"Oh, boo-f'ing-hoo, poor you, did you have a bad day today?" the guy snickered, and turned his attention back to verbally attacking the cashier.

With that, John completely snapped. Six months of anger, fear, exhaustion and frustration came raging out at that moment. He had been suffering physically and emotionally every day for months trying to keep his son alive, trying to keep his family intact, trying to please his company, trying to be there for his emotionally distressed wife, trying to be the best father in the world, trying to do it all while being completely sleep-deprived, and here he was listening to some jackass take out his "bad day" on an innocent woman! John grabbed the man tightly around the collar and literally picked him up off the ground and shoved his body against the wall. With his face burning red and gritting his teeth, John yelled, "Leave her alone!"

The man's mother began to scream. "Please stop! Don't hurt him! Let him go, please!" she pleaded. Realizing for the first time what he was doing, John let go and the guy tumbled to the floor. Instead of fighting back, he rose to his feet and extended his hand to John as if to apologize.

"I don't want to shake your hand, just get out of my face," John demanded. He had hit his breaking point. Watching his son suffer, not only that day but for all those months, had just built up inside him.

When he got home he described the scene to me in frustration. "I don't know what was going on inside me; I just lost it!"

"I think I know what drove you over the edge – our life! This is not a normal way to live," I chimed in. I wasn't happy that he'd almost been in a fight, but I completely understood why he had reacted that way.

The Great Cape Escape

Ever since Charlie began treatment, we had kept our fingers crossed that we would still be able to go on our annual family vacation to Cape Cod with our best friends. What started off as five college women partying for a week at a beach front home turned into five couples, four cottages, and thirteen kids, all under the age of six. No, it was never a restful vacation, but we counted the days until it arrived, and it created lasting memories for all of us each year.

We were so thrilled that Dr. Kretschmar allowed us to go. By some miracle, it worked out we did not have chemo that week. And aside from the dressing changes, flushes, six medications, and the heart-shaped bandage on Charlie's head that we had to change daily, we were about as far away from cancer as we could be. What a gift! To cross over the Sagamore Bridge onto the Cape was to finally escape from our new lives as a cancer family. We had lobsters, took the kids clamming, went mini-golfing, went to the beach every day, cooked out, and just laughed with our friends. Jay enjoyed every single minute being around friends, and for the most part, Charlie was a normal 11-month-old, eating sand, dripping Popsicles down his chest, and giggling. The only reminders of our "other life" were that he couldn't go near the water, because he was at risk of getting an infection from the "live" bacteria and organisms; he couldn't wear a bathing suit without a shirt, because we had to keep his line clean; and he had to wear a hat to cover his bald, freshly scarred head.

On the last night of our vacation, we all headed down to the beach to watch the sunset. The kids were racing up and down the sand dunes, getting dirty and chasing each other. Everybody took family photos. We had our backs to the sunset as Jane snapped our family shot. I noticed a man and a woman watching us while we had our pictures taken. As we gathered up the kids to head back to the cottage, the woman, who was sitting on a log, leaned over and smiled directly at me.

"Is he sick?" she asked sweetly. She'd obviously noticed his head was bandaged, and even though he looked okay, it was evident by his pale skin, sunken eyes and bald head that he wasn't healthy.

"Yes," I smiled back at her.

"Is it, is it..." She couldn't bring herself to finish her sentence. I didn't feel she was being nosey, just curious and sincere in her concern.

"Yeah, it is cancer. A brain tumor," I answered her, as I continued to gather our blankets and shoes.

"Oh, I'm so, so sorry," she whispered as her eyes filled quickly with tears.

"Don't be sorry. He's alive. He's doing really well. In fact, he's a little miracle, this one. But you know what? If you would, I'd really appreciate it if you could keep him in your prayers. His name is Charlie," I said, as I walked him over to shake her hand.

"Oh, I will absolutely do that. Absolutely. God bless you, Charlie."

"Oh, He already has, believe me!" I grinned.

Packing up on our last day of vacation was sad. You never want to go home from a great vacation, but given Charlie's situation, it was even more difficult. I didn't want to go back to "reality." I wanted to stay on the Cape in our little fantasy world. I wanted to hide from the hospital, the doctors, the nurses, and the clinic. But it was time to face facts and head back over the bridge. Back to life. Back to cancerville. Sigh.

The First Annual Charlie Bear Fund Fest

Our family and friends spent months planning the First Annual Charlie Bear fundraising event for our family. The money raised was to assist John and me financially so that we could focus on what was most important, curing Charlie and keeping our life intact. What started as an idea ballooned into the event of the century. The selected venue was a beautiful, sprawling farm in Canton, Massachusetts.

People from all walks of life donated well over 300 prizes for the raffle, and over 250 silent auction items ranging from autographed sports memorabilia to airline tickets, to handmade quilts, to professional teeth whitening and will-writing services. John and I were just blown away by the thoughtfulness and generosity behind the donations. Jill was the project leader, but a great many hands were involved in the planning process. My mom, Joanne, is an event planner by nature, and she dove right into the planning, hitting up every person she ever met over her 67 years for a contribution!

As we watched the pieces for the event fall into place, we occasionally became overwhelmed. "This is too much," John and I would say. "Who *are* half of these people, do they even know us?" Raffle and event tickets were sold everywhere, church, the schools, at businesses and elsewhere!

The goal was to have 300 people in attendance. Roche Brothers Supermarkets, where I had been a cashier for nine years during high school and college, generously donated all of the food including chicken, hot dogs, hamburgers, chips, condiments, soda, water – everything!

Regretfully, when we all woke the morning of the event, we were deeply saddened to see it was a monsoon outside.

"Oh my God, what are we going to do with all the people?" John asked, staring out the window at the pouring rain, hearing the thunder clapping in the distance.

We did have a tent, but there were also numerous activities planned, such as a whiffle ball tournament, face painting, and relay races.

"What will we do with all the food?" I asked.

But as each minute of the event drew closer, the sky slowly, almost deliberately, cleared for us. By the time we pulled into the parking lot at the farm, it was down right hot, sticky and sunny!

The event was scheduled to start at noon, and by 11:00 a.m., throngs of people started to arrive. Work friends, old high school friends we hadn't seen since graduation, childhood friends we couldn't even recognize. It seemed as if every person who had ever touched our lives showed up to lend their support. Even people we didn't know came because they were a friend of a friend, heard about the event, and wanted to help out. People spent the entire day eating, hanging out, listening to music, and bidding on auction items.

We ran out of food halfway through the day! A friend jumped into his car and raced back to Roche Brothers with a handful of money we'd raised. We did NOT want people to be without food! The store manager at Roche Brothers told our friend to put the money back into his pocket. "It's on us," he said, as he helped load the food into the back of the truck.

Toward the end of the event, a group of friends from Carat Freeman, the media-buying agency I was working at when Charlie was diagnosed, made their way up to the microphone. Through the combined efforts of the magazine publication companies from which we bought ad space for our clients, my friends at Carat reached their goal to raise enough money to cover my salary for one year, which they did and more! These companies did not even know me or my family. But they heard our story from the Carat reps and jumped at the opportunity to help. People gasped out loud as the announcement was made. I shook with joy. My dad began to weep. In total, over 500 people shared in our glorious day. We didn't want the day to end. It was like we were removed from our situation, and we were just having a ball! Obviously we were elated with the money that was raised to ease our financial burdens, but it was the love, thoughtfulness and caring people that showered us with love and attention that day that was truly inspiring.

Chapter 9
Anybody There?

....

Windows to the World

On average, Charlie and I would get about four hours of sleep in the hospital, broken by episodes of vomiting, the nurse's hourly checks, and his endless bedwetting which was a result of the tremendous amount of fluids they flushed into him 24/7. There wasn't a diaper on the planet that could have kept that amount of urine at bay.

Without fail, Charlie would wake up at 5:00 a.m., before dawn broke over the city of Boston. I always took him out of the room at that early hour, so as to not wake our sleeping roommates. Usually smelling like vomit or sour formula, Charlie and I would venture out into the hallway to chat with the nurses and to begin what would be hours upon hours of pacing the halls.

There was an enormous wall of windows on the 7th floor that overlooks the Expressway, and beyond that, Logan Airport. There we stood, morning after morning, watching the world below begin its new day. We'd watch the sunrise, the traffic jams, the construction cranes swinging into motion, and the trains pulling in and out of South Station, and, of course, the planes taking off from Logan to destinations unknown. Many times, I'd think, "Man, Chooch, I wish we were on one of those planes, going somewhere really fun and sunny." I'd daydream of where the commuters and travelers were going, to business meetings, to their offices, to exotic vacations. Since we had started our inpatient treatments, we'd watched a huge new building appear, going from a gigantic hole in the ground to a 30-story tower.

During these morning shuffles, we'd greet all of our new friends: cleaning people, construction workers, the medical staff and personnel and the security folks. They all loved Charlie, knew him by name, knew why he was there, and always wanted an update on how he was doing. "That kid's the mayor of this place," Winston, the head of maintenance, would say. The room service deliveryman always greeted us the same way: "I see Charlie, and I forget about my own troubles. What do I have to complain about? Look at him, fighting for his life, with the energy of a hundred strong men!"

Our Prayers Were Being Heard and Answered

During the late July treatment we were awaiting results of an MRI and spinal that had been done a few days prior. As always, I was anxious, but trying to remember what Dr. Wolfe said: "It takes time to have all the appropriate people read the scans before we can tell you." John had arrived at around noontime and had gone to grab a slice of pizza outside the hospital. My dad had been there earlier, but needed to attend a doctor's appointment himself. So, as usual, I was strolling with Charlie when I heard someone yell my name.

"Mrs. Capodanno," the voice said, completely out of breath. It was Jen, one of the resident doctors. She was running toward us as fast as she could down the hall. "Ah, I, I found you! I've been looking everywhere!" she said as she stopped to swallow. "The spinal fluid is *clear*! I had to find you to tell you. It's *clear*, Mrs. Capodanno!" I stood silent for a split second trying to comprehend what she was saying.

"Clear, as in no malignant cells?" I questioned calmly.

"Yes, no malignant cells, that's right. It's clear! This is what you've been waiting to hear!" she yelled. It was very evident that she was overjoyed to share this news with me.

"Are, are you sure? Did you talk to Dr. Kretschmar?" I was still calm. Dr. Kretschmar had warned us in the very beginning not to rely on any test results or information that she did not deliver to us.

"Oh yeah, I just got off the phone with her five minutes ago. She called up to have me find you because she's tied up in a procedure and she knows how much you would want to hear this."

"Oh my God, are you kidding me? I can't believe it! Thank you, God!" I grabbed her hand and squeezed it. "I, I just can't believe it, this is the best news, and I just can't believe it!" I shrieked, jumping up and down. I could feel the tears welling in my eyes, and noticed Jen was tearing up too. "Thanks so much for finding me; you made my day; no you made my life!"

"Mrs. Capodanno, it's my pleasure. I'm just as thrilled; we love Charlie, you know that, we all love Charlie," she said with a wink.

I couldn't wait to tell John the incredible news. Charlie and I paced back and forth between the two elevator shafts, anxiously awaiting his return.

The second the doors opened and I spotted him inside, I blurted out, "It's clear! The fluid's clear!" I was screaming it as loud as I could.

"Oh my God, that's awesome!" He leaned over to kiss Charlie on the forehead. "I knew it; I just knew it. He's amazing," John said, as he took Charlie in his arms and leaned over and kissed me.

"Tell me our prayers aren't being heard! Thank you, Jesus!" I yelled, turning my eyes toward the ceiling.

We raced back to the room to call everyone we could to share this miraculous news. I first called my dad, but he hadn't arrived home yet. "Hello," Bebe answered cheerfully. "Bebe, it's…" I started, but was overcome with emotion. "Hello?" she said again. I cleared my throat. "Sorry Bebe, it's Deirdre, um, I just wanted you both to know that the spinal fluid is clear. It came back clear…meaning they can't detect any cancer cells in his spinal fluid! Can you believe it?" I said, trying as best I could to be coherent.

"Oh, oh, Sweetheart, Deirdre!" she said, choking on her words. Her voice lowered. "That's the best news I've ever heard in my life. Thank God. It's a miracle. It's just unbelievable." We talked for a while, and I made a few more calls. Minutes later the phone rang and I could hardly hear who it was. I heard a deep breath, a signature trait of my dad's.

"Dad?" I said. "Dad, is that you?" He was completely overwhelmed with emotion.

"Yeah, hi, I, I'm just so thrilled. God's definitely listening," was all he could muster up to say.

"I know," I whispered. Hearing my dad cry was tough. I'd seen it a few times over the past few months, but it never gets easier. My dad is an emotional person anyway, but as strong as he tried to be through all of this, sometimes it was just too difficult to even try to control his emotions. I could only imagine the pain both sets of parents felt as they watched, helplessly, as their children struggled every day to do whatever it took to save their grandson's life.

John, Charlie and I walked the halls again, telling everyone we came in contact with about Charlie's news. It felt like our feet weren't touching the ground. Yes, the chemotherapy, the modern science that was being used to combat Charlie's disease was working. But we also believed, without any shadow of a doubt, that the prayers that were being said for Charlie across the country and around the world were being heard, and answered.

The Power of Prayer

We knew moments after Charlie's initial diagnosis that it would take more than modern medicines, cutting-edge surgical procedures, and ingenious doctors and devoted nurses to save our son's life. We already had all that on our side fighting for us. We knew that Charlie's chances of survival were slim. The odds were stacked against us. We knew beyond a shadow of a doubt that it would take a true miracle for Charlie to live. And the only one who could grant us this miracle was God. This is all we had to hold onto – our faith and our hope in a miracle. We needed all the voices we could gather to share in our quest to ask God, and all the angels in heaven, to cure Charlie of his disease. For we were all in agreement that Charlie's fate was in God's hands. Only He could make the final decision.

People were constantly calling to ask, "What can we do? How can we help?" And our immediate response was always the same: "Please ask everyone you know to pray for Charlie; that's all we ask for. That's all we want from anyone."

Now, I don't preach religion to anyone. I believe it is a very personal choice, and I wouldn't jam it down anyone's throat. But in this time of crisis, I asked everyone, even those who didn't necessarily believe in God, to join us in praying to whomever it was that they believed in to ask for a cure for Charlie's disease. Everyone obliged. No one was going to deny our special request because they knew that, in our eyes, Charlie's life depended on it.

People let us know through voice mail, e-mail, cards and letters that they were praying for little Charlie. It's difficult to even begin to describe how profound and incredibly overwhelming this outpouring of support and love was to us. It was incredibly uplifting. It gave us a new sense of hope. It renewed our faith in mankind. It gave us a great deal of comfort and peace. It energized and motivated us to never give up. It let us know that our world is still a beautiful place.

It was amazing to us that, as the months passed, individuals who said they no longer believed in prayer or God or the church were slowly turning back to God and to prayer. As our prayers were answered, one by one, they began to believe again.

It became obvious that Charlie's story was affecting many people, in many different ways. For instance, John has a good buddy from Franklin named Steve Killoy. Steve owns his own plumbing company. He's just a super nice, regular guy with a wife and four kids. But he's the type of guy who would do just about anything for anybody without giving it a second thought. One afternoon about five months after Charlie was diagnosed, Steve casually mentioned in a conversation to John that the pastor at their church had asked him to deliver a sermon the next day and that he was very nervous about it. He didn't say what the topic would be. "Maybe we'll come to give you support," John said jokingly. Steve didn't reply.

So the next morning, John decided we should take the kids to Steve's church. Steve didn't know we were going to be there. The pastor introduced Steve, who stepped on stage with a terrified look in his eyes. I immediately felt very nervous for him. It took him a solid few minutes to gather his strength and he didn't utter a word the first two minutes he was on the stage. He just continued to clear his throat and shift his body weight back and forth. He was really struggling. John and I stared at each other nervously. Finally, Steve cleared his throat one last time, looked down at his wife in the first row, and began.

"*A couple of weeks ago Pastor Chris asked me if I would be interested in speaking in church about how God is working in my life. Being a semi-devoted Christian, my first thought was how I can get out of this one. Not being able to come up with a semi-decent excuse, I had no choice. I said yes. And here I am. I think for the best way to explain how God was working in my life is to share some things about myself.* (Steve stopped and took a long, deliberate pause before he could continue to speak.)

"*A few months ago, everything was going pretty good. My job was going good. My family was getting along. Not a lot of problems, or should I say not a lot of problems I couldn't handle. You see, I was the kind of person who liked to have it all under control. I always thought by doing things my way, I could get anything done. Or at least take care of anything I needed to.* (Again Steve took a long pause and lowered his head. As he again began to speak, his voice cracked and he started trembling.)

"*One day I came home from work, said hi to my family, and the phone rang. When I answered, it was my friend. His voice sounded distraught, so I went in the other room to talk. When I asked him what's up, he said he was in the hospital with his second son, who was only six months old. He said the baby was very sick. I asked what was wrong. He answered me crying and he said they found a large tumor in the baby's brain that might be cancerous.*

"*Not knowing what to do or say, I asked how bad it was. He said the doctors said he had less than a 20% chance of living. Hearing this* (Steve caught himself choking up and took a breath), *I immediately fell to my knees and the only thing I could say was I'm sorry. My friend said he had to go, but before he hung up the phone he asked me, 'Please pray for us tonight.'*

"*When I got off the phone, I tried to get myself under control. I wiped the tears from my eyes and went to go tell my family. When my wife saw my face, she knew something was wrong. At that point, I completely broke down and started to cry uncontrollably. My kids were in complete shock. This was the first time they had ever seen their dad cry. You see, I was always the type of person who kept his emotions under control. That didn't work this time.*

"Later that night, after everyone was asleep, I got on my knees to pray. Not because I believed that strongly in prayer, but because I promised my friend that I would. When I started to pray, I felt lost. I didn't know what I was doing and I had no control over what was going on. I could only look to God and ask why. For the first time in my life, I knew I didn't have all the answers. I think this was the first time I opened my heart and my mind to God.

"Well, this little boy had surgery to remove the tumor, which was cancerous. The doctors said it would probably be a while before he could do anything. But that same night, he was so active they actually had to tie him to his bed so he wouldn't hurt himself. He has made it through the tough parts and is still taking chemo but he is coming up on his first birthday.

"My friend had a miracle happen in his life, but somehow it affected me deeply. I suddenly found myself seeking God. I think I've always known there was a God, but now I wanted to know Him personally. Until this point in my life, I've lived life very closed emotionally. I never trusted anyone but myself. Since I've opened my heart to God, I've learned so much more about myself.

"Since I've opened my heart to God I've also experienced a true joy that I've never felt before. It is a joy in the simple everyday things that somehow I used to miss; in the everyday blessings that through life's distractions, I used to look right past. I have been blessed with four beautiful children and a beautiful wife, and I don't want one day to go by without telling them that I love them very much. This is just one simple thing but it brings me so much joy.

"I'm not afraid anymore to say I'm scared or that I need God in my life. In fact, it's much easier to turn to Him and ask for His help and to receive his blessings."

John and I were both in tears by the time Steve finished. For a grown man to get up in front of a church full of parishioners to share this remarkable story was intensely moving to us. And it reinforced our feelings and beliefs that Charlie had not gone through this experience in vain. People from all walks of life have learned much from Charlie's life and his battle to stay here on earth.

Look Who's Turning One!

"Franklin Boy Celebrates First Birthday, And His Life, Today" was the headline of our local paper on Saturday, August 26, 2000. And there was a pretty unflattering picture of the four of us on the cover. The newspaper reporter had gotten John's name from the public relations folks handling the Pan Mass Challenge, which is a 200-mile bike-ride he and five other family members rode in to raise money for cancer research and the Jimmy Fund Clinic at the Dana-Farber. "Why'd you get involved in the PMC?" the reporter asked John over the phone. "Well, my one-year-old son has a rare form of brain cancer and he was originally a patient at the Dana-Farber. So we rode for him and for the thousands of others who are battling cancer," he answered. That was the end of the story on the PMC. Then the article took a completely new spin about a miracle right here in Franklin.

Little Charlie John Capodanno was turning one year old. To celebrate, we rented a big castle-shaped "moonwalk" for the back yard, and had close to 60 people join us in a birthday bash. Our theme was the "yellow smiley face," because it just reminded me of Charlie, a life-sized smiley face with a bald head!

Before the guests arrived, I did something I probably shouldn't have done. I pulled out the photo album from the day Charlie was born. He was gorgeous from the minute he was delivered by C-section. He had a mop of thick black hair; he was so Italian-looking at birth.

It seemed like a lifetime had already passed. He'd been through so much in the first year of his young life, more than many people would endure in a lifetime. Months earlier we had no idea if he'd ever see his first birthday, and here he was, preparing to blow out, or at least drool on, the candles on his cake. I got a little choked up, and decided to put the pictures away.

That was then; this is now. And look how far we'd come. Nothing was slowing him down. Nothing. He was developing right along with all the rest of the one-year-olds we knew. He was not delayed in any way, shape or form. I practiced singing *Happy Birthday* to him so that I wouldn't lose it in front of everyone during the real event. It was more than a birthday celebration; it was undoubtedly a celebration of the gift of his precious life. We were thrilled to have all our friends and family around to share in Charlie's special day. It helped to distract us from the fact that, three days later, Charlie would once again go under the knife, for his fifth surgery, to place a shunt in his brain.

Surgery Number Five

Yes, the dreaded shunt was no longer an option. The pooling had caused Charlie's head to swell around the new incision and the catheter was not capable of alleviating the problem. We had a CT scan done at Children's, and the Thursday before the party, I had brought the scans, as well as Charlie, to Dr. G's office.

She took one look at both, and said, "It's not good." I thought I was going to fall on the floor.

"What's not good?" I said, feeling the hair on my neck beginning to stand up.

"Oh, the ventricle pooling isn't good," she clarified.

"Cripes!" I swallowed hard. "You might want to use another phrase than 'not good.' I thought you meant the cancer was not good, like you saw growth or something on the scan!" Don't doctors know that certain word choices like that can take years off a mother's life?

So, once again, we checked into Children's Hospital for Monday morning surgery with Dr. G. In a way, we were getting used to it. You don't have the same fears you do when your child first has surgery, such as panicking that he's going to be sedated, panicking that something could go wrong. Especially after his lengthy brain surgery, this stuff just seemed to be routine. But it was still a drag that he'd have to endure it and even more of a drag because we'd only had two and a half weeks at home since the last chemo. So this was cutting into our "home time" and it also meant more time away from Jay Bird. Dr. G informed us that Charlie could experience more pain after this surgery because the shunt is implanted in the brain, then threaded down through his neck and into his stomach, where another incision is made. John volunteered to stay that night. We were told Charlie would be sedated for the entire night, and he would need to lay flat for 24 hours after the surgery — which we all knew was going to be next to impossible for him, regardless of the pain. But in true Charlie style, we were in and out of the hospital in record time.

After the Shock – Annoyance Sets In

I must say I was a complete crank for pretty much the entire month of August. I wasn't sure exactly why. I couldn't honestly pinpoint what it was that was bothering me. Well, okay, maybe that my one-year-old was battling brain cancer — but other than that, I'm not sure what my problem was. Why was this month particularly difficult? His two inpatient treatments went well, and his MRIs and spinals had shown great results. Then I thought maybe it was his birthday that was bothering me. This certainly wasn't what I had dreamed the first year of his life would be about. I wasn't feeling great about myself; perhaps that was it. Having fabulous, lip-smacking meals made for us for over four months was awesome, but my gut and my butt were wearing every last bite! None of my clothes fit. And I was in desperate need of a haircut. I was looking like Mackenzie Phillips during her days on *One Day at a Time*. I let my worried friends know that I wasn't going to take a swan dive off the John Hancock Tower or anything, but I really needed to find some time just for me.

I decided to join the gym for a three-month special and quickly learned it would have been just as much a waste of money if I had rolled down the window of my Toyota Camry on Route 495 and tossed the $199 into the wind.

But I tried. Well, sort of. The first day, I worked out on the equipment for a good solid 15 minutes, then I grabbed a magazine and sat by the pool reading an article on Kel Preston and the insecurity she felt when she first married John Travolta. "Well, that was a good workout," I laughed. "I'll do better next time." The next time I joined the "Guts and Butts" class. This was what I needed. Come to find out, the class was canceled. Okay, I'll try the "Mix it up" class, which turned out to be kickboxing. All I could think of was that I looked like an uncoordinated woman trying to violently shake seaweed off her leg at the beach. Plus,

I felt like I was surrounded by some pretty angry women punching out their frustrations at imaginary people in front of them! So I found my niche in Aqua Aerobics, along with about ten other women, all over the age of 60. I stuck with this class for, oh, about three weeks. That was it. I didn't lose an ounce. Instead, I went to the mall and bought some new clothes and vowed to dress nicely whenever we had clinic visits. I thought if I felt better about my appearance, I'd feel better all around. Of course, I just bought bigger sizes this time!

The Central Line from Hell

Our September inpatient treatment was a drag. Tuesday and Wednesday night he did okay, but Thursday night was just horrible. First, I had noticed what looked like a bubble in Charlie's central line. "I swear," I complained to John, "this central line will be the death of me." The nurse paged the surgeon on call. While waiting for the general surgeon to arrive, Dr. Heilman, the neurosurgeon, stopped in to remove the bandages and the stitches left over from the shunt surgery. As gentle of a man as Dr. Heilman is, he didn't give us any warning. He placed one hand on Charlie's head, and with quick and precise force, he ripped the bandage right off. My eyes popped out of my head. "*Ouch!*" I yelled. "That had to have hurt!"

Charlie, who was sitting on John's lap, was screaming. "I know, I'm sorry, but there's no other way; to peel it off slowly would be agony for him," Dr. Heilman said. He proceeded to remove the stitches, first from Charlie's head, then his stomach. Charlie wailed in protest and pain. My poor little baby. As a parent, you never, ever get used to seeing your child in pain, even when it becomes a normal part of your life. So that was at 6:30 p.m. At 7:00 the surgeon came down to once again repair the central line. Charlie was tied down to a board for a half hour, completely alert, as they repaired the line. And because we could not use the repaired line for 12 hours, they needed to run an IV needle through his arm. This was one of the most grueling periods John and I had experienced in a long time, not to mention how completely agonizing it was for precious Charlie. "I wish he could just be a normal one-year-old," I whimpered through my exhaustion.

We were finally discharged on Friday, but things didn't seem to improve at home. For five straight mornings in a row, Charlie threw up his morning bottle. In Brain Tumor Land, this is not good. Morning vomiting is a symptom of a brain tumor. Or the shunt could be backing up. I had Dr. Kretschmar paged. Fortunately, she was on call that weekend. I explained the situation. "Oh, that's not good," she said. She told us to meet her in the in the ER for a CT scans and X-rays.

See, in Cancerville, you absolutely have to rule every possible scenario out. You can't leave any room for error. If this was Jay, and he was throwing up, we'd all know he had a bug. But with Charlie, it sends everyone into a tailspin.

We weren't overly concerned this time, because Dr. Kretschmar did not seem alarmed at all. Both the CT scan and the X-ray looked okay. He must have caught the bug. Phew. For us it was just another unplanned, unwanted visit to the ER. "Oh well," John smiled, "as always, it could have been worse, right?"

We Go Up! We Go Down.

By Monday morning at the clinic, Charlie was feeling better. We sat coloring at the arts and crafts table. When Dr. Kretschmar came in, I stood up to let her know he was feeling better.

"Well, that's good, because I just got the cytology from the surgery at Children's. It appears, well the fax indicates, that they see some abnormal cells in his cerebrospinal fluid." Her words caught me completely off guard. I felt my knees buckle, and I had to put my hand down on the reception desk to catch my balance.

"What, what does that mean?" I asked, my voice shaking.

"Now, I don't know exactly, and I'm only reading it off a fax. They're saying they see abnormal cells again. But I'm trying to get Dr. Goumnerova on the phone right now. I don't know where the cells were taken from, his brain or his spine. Let me find out more information and then we can talk. Please, Mrs. Capodanno," she said calmly, obviously seeing the fear in my eyes growing, "don't panic yet."

The nurse came down the hall and ushered Charlie into a treatment room to access his line. My whole body was shaking. Every last muscle and joint tightened. I could feel my throat begin to close and tears welled in my eyes. After Charlie was hooked up to his pre-medication, I picked him up off the chair, dragging the IV pole behind us. I must have looked as if I had just seen a ghost. One of the mothers came over to me to ask if I needed help. I couldn't respond to her. I just shook my head as the tears began to roll down my cheeks. I walked out into the hall, clutching Charlie close to my chest, and walked over to the wall of windows.

"This can't be happening to him; please Jesus, don't let this happen. We've come so far, please," I pleaded.

"Mrs. Capodanno," Cathy yelled down to me from the clinic doorway, "we're ready; I've got the chemo all set." I shuffled slowly back to the clinic in a zombie-like state. She could tell I was upset, but she remained calm.

"Cathy, how can this be? What could this mean?" At this point I was completely dazed as she performed Charlie's exam.

"I know you're scared, but don't panic. Dr. K hasn't even talked to Dr. G yet. Stay calm, okay? Let those two talk first," she said calmly.

We hung around the clinic for four hours and I stayed close to the trash barrel because I was on the verge of dry-heaving the entire time. Finally Dr. K came out, but she still hadn't heard back from Children's. "Please, go home. I promise I'll call you the minute I hear from her," she instructed us.

"Are you worried?" I asked, with a complete look of despair on my face.

"No. Not yet. I'm not sure. This report isn't clear. It doesn't...." she went on and on, way beyond my mental capacity at that point. I just kept shaking my head in disbelief.

"Please, I don't care what time it is; please give me a call once you've heard, please," I asked her repeatedly. I didn't want to leave, but I knew it could take hours, or even days, before she connected with Children's.

So here we were again, and the roller coaster we were on was spiraling downward just as it had done before, with no one at the controls.

Isn't Anybody Listening?

I packed up our bags and slowly shuffled through the halls to the garage. My mind was racing, but my body was completely numb. I was clutching Charlie's body so tightly as I carried him, I actually felt him wince. The hallway from the clinic to the garage was exceptionally long. And on the days when my head was clouded with terrifying thoughts, it was even longer. "How could this be happening?" I said out loud. "How could they see bad cells again? Why? How?" I questioned myself, as I continued down the hall and up seven flights of stairs, carrying Charlie on my waist and frequently bumping into people along the way.

Once we reached the car, I opened the door and strapped him in his car seat. He was smiling gleefully, and I just knelt down next to him outside the car. I knelt still, in silence, for what seemed to be forever, just staring at his precious and innocent face. He had no idea, at the age of one, what he was up against. No idea that he had a disease that could claim his young life. He didn't have the fear John and I lived with every day. He just sat there, smiling and giggling at me. "How...we'd come so far...how could this be happening to us again?" I said, burying my face against his tiny body. I tried to regain my composure but was unsuccessful. I thought out loud, "I love this child more with every breath I take." He and Jay were my life. They were a part of me. And once again, we were facing a battle to save Charlie's precious life here on earth. I couldn't lose him. I was *not* going to let him leave us. He was not going to lose his life to this horrific disease.

I finally got off my knees and climbed into the driver's seat. The drive to the day care to pick up Jay was always long, but even longer after receiving such frightening news. I adjusted the rearview mirror to catch another glimpse of Charlie. Chewing on his teething toy, and with a huge drool running down his cheek, he laughed out loud. Within five minutes of leaving the parking lot, Charlie was sound asleep.

There I was, once again alone with only my thoughts. As I wept openly, I recited over and over in my head the news that Dr. K had delivered to me: "Children's saw some abnormal cells in his CSF." My sadness quickly turned to anger, then hysteria.

"Why, why is this happening, God, why?" I screamed. It was the first time I'd *ever* questioned God and showed Him my anger. I was crying and screaming at the top of my lungs. At one point I completely startled Charlie, but then he dozed back off. My face was drenched with tears.

"I can't understand...we've come so far...he's done so well...why is this happening again? How could the cancer be back? He's a little boy... just a baby...he deserves to grow up and have fun, and get married and be a daddy...why is he spending his young life in a friggin' hospital fighting for his survival every day?" My voiced rose to a pitch I'd never heard before.

"*Jesus, aren't You listening to me? Please don't take him from me. Please, please, please. We love him so much. Please, don't You hear us? Doesn't anybody hear us praying? Any of you? Saint Jude, Saint Anthony, Saint Theresa? Our guardian angels? Anyone?*" I cried, slamming my fist against the steering wheel. I leaned over and looked up to the sky.

"*Can't You hear me begging You to save my son's life on this earth? Is anyone listening?*" I sobbed, wiping the tears with my shirtsleeve.

I glanced out my driver's side window. Within a split second, a *Boston Globe* delivery truck passed me, immediately followed by a Staples Office Supply truck. My left hand immediately went up over my mouth as I gasped. Instinctively, I tugged at the wheel as I caught myself swerving into the next lane. Although I was still crying, a huge smile engulfed my face. I wasn't crazy; in fact I was in complete shock over what had just happened.

Since Charlie was diagnosed, I had been praying not only to God and my patron saints, but also to a few people that I had known who had lost their lives to cancer. Wonderful people like "Aunt Paula" Fellows (an aunt of my childhood friend's), Theresa Carroll, Mr. McCafferty and Mr. Coakley (all parents of dear friends of mine), John Kavanaugh (a junior high classmate), "Mary Katherine" (that's what I decided to name the woman in the gray suit who appeared to me on Good Friday), Bradley Andrews* (the young boy from our pediatrician's office who passed away because of a brain tumor), and a very special friend and old boss from Hill, Holliday, Tom Woodard.

Tom was a great man, a nice guy, dedicated to his family. He battled cancer for a long time, went into remission, relapsed, and finally succumbed to the disease about three years earlier. I knew Tom understood how horrible cancer was, and how much strength someone

*Name changed to protect privacy.

248

would need to battle the disease. He was a thoughtful and caring man, and I knew he'd be willing to hear my prayers and help Charlie out if he could. That's the type of man he was. I called upon Tom to be one of Charlie's guardian angels in heaven. I asked him to plead with God to cure Charlie of his disease, so that he could live a normal and happy life here on earth. So, as I was ranting and raving, screaming and crying and swearing, slamming my fist, and hollering at the sky asking, *"Don't any of you hear me?"* Tom sent me a sign that he did. He heard me loud and clear.

I had worked for Tom on three accounts at the advertising agency. Two of the three accounts were The Boston Globe and Staples Office Supplies. (The third account was Killington Mountain, and it would have been pretty difficult for him to send the mountain barreling down the highway as well that day.) Having those two trucks pass by me simultaneously during my tirade was Tom's polite and clever way of saying, "Yes, Deirdre, I hear you. We all hear you. We are up here, and we do hear your prayers."

"Thank you, Tom," I whispered. I felt humbled. I felt embarrassed by my tirade. I knew someone was hearing our prayers and our pleas and it was very comforting. But also pretty bizarre. I wanted to tell Kristine about it as I went to pick up Jay, but I think I felt, at that point, everyone might think I was losing my marbles given the situation I was in. It's not like on an average day you can walk up to your friends and neighbors and say, "Hey, this really cool thing happened on the way home from the hospital. See, I just got a sign from my old boss. You remember Tom? He died of cancer, remember? Anyway, he's in heaven now, and while I was having a mental breakdown on the highway, well, he sent me a sign that he's hearing my prayers."

Or in the case of the mysterious woman in the gray suit, "Hey, listen to this! One day while I was dozing off at the hospital, a woman appeared to me to say that Charlie is not going to Jesus yet." Let's face it, this stuff doesn't happen to people every day, and if it does, it's not like you run around shouting it from the mountaintops. I didn't want people to think I was nuts. There are people who would believe me, and people who wouldn't. I would swear on the heads of both my children, and on my own life, these events actually happened. But since the signs seemed to happen only to me, I decided I'd hold off on mentioning them to anyone until a more appropriate time. Like when people wouldn't look at me as if I had three heads. For now, these signs were safe inside me.

When John walked in the door that night, he could tell I had been upset. I explained what Dr. K had said, including that she wanted to wait to talk to Dr. G herself to get a better understanding of how the test was done, where the fluid was taken from, etc.

"Good. I agree with her. Let's not panic until she has more information," he said, grabbing a Mountain Dew from the refrigerator.

"I know, but I'm so scared."

"Why freak out before we know?"

"Because I'm a freak," I said, grabbing Charlie to feed him his bottle. "I guess it's my nature now, to freak out when people tell me that my son's cancer might be back in his spine!" And since we were on the subject that I was a freak, I subtly mentioned to John the sign Tom had given during my temper tantrum. We were sitting on the couch, watching the kids dance around to a *Grease* CD (mommy's choice, of course). I shared the experience with him as if I was telling him about something totally normal. He listened, and replied in true John fashion.

"Wow. That's weird, huh?" was all he said. He never made a big deal out of anything!

I frantically spent the next two days on the phone, back and forth with Children's and the Floating, trying to get answers regarding the CSF issue. I wasn't going to wait for the two doctors to connect by themselves.

I was going to intervene myself. I finally got Dr. Goumnerova on the phone.

"Hi, Dr. Goumnerova, it's Deirdre Capodanno," I said.

"Yes, yes, I understand you've been trying to get in touch with me," she said. Okay, so I must have left seven messages with her assistant Sandi all on the same day. "I've been in surgery today," she explained. It was her polite way of saying she'd gotten my messages, and she had planned to call me back as soon as she had a free minute.

"I know, I'm sorry, but I'm panicking about the report you sent to the Floating that you saw abnormal cells in the fluid," I said anxiously.

"Yes, yes, we do see some abnormal cells, that is correct," she replied.

"Well, where did you take them from, his brain or his spine?"

Dr. K had said that if the abnormal cells had been taken from his brain, that could make sense because there were still two "spots" there that could have been remaining tumor tissue. If they had taken it from his spine this would be more of a concern since previous reports had shown the CSF was clear.

"No, no, we took the fluid from his brain while we were doing the shunt placement," she answered.

"Okay, so it was from his head. Then what do you think about this finding?" I asked her.

"Well, we didn't say it was a malignancy, just abnormal cells. I believe we just need to be aware of it, and to keep our eye on it, okay?" She was trying to sound upbeat and she was doing her best not to freak me out, which at this point was useless.

"Well, they're going to re-test him next week," I informed her.

"Very good then, let me know how things go. And if you have any questions, you know where to find me, okay?" she said, ending our conversation.

Self-Diagnosing

I was trying to feel better after our conversation, but I was still a basket case. In hopes of calming my nerves, Dr. Kretschmar bumped up the appointment for the next lumbar puncture.

"I'm really not worried," she kept telling me. But I was relentless, calling her constantly to ask her questions. She was very gracious, trying as best she could to explain to me, over and over, how the CSF around the brain could show different things. Finally, after my sixth call, she said, "Mrs. Capodanno, please, let's just wait to see what the results say, okay?" She certainly knew how to put me in my place, graciously at that.

I took many deep breaths that day. And after putting the boys to sleep, I climbed into bed and prayed. "Please, God, please send us good news after the next test, please." I continued praying and pleading, and at some point I dozed off. During the early morning hours I dreamed about the abnormal cells in Charlie's head dripping cancerous cells through his newly implanted shunt and dumping them into his belly. With a jolt I awoke covered in sweat. Once again, my wheels were spinning out of control. I jumped out of bed and immediately paged John.

"Honey, listen, I'm freaking out about something," I gasped.

"That's a shock," John joked. I didn't find his comment amusing, but wasn't going to address it at that time. I had other things on my mind.

"Okay, so we know that there may possibly be abnormal cells in his brain, right?"

"Yeah," he answered, wondering where I was going with this line of questioning.

"And the purpose of the shunt is to help drain the fluid that's backing up in his brain, by sending it down the shunt into his stomach, right?"

"I guess, yeah, that's what the shunt does."

"Well then, it must be dumping abnormal cells into his stomach. If so, then what on earth is preventing it from spreading cancer to his belly? That's what the shunt does!" I screamed at the top of my lungs.

"Honey, I don't know. It's a good question," he said, not sounding the least bit alarmed. John had such an amazing way of handling my self-diagnoses and me. "Call the clinic and ask them, and let me know what they say. I gotta go," he said, needing to end the conversation.

It wasn't at all that he didn't care; it's just that he constantly had to put up with hearing these things that I conjured up in my own head, some of them valid, some of them downright crazy. But I was really scared about what I had concluded to be happening in Charlie's body. This was the person I became, a person obsessed with finding a cure, or finding a reason, or self-diagnosing things. When your child has a life-threatening disease, you can become insane.

As usual, I dialed the clinic at 8:31 a.m. "Cathy, it's Deirdre Capodanno." I was breathless. I went on to explain my discovery.

"Well, Mrs. Capodanno, I don't have the answer for that one. It is very interesting. We've had tons of kids here with shunts, and I've never known that to be a problem. But it's definitely worth asking the doctor," she replied.

"Promise me you'll call me back as soon as you talk to her," I begged.

"You know I will! I know you, and I know you won't rest until I do," she laughed. I'm sure she thought I was making a mountain out of a molehill, but I honestly didn't care. I was Charlie's mother, I was his advocate, and I intended to do whatever it took to help him survive. I hung up from that conversation and quickly dialed Children's. There was no way I was going to wait to hear back from the clinic. That could take all day. Luckily, Dr. G was available.

"What's preventing the shunt from dripping cancer into his stomach?" I said anxiously.

"Wow. You really have been thinking about this, haven't you?" she laughed.

"Yes, I have," I answered, slightly embarrassed.

"Well, it's a good question, although no one has ever mentioned it before. You see, the shunt acts like a filter with a tiny drain, and any abnormal cells, which are different shapes than healthy ones, will get caught in the filter, so they can't pass through to his intestines. I wouldn't worry about this. It was a good question. You're very thorough, Mrs. Capodanno," she added. But I felt like a loser.

"I'm sorry to have bothered you, it's just..." I could feel myself choking up. "I just want him to live. I want the cancer to be gone. I'm just doing my best to...." I said as my voice trailed off.

"I know you are," she said gently.

I paged John. "My theory got squashed. I was wrong," I informed him.

"That's good," he answered.

"I way over-think things, don't I?"

"Definitely," he laughed.

I couldn't help it, or control it. This was the way I was. Thank God for John. We were a good balance for the doctors and nurses. I am pushy. He is patient. I panic. He stays calm. When I question things, he's the voice of reason.

I have a distant cousin whose child had a brain tumor. Fortunately, her daughter has been in remission for about five years. One day she told me that she'd been talking to a specialist who insisted that she never feed her daughter hot dogs ever again, due to all the nitrates they have inside them. These nitrates could bring the cancer back. I got off the phone and immediately informed John that Charlie would never eat another hot dog again. He laughed in my face and said, "Hot dogs are part of being American. What good would living be without a hot dog?" After his wise-cracking comment, my hot dog strike only lasted one day.

Chapter 10
The Greatest Gift of All

···

Boy in the Bubble

Occasionally during the first year of treatment, we called Charlie the "bubble boy," because if we weren't at the hospital, we were trapped inside our house. All we ever saw of the outside world was the hospital and the Mass Pike. Given that chemotherapy weakened his immune system, we had to be very cautious of germs. And when you are a one-year-old, you put everything in your mouth. I was obsessed, because even a common cold could wreak havoc for us. Poor Charlie. For one full year he could only play with his brother, and occasionally the two neighborhood boys, KJ and Colin, as long as they were outside.

But since I was so stressed about the spinal fluid issue, and before I diagnosed him with something else, I decided it was time to break out. Fred and Ginger, our two beagles, had torn apart the comforter on our bed. I'm guessing they were acting out due to lack of attention — what a surprise! So Charlie and I went to Linens and Things to search for a new comforter. You should have seen the looks I got from fellow shoppers as I completely scrubbed the shopping cart handle and seat with antibacterial wipes before I plopped Charlie in. "Germs, yucky," I said as I smiled and winked at one woman.

It felt wonderful to be out and about with him! This was a new and very exciting experience for him as well. He hadn't been in a store since he was about five months old. And he sure as heck had no recollection of that. He was thrilled to be in the seat of the carriage, checking things out, although that lasted for all of seven minutes. "Up, up," he said, pointing into the carriage. He wanted to sit inside. "Only if you will sit down," I instructed him. "Sit, I sit," he replied.

I hoisted him up into the body of the carriage and again began wheeling him around. Of course, he immediately stood up, facing outward. "Wheeee," he squealed, bending his knees up and down in excitement. He was having a ball. He was free! He was seeing things literally for the first time! This was a whole new world for him. People in the store couldn't stop laughing and smiling at him.

"He's precious, but you better watch him," a young mother warned me.

"Oh, I don't take my eyes off him, trust me. He just thinks he's Leonardo DiCaprio in that scene from *Titanic* – 'I'm king of the world.'" We both laughed.

I dreaded bringing him home, so off we headed to the crafts store. He ran like a madman up and down the aisles. It was as if he'd been released from prison and was seeing things he'd never seen before. It was amazing for me to witness this revelation. "Okay, pumpkin, let's go," I told him. At the checkout, the woman behind the counter leaned over to get a closer look at him.

"Oh, he's precious!" She smiled until she noticed his scar and his pale coloring. A very strange look came over her face. "Oh, oh my, what happened to his head?" she asked, placing a hand to her mouth.

"Surgery," I answered, shuffling through my cash.

"Oh, dear, it wasn't a tumor, was it?" Her voice grew louder. At this point, she had attracted the attention of all the customers and clerks around us. I gave her a semi-uncomfortable smile.

"Yes, yes, it was a tumor," I answered matter-of-factly.

"It wasn't *cancer*, was it?" she shrieked.

"Yup," I replied, placing my change on the counter and giving her a semi-sarcastic grin.

"He is gonna live, isn't he?" she asked directly.

"I surely hope so! That's what we're praying for," I said, grabbing Charlie and heading out the door. "Say a prayer for him; his name is Charlie."

And with that, we left. I was glad I could finally make it through an encounter like that without falling to pieces. This was an enormous step for me.

Inquiring Minds Want to Know

Now that I was comfortable with bringing Charlie out into the germ-infested world, we both felt like new people. Still, everywhere we went, someone asked, "What happened to his head?" I guess I could have forced him to wear a hat to avoid these confrontations, but he didn't like hats at all. A week after the crafts store, we were in line at the bank with about six other people. I had mastered the art of pinpointing the exact kind of person who was going to ask about the scars. They weren't of a certain gender, color, or social status. They were just the ones who, once they spotted the scars, would shift around, rearranging their position, to try to check it out from every angle. Then they'd finally ask. We were in the middle of the line, and as usual, I could see this guy shifting his body weight back and forth, trying to catch a glimpse of Charlie's head.

"Mercy, what the heck happened to his head?" the stranger asked bluntly.

"Brain surgery," I replied.

"Was it cancer?"

"Yes, but he's doing amazingly well," I said, stroking the 18 strands of hair Charlie still had left on his head.

"God bless him," the guy mumbled under his breath.

"Oh, He already has, but feel free to say a prayer for him!"

The Spots

On Wednesday, September 26, Charlie underwent another MRI and lumbar puncture. As always, the waiting part was stressful. And as usual, we waited and waited and waited. John (believe it or not) and I were both anxious about these results because it was the first LP he'd had since Children's detected the abnormal cells. By mid-afternoon on Friday, we still hadn't heard. I called the clinic again.

"Mary Jo, its Deirdre Capodanno. I know I'm a bother, but I don't want to sweat this out the entire weekend. Please, for my sanity, and for a relaxing weekend for my family, could you check and see if the results are in," I begged.

"Sorry, I just checked. I knew you'd be calling. I promise, if we know by 5:00, I'll call," she replied.

"Okay, here's John's cell number. We have a meeting with a lawyer to discuss a trust we're setting up for the boys with some of the money raised from the fundraiser that was held in July for our family," I rambled. "Anyway, please give us a call, please."

We were still at the attorney's office at 5:30 when the cell phone rang.

"Hey, Mary Jo, how are you?" John asked. He was silent, but was raising his eyebrows and had a smile on his face. "Great, that's great news," he said. I started waving my hands in the air. "Wait, the boss wants to talk to you. If I relay the info, she'll quiz me for the next hour about the tone in your voice and stuff like that," he said as he handed me the phone.

"What's up? What's the story?" I asked impatiently.

"Good news," she answered. "The initial report on the spinal fluid is clear, which is what we were hoping for. And we don't expect the final report will be any different. Now, the MRI showed no change in the two spots on his brain." I slumped back in my chair. "Now remember," she continued, "no change is good. It means the chemo is working, right?"

"Oh," I sighed, "I know, I just want to see it shrink. I want them *gone*. I don't want them there at all."

"Remember, this is still very positive news," she concluded.

After we finished a very uncomfortable conversation with our attorney about how our children's trust should be worded in the event "Charlie didn't make it," we got back in the car.

"It's been nine weeks since they've seen any shrinkage," I sighed.

"So what! I'm psyched," John responded. "No growth is awesome!"

He was right, but in the back of my mind, I just wanted those spots to go away. Forever. They just seemed to be lingering there, idling, like a ticking bomb. All I could say to myself was, "What could they be, and why weren't they shrinking? Will they ever disappear? The doctors were so excited in the beginning to see them shrinking; now they're not, but they don't seem to be concerned. Why can't they go away?" I couldn't imagine going on knowing those spots were there, and wondering, when, just when, they would start growing.

Sleep Deprivation Is Not a Good Thing

We had two scheduled admissions for chemo in November. Both, fortunately, were uneventful. John and I had been trying for weeks to get Charlie to sleep alone in his bed. And of course there was a lot of crying going on as we tried "training" him. Now mind you, listening to a child scream and cry at night is torture for any parent. Try doing this with a child who has a life-threatening illness! It's absolutely excruciating. But we desperately needed sleep ourselves in order to function as semi-normal human beings – well, as normal as we could possibly be. So we tried, and tried, and tried.

We even tried, in vain, to put him back in the crib in the hospital after the nurses had awakened him. There was one nurse in particular whom John and I dubbed "The Slammer." She had no concept of closing and opening the door quietly. She barged in and barged out, slamming the door every single time. She didn't even try to keep quiet. I was pretty sure I was going to kill her. On this particular night, I was so determined not to let her wake Charlie that I didn't sleep a wink. The minute the nurse came in to change his diaper, I jumped out of bed. "I'll do that," I insisted, lowering the side of the crib ever so slowly in order to not awaken him. It took me about 10 minutes to change him, but I didn't care how slow I was going; I was *not* going to wake him up. I saw every single hour on the clock turn. Charlie slept well from 10:15 p.m. to 3:00 a.m. I thought this was a marked improvement. He woke briefly, but we both dozed off at around 4:00 a.m., and Charlie was bright-eyed and bushy tailed at 5:00 on the nose. I, on the other hand, was beat.

The next night was John's night to stay. "Good luck," I said, kissing him on the cheek and yawning. "I hope you get more sleep than I did." I was so incredibly exhausted, I almost drove off the Mass Pike – twice.

Back at the hospital, with Daddy's magic touch, Charlie fell asleep around 8:30 p.m. and slept straight through until 5:00 a.m. This was unbelievable. Luckily for John, Heather, one of our favorite nurses, was on that night. She crept into the room ever-so-quietly, took extra care and time changing Charlie so as not to wake him, tip-toed around the room, and amazingly, managed to get to the IV pump just minutes before it was to beep so that John and Charlie wouldn't be awakened. Charlie didn't finally wake up until Heather needed to take his blood.

"Is it okay if I take him for a walk?" she offered.

"Sure," John said, wiping the sleep from his eyes. In true John style, he instantly fell back to sleep. Heather and the other nurses took care of Charlie for the next three and a half hours while Sleeping-Beauty John snoozed away! They finally returned Charlie when he needed to nap at 8:30 a.m. I strolled in at 9:45 with a box of munchkins, and the two of them were fast asleep!

"Ahhh, my back's killing me from lying in this bed so long," John said seriously upon awakening.

"Very funny, Honey!" I said with more than a touch of sarcasm in my voice.

Losing Julia

November 12 was a horrible day. John was napping when the phone rang.

"Hello, Mrs. Capodanno, it's Katie from the clinic," the voice said.

"Hey, Katie, what's up?" I replied.

Katie is the social worker at the clinic. I was surprised to hear from her and was very curious why she was calling.

"I've got some sad news, I'm afraid," she said. "Julia passed away last night." I was in complete shock. Julia was a beautiful little girl who had been battling leukemia since she was two years old. She was to turn five that very week. She had gone into remission three separate times, but only to continue to relapse. Since July she'd been in isolation at the hospital, meaning no visitors except for her mom and her docs and nurses. She was holed up in that room for almost four months, but on November 11, she was finally going to be able to go home for her birthday.

I had become very close to her mom Isabel. We'd spend lots of time just talking. Like John and me, Isabel didn't focus on the "why us" stuff. She just dealt with it. She, too, had an amazingly strong faith that kept her going every day. She was, in my eyes, the strongest woman I'd ever met, but in a very gracious and special way. John and I bought Isabel a celebratory lunch the afternoon Julia was leaving the hospital: shrimp cocktail and a lobster salad sandwich from Legal Seafood. We wanted her to know how excited we were for her that Julia was finally going home.

Like her mom, Julia was amazingly strong, and boy, she was a fighter! Yet understandably, she grew depressed after being in isolation for so long. She wanted to go home. Only this time, home wasn't her Groveland, Mass., home. It was heaven. Julia had only been home a few hours when she died.

At the wake, Julia's mom told us that she believed Julia knew she was going to die, and that there was no way she was going to die in that dreaded hospital room. Nights earlier, when a nurse asked her who she was talking to when she was alone in her bed, she had said "her angels." Imagine, at only five years old, this brave little princess having the determination to leave this earth the way she had chosen, not at the hospital, but at her own home. John and I fell to pieces at the wake, and continued to cry the entire ride home. This was terrifying to us. Our hearts were crushed for this beautiful family that now had to somehow continue their lives without their precious child. And what was equally painful was that this could be us some day.

"Babies aren't supposed to be born and suffer for three years to remain alive and then die," I cried.

"I know," John wept. "It's just not right, those poor parents…How are they supposed to go on?…And their son…What's his life going to be like without his sister?…It's just so wrong.…I just want to go home…I don't care if the kids are asleep…we're waking them up…I just want to hold them, and kiss them." He sobbed uncontrollably. This was just the grim reality we as parents of cancer children face: the fear of the unknown. As brave as we were, and as optimistic as we continued to be, watching a little one lose her life to this disease is nothing less than excruciating. And in the back of our minds, we thought, "Could this be us?" You never want to think it, or discuss it, but the mind plays evil tricks on you, and you have no control over it. As we were leaving Julia's wake, our minds were playing these brutal tricks on both of us. Would that happen to us? Would we be standing by a tiny casket? Would our lives be destroyed? My body shuddered at the thought.

No Crystal Ball

Given what we saw Julia go through, John and I decided we both wanted to sit down with Dr. K and discuss as much as we could about Charlie's future treatments.

"I don't have a crystal ball," she said. "I wish I did. I wish I could tell you he'll be fine, he'll be cured, but I just can't say that. I hope you understand. But," she went on, "let me tell you something – kids like Charlie don't grow on trees. He's an amazingly strong little boy."

She was being honest, and that's what we respected most about her. We all agreed Charlie was amazing. Every doctor, nurse and specialist we'd come in contact with was just in awe of his strength and determination. "This kid's a fighter," she continued. "I do want to tell you that I believe the remaining spots on his brain are just dead scar tissue," she said, matter-of-factly.

"What do you mean?" I asked, not quite understanding her.

"Well, let's see, it's been nine months since his surgery, and aside from the first month or so of seeing shrinkage, we haven't seen any change in those spots at all," she explained. "So, my guess is if this was a viable, live tumor, it would do one of two things – it would either grow or shrink. And in this case, the spots are indicating it's doing neither. So I'd say what we're seeing in those two spots is either dead tissue, or it's just scarring."

John and I looked at each other and beamed. "Wow. That's great news!" John chimed in.

"So...if nothing changes from now until March, which would be a year since he started treatment, do, you think he'll be done then?" I asked excitedly. At this point, we were both at the edge of our chairs.

"No, probably not," she said, scrunching up her nose and shaking her head. I slumped back in the chair. "Now," she began, "you've got to understand, most of the children on this protocol get a year of chemo and radiation. But remember, we can't radiate Charlie without causing major damage to his brain, so we need to be aggressive with the chemo."

I looked over at John and rolled my eyes. These conversations were never pleasant to hear.

"So to be safe, we will more than likely continue him on chemo. Not the stuff he's on now; we'll probably do Ironotechian. It's done in the clinic, all outpatient," she continued.

"You mean we won't have to sleep here?" I almost jumped out of my chair.

So, all in all, our meeting went very well. It felt like the roller coaster was hitching back on the uphill track again. We were excited about the possibility of switching him off this really harsh chemo. And it would be awesome to do it on an outpatient basis. The thought of not having to sleep in the hospital was the best! To have us all home together under the same roof every night was definitely something to look forward to. It would be better for all of us, but especially Jay. Although we'd hoped in the beginning of treatment that one of us would always be home to put Jay to bed at night, given that John worked long hours and still wanted to share in Charlie's overnight treatment, Jay usually ended up sleeping at his grandparents' house for one night during treatment. And they enjoyed every minute of having him there.

"Now, one last thing I want to mention," she added, "Charlie's lost about a pound. Not sure why. It's nothing to be alarmed about," she said, turning toward me. I got the message: don't freak out about this. "We're going to hook him up to some lipids and fat during this week's treatments to see if we can put a little weight back on him."

Once we were admitted, they hung a bottle to his line that was labeled "fat and lipids." It was white, and it looked like milk. "That's gross, isn't it?" I said to John.

"Nasty," he replied.

"Listen," I said to one of the resident doctors walking by, "I know people can donate blood and platelets, but is there any way I can donate some fat? I've got plenty on either side of my hips and my gut that I'd be more than willing to have someone suck out for the good of medical science and mankind," I laughed.

Just nights before, I had gone to my high-school reunion, where I was approached by a former classmate. "Hey, Miss Carey," this guy said, addressing me by my maiden name. "Looks like you're expecting, huh?" he said joyfully. I felt my face blush in embarrassment. "No, David, actually, I had my last child 15 months ago, but that's just the reality smack I need to get my butt back on the treadmill." I smiled and walked away. Hey, you've gotta laugh, or else you'll cry, right?

A Dangerous MRI

Our November MRI was a bit harrowing, to put it mildly. As always, I insisted on going into the MRI room with Charlie. With much hesitation, the doctor agreed. We were about one hour into the scan and I was saying my usual prayers, chatting with our guardian angels, and sending Charlie all the positive vibes I could. I was guessing we had about 10-15 more minutes until the exam was finished when I heard him whimper. I turned and looked through the two-way window to see if anyone was going to respond to his cry. No one was there.

"Waah," I heard a muffled Charlie begin to cry, and I could see his arms and legs, which were both strapped down, begin to twitch. Although I was forbidden to get out of the chair during the exams, I jumped up and began banging on the window. No one responded. At this point, through what was left of the sedation, Charlie somehow managed to completely flip his entire body over while still strapped down. He was now facing down on the table, with the oxygen mask pressing sharply up against his tiny face. I ran to the door but could not open it. It may have been locked from the outside. I jiggled the handle as hard and as fast as I could. I began pounding frantically, yelling, "Help!" John, who was waiting in a chair right outside the door, heard the banging. He spotted the doctor and three nurses chit-chatting outside the other MRI room.

"Hey, I think someone's trying to get out of that room," he said, raising his voice in confusion.

"Oh no!" The nurses and doctor scurried over and opened the door. They could all see the fury in my eyes.

"He's awake in there, and he's flipped himself over," I said, hovering as close to Charlie as I could. "He's probably terrified in there!" I was mad as hell. They unhooked and unstrapped my baby and I grabbed him immediately out of the nurse's arms. Obviously they did not give him enough anesthesias to get him through the entire exam.

"Gosh, that's never happened before; that's one strong kid you've got there," the nurse remarked. I couldn't even acknowledge her because I was so furious. So was John. He could see how visibly shaken both Charlie and I were.

"He could have seriously injured himself in there! What on earth were they doing out here?" I asked John as he huddled both of us in his arms.

"They were looking at someone's baby pictures!"

"I'll tell you right now, I will *never* not go into that room with him, ever!" I yelled, loud enough so that everyone within earshot could hear me.

Rejoicing at the Holidays

We were so looking forward to the Christmas season. After all, the Grim Reaper had bluntly informed us that if Charlie's cancer continued to progress as it had, he wouldn't see this Christmas.

Charlie was the source of most of our strength. He was the one going through the treatments, and he continued to persevere. He didn't feel sad, he didn't complain, he just kept on going. So who the heck were we to complain?

I spent a great deal of time preparing for the holiday and reflecting on the past year. We'd gone through hell, that's for sure. But especially at this point in our lives, we felt that we were on our way back. We were on the road to recovery. The roller coaster was on track, and going at a steady pace. Sure, we had cried a lot. We'd found ourselves (okay, I found myself) curled up in a fetal position a few times, and there were a few days when we weren't so sure we were still breathing, and had to actually remind ourselves to exhale. But we'd also learned so much in the year about courage, faith, unconditional love, and just how blessed we are to have the friends and family that we do. Without a doubt, we could not have survived without them.

I often think about the poem *Footprints*, and the man walking on the beach who sees only one set of footprints in the sand. He's questioning where God was as the man faced many difficult challenges throughout his life. And God replies that those are His footprints, as He is carrying the man. And I often thought about my own life, what we'd gone through, and how God, my family and friends figuratively and literally carried me through the past year. Our parents did, our sisters and brothers did, my husband did, our friends and neighbors did, our church did, and even complete strangers did. They all carried us from one challenge to the next. We continued to feel truly blessed. Even faced with tragedy, goodness always found a way to shine through.

Our December inpatient chemo treatments went very well. It was five days before Christmas. Some way, somehow, we managed to swing a single room, which made the admission a hundred times more bearable. The Boston Bruins came in for a visit, passing out beautiful toys to all the kids. Camera crews from three different television stations were there, covering the event. Of course, given that Charlie was the youngest patient, everyone wanted to interview us.

"You never expect to be spending Christmas week in the hospital with your baby," John told the interviewer as the camera rolled, "but here we are. And he's doing great. He's a little miracle!" he beamed. Off camera the reporter asked us what was wrong with Charlie. When we told him he had cancer, the man's face just went blank.

"Oh my God, I'm so sorry. He's precious, look at him," he said as we all watched Charlie lick the frosting off a gingerbread man cookie.

"I will absolutely keep him in my prayers; God bless all of you," he said, extending his hand to John.

As we watched the news that night, the sports anchor said sweetly, "Man, I just can't get that little Charlie off my mind, what a tough kid. I wish him all the best."

We attended the clinic's Christmas party on Sunday afternoon. It felt strange. As attached as we were to these families, especially their children, it felt a bit sad to be there. There were families there whose kids were still on treatment, and kids who were off treatment. The staff did a wonderful job of making the cafeteria look festive, with lots of decorations, food, music and gifts not only for the patients, but also for their siblings. But in my heart, it made me sad to think that all these precious children and all these amazing families were there because we shared a common bond – our children were battling a life-threatening disease. It was nice to be able to socialize with the other families outside the confined walls of the clinic, and the 7th Floor. And it was great to see how well the kids who were off chemo were doing, and to reconnect with their families. Still, the minute I got there was the minute I wanted to go home.

I felt claustrophobic. I just *never* wanted to be in that hospital a minute longer than I had too. Because when we were there, we had no control. And every minute I was there, I was missing Jay terribly, and worried about how he was doing. Every minute there robbed me of the semi-normal life we tried to lead in the comfort of our own home.

"I want to go home," I whispered in John's ear after only being there about a half hour.

"Why?" he questioned.

"I just do," was the only explanation I gave.

"Can we wait for Santa to come?" he asked, looking at me oddly.

"All right, and then let's just go, please."

The kids were so excited to see Santa arrive. He had a gift for each child, and he posed for pictures with each of the patients and their siblings. "Charlie and Jay Capodanno," Santa said, summoning the boys to his lap. Jay had *no* interest in going anywhere near Santa. So I carried Charlie up to him and placed him on his lap. Charlie wasn't going to let go of my sweater, so I knelt down beside him for the photo. Just as the Polaroid snapped, Charlie yanked my V-neck sweater down over one entire side of my chest, exposing my bra for all to see! My face went completely red! My flashing episode appeared to be a crowd pleaser, since I heard all sorts of laughs and cheers. John started calling me "Nip," stealing the famous line from a Seinfeld episode when Elaine sent out a holiday card with a picture of herself that accidentally exposed her breast.

I wanted our Christmas cards to be extra special that year. So I wrapped a humungous cardboard box with festive green and red wrapping paper, positioned Jay and Charlie inside of it wearing their PJs, and wrote on the front of it in big red letters, "The Greatest Gift of All." We sent out over 125 cards, and I bet we got over 75 calls or emails from people saying it was the most touching and heartwarming card they had received. But it was so true – our two boys were the only things we wanted for Christmas. They were our greatest gift.

We had a photographer from our local paper "shadow" us for an entire day during our pre-Christmas chemo. Since the first article had been written about Charlie back in August, the paper had received many calls asking how "little Charlie" was doing. So, due to the overwhelming response, the paper asked if they could do an "inspirational" story on Charlie for Christmas. Needless to say, when the paper arrived with the cover photo of Charlie wearing John's baseball hat and staring lovingly into John's eyes, we almost melted. The article was titled "Gift of Hope." It was a wonderful article, but what was even more moving was the full-page spread of pictures inside. One of them was of me in my PJs, sporting morning bed-head, reading Charlie a book in his crib.

Charlie had been filmed early in the month for a public service announcement for the Cam Neely Foundation, which supports cancer research. Cam, a former Bruins hockey star, lost both his parents to cancer. He and his family, as well as a host of celebrity friends, started the Foundation and created the Neely House, which is a "home" within the hospital where families of cancer patients can stay as their loved ones go through treatments nearby. As we were packing up to leave for Christmas, Jeanie, the Child Life specialist, came over and handed me a copy of the taped PSA. "Oh gosh, wait until you see Charlie on this tape," she smiled. When we got home, I popped it into the VCR. It was a very beautiful and touching video, but as the scene panned over to Charlie, I suddenly started shaking. It's just too painful to see your one-year-old child in a commercial for cancer research. He looked angelic, innocent, beautiful, and sickly. He looked like the epitome of a pediatric cancer patient. I refused to watch it ever again.

We spent Christmas Eve with my in-laws at our house, and went to Mass as a family. I couldn't make it through *Silent Night* without shedding a tear, and neither could my mother-in-law. My father-in-law spent just about the entire Mass staring at Charlie. It was as if he just couldn't believe he was there. Jay bounced around from one family member's knee to the next, savoring every minute of the excitement.

We had Christmas brunch at my sister's with her kids. Then it was off to Jill and Matt's for Christmas dinner. And as we all gathered around the table, we held hands as my father-in-law said grace. He thanked God for all our blessings, and for the fact that we were all there together, as a family. The thought that was going through everyone's mind was the same: "Thank You, God that Charlie is here at this table with us. Thank

You, Jesus." We spoke not a word, but each of us squeezed the other's hand.

Charlie Plays Tricks

One snowy morning between Christmas and New Year's, Kristine pulled into our driveway to pick Jay up for day care. Our front steps were very slippery, so I motioned to Kristine for her to stay in the car. I scooped Jay up in my arms and walked him slowly out to Kristine's minivan. I spent a few minutes smothering him with kisses and hugs. It was snowing lightly outside, and our front yard was glistening with a blanket of snow cover.

"What a gorgeous morning," I said to Kristine, as I breathed in the fresh, cold air.

I was only 20 steps away from the house, and Charlie, who was standing at the glass front door, kept waving away. After I tucked Jay into his car seat, I walked back toward the house to a grinning Charlie. As I reached the top step, he slammed the door shut – locking me out! I rattled the doorknob to no avail!

I began frantically running around the outside of the house, wearing only my PJs and shuffling around in John's old sneakers. I checked every window and every door. I climbed up on our deck table and tried to pry open my kitchen window from the outside, but it was frozen shut. I caught a glimpse of Charlie, who jumped up and down, and then with a huge smile on his face, he dashed out of the kitchen. I flew back to the front yard, and met up with Kristine at our front door. "Charlie, Charlie!" the two of us yelled, listening for him to make some noise so we knew he was safe. After about two minutes of silence, we both grew concerned. I raced as fast as I could across the street to my neighbor Anne's house, since she had our spare key. It was only 7:00 in the morning, and I began frantically banging on the front door. Anne's husband Rob appeared baffled at the front door. He grabbed the key from his kitchen drawer and tossed it to me.

"Can you hear anything?" I yelled to Kristine as I darted across the street.

"NO!" she said with concern, with her frozen ear pressed against our front door.

"Where the hell is he?" I screeched. As my cold hand shook, I dropped the key. Kristine and I were now on our hands and knees in the snow searching for the key.

SMASH! We both looked up at each other in a panic. CRASH! SMASH!

"What...what is that?" Kristine asked.

"Sounds like breaking glass!" I yelled. I finally found the key and scrambled to open the door. There under my Christmas tree were a dozen smashed glass ornaments.

"Charlie John Capodanno, where are you?" I yelled out loud. Again, silence. "Charlie!"

I heard a faint giggle and followed its trail. I swung the bathroom door open, and there was my little prince hiding in the tub, behind the shower curtain. I couldn't help but laugh.

"What is it with you, little man? Must you play these tricks on me?!"

See You Later, Millennium!

John and I had enough of the millennium. To quote my husband, "The year 2000 blew!" We were looking forward to, and praying for, an easier, less stressful, less challenging, more sleep-filled, fat-free, and most important, cancer-free 2001!

We absolutely felt that things were headed in the right direction for us. Charlie was still going strong, and he was braver than ever. Jay continued to bring us endless days filled with laughter and smiles. He really was the one, without even knowing it, who kept John and me focused. In his eyes, life was great, and we desperately wanted to keep it that way. My goal was to ring in the New Year with a two-pound lobster, some drawn butter, and the three beautiful men in my life sitting by my side. "Please, God," I prayed at midnight on New Year's Eve, "let this year bring us peace, happiness and a cure for Charlie."

The Battle with the Shower Hose

Charlie's first January inpatient treatment was tough. We were in for a grueling four-day treatment. To make matters worse, the nurse didn't give him his anti-nausea medication when it was due. So needless to say, it was a horrible night of vomiting. I gave up on trying to get him to throw up in the little plastic dish, and just ended up draping myself with towels as he buried his face in my lap.

But as always, he was as happy as a clam at five o'clock the next morning, wanting to do his usual meet-and-greet out in the lobby. He sat in his highchair, munching away on Cheerios and a cut-up pancake, waving at everyone who walked by. "Morning," everyone waved back.

"Oh mom, you don't look so good," one of the night nurses said.

"I don't smell too good either," I said, rolling my eyes. Given that I was puked on numerous times the previous night, I reeked! Although I almost always waited for John to arrive mid-morning before I showered, this had to be an exception, so I entrusted Charlie to Jamie, one of our favorite nurses. Regrettably, the room we were staying in did not have a shower, which meant I would have to use the "community tub room." The thought of the germ-party that must go on in that room turned my stomach. But I had no choice – I desperately needed to bathe. The tub room is a giant room with a tub, three showerheads, a toilet and a sink. The shower curtain was the size of a Kleenex. With the tips of my fingernails, I pulled the curtain open and stepped hesitantly into the shower on my tippy-toes. "*Uugghh!*" I groaned, thinking about all the germs below.

There were three knobs in front of me; I had no idea which one turned on what. So I picked a knob, and turned it. Bam! Whoever had used the shower last had stuck the "hand-held" shower head on the safety guard rail facing straight out, and the thing started thrashing around like a wild snake and shooting water straight at me and across the room — at full blast. It began swirling around in the air furiously as if it were alive! I swear, by the time I wrestled the homicidal showerhead to the ground I, as well as the entire room, was drenched. There were a good two inches of water all over the floor, heading straight under the door, and my entire bag of clean clothes was soaked. I'm pretty sure I yelled every profanity in the book and, catching a glimpse of myself in the mirror, I just burst out laughing. "What a way to start my day," I gasped.

The New Year Starts on the Wrong Foot

Although Charlie seemed to handle the rest of his four-day treatment okay, he felt incredibly sick once we got home, and he stayed very sick for five straight days. We continued to do our best to keep things as normal as possible, but during this week, there wasn't a towel, blanket, rug or piece of furniture in our family room that didn't feel the aftermath of the chemo. Charlie threw up on everything. Even John was worried. And if he worried, I worried even more. We were very concerned about Charlie losing weight with all his throwing up. We were scared he'd have to be fed, like the majority of the kids at the clinic, intravenously.

And poor little Jay. Although he was used to seeing his brother throw up, it wasn't ever pleasant for him. There was no warning when Charlie got sick — he'd be on the floor playing with Jay one minute, and all hell would break loose the next. The second Jay heard Charlie make the heaving noise, he'd put his hands over his ears and would jump head first onto the couch until it was over.

Since he was only three, Jay didn't understand what cancer was. Nor did we ever try to explain it to him. He knew Charlie had "boo-boos" in his head, and needed to get special medicine at the hospital to help the boo-boos go away. In Jay's eyes, he associated Charlie's being "sick" with vomiting. So, after three days of watching his baby brother throw up, Jay asked, "Mom, doesn't he go to the hospital to get medicine to make him feel better?"

"Yes, the medicine is helping him get better," I answered.

"Then why is he getting so sick?" What a good question! It was difficult, if not impossible, to explain to our three-year-old that, yes, in fact, the medicine that Charlie was getting would, in the long run, God willing, make him better. But it also would make him really sick. "I never want medicine again," Jay said, covering his mouth with his hand.

"Okay," I said to myself, erasing the month of January off our enormous wall calendar one week earlier than I should have. "Enough with the month of January; let's see if February will be a bit easier." I was also anxious to have February begin because John and I were hoping for some good news about finishing Charlie's inpatient chemo. And maybe, just maybe, we were holding out for the hope that Dr. K was so happy with the way he was doing, she'd just decide to stop his treatments altogether.

Disturbing News

Charlie's early February treatments were stressful. First, we arrived Monday morning to be admitted for three days, but after hanging around the clinic until mid-afternoon, we were informed that we needed to go home because there weren't enough beds available on the floor. This bummed me out at first, but I tried to look on the bright side. If Charlie was really, really in desperate need of a treatment that night, they wouldn't let him go home. They would have sent someone else. And if I had the option of going home, I took it.

We went back to the hospital on Tuesday and stayed until Friday morning. Over the course of those four days, Charlie went through an MRI, a spinal, a chest X-ray and an abdominal X-ray (to see if he had some blockage), and on Wednesday night, he spiked a 104-degree fever. One minute he was running around the halls like a madman; the next minute he was curled up in a ball, shivering in my arms. This fever landed us in an isolation room for 24 hours. The resident doctor cut us a break. Normally, any fever would result in an automatic 72-hour stay in isolation, but they went easy on us.

As we prepared to stay an unexpected extra night, Dr. Wolfe poked his head in. I shot John a look as if to say, "What the heck is he doing here at 8:30 at night, and why is he coming to visit us?"

"Well, Mr. and Mrs. Capodanno, the MRI looks terrific, no changes, just what we want," Dr Wolfe said, shaking his fists in the air. "Now, they did detect some abnormal cells in the CSF." His words stung me.

"What?" I said, feeling my head flip backwards.

"It appears they found one abnormal cell. That's not to say it's malignant, it's just abnormal. Now, my wife is a cytologist, so I called her before I came up to talk to you. She's seen this before, and says it doesn't mean it's malignant, just abnormal," he repeated. "Let me talk to Dr. K in the morning, to get her opinion on this. It's no reason to panic. Okay?"

"Thanks for stopping in; we'll talk to Dr. K in the morning," John said, walking the doctor to the door. Jay was with us, so I couldn't fall apart too much.

"I swear, John, I don't know how much more my heart can take. Just when things look good, something like this always happens to remind us we're not out of the woods. I can't take it," I said, fighting back tears.

"Lets just talk to Dr. K in the morning, okay? Please, Honey, don't freak out about this just yet."

Elbows, Knees and Other Body Parts

John was planning to spend the night with Charlie, since I had already stayed twice that week, and I would be staying with Jay at the Neely House. When we arrived, Jay was tired, but excited to be there. It was incredibly quiet, and I asked Jay to keep his voice down. Patricia, the housemother, greeted us at the door. She gave us a brief tour of the house. As we strolled, Jay spotted the playroom.

"You can go in," Patricia smiled. Jay opened the door and looked around. The room was filled with brand new toys and games. On the windowsills must have been over a hundred stuffed animals, dolls, teddy bears, Disney characters, cartoon characters, you name it! "Go ahead," Patricia said to Jay, "you can pick one out, for keeps!" Jay's eyes lit up, and he turned to me for approval.

"Are you sure? He's got lots of stuffed animals. Maybe we should save them for the kids who come from really far away to stay here," I suggested.

"No really. We have plenty. They're for kids just like Jay, whose siblings are in the hospital. Go ahead, take your time making your selection," she grinned. Jay ever so slowly checked out every single, solitary stuffed toy. He would linger over the ones that interested him, and then he'd move on to the next. After about five minutes he went back to one of the first ones he laid eyes on. With a huge smile on his face, Jay grabbed a stuffed animal that had the face of a teddy bear, but with a body that looked like it was tucked into a sleeping bag. It was the kind of stuffed animal that was crib-safe for a baby, because everything was embroidered, with no removable eyes or buttons. It certainly wasn't the cutest or most cuddly-looking one, but he really was taken by it.

"Really, that's the one you want?" I asked, surprised by his selection.

"Yup," he smiled.

"What do you say to Patricia?" I asked.

"Thank you," he said, shyly burying his face in my leg.

Patricia handed us our key, and wished us a good night. Jay Bird and I started slowly down the long hallway holding hands.

"Why'd you pick that nice bear?" I asked him.

"Look," he said, pulling my arm so I'd bend down next to him. He pointed at the bear's head.

"Look," he beamed, "he's got a boo-boo on his head, just like Choochie!" It was true. This stuffed bear had a quilted patch on his head and a little, tiny blue tear in one eye. I hadn't noticed it before. So out of over 100 stuffed toys to choose from, he selected the one that reminded him of his brother, because it had a boo-boo on his head. I gave him a big, long hug, and kissed his forehead. But for a minute, I was speechless. I didn't want him to see I was getting choked up, so I stood up quickly and cleared my throat.

"What should we name him?"

"Scud, like the bad dog in *Toy Story 2*. No, how about Scott?" he decided.

"Scott it is!" I agreed.

Our room at the Neely House was small but very quaint. Everything was brand new and squeaky clean. I loved it. It had a little kitchenette, a bright and clean bathroom, and twin beds. I got both of us into our jammies and read Jay a few books, then went over to tuck him in. He looked sad. I thought it was because of Charlie being sick, or that he'd just wanted to go home.

"Sweetie pie, what's wrong?" I asked, stroking his head.

"I'm scared," he said sheepishly.

"Want to climb into bed with me?" I asked, giggling.

"Ya-hoo," he yelled, jumping out of bed.

It was about ten o'clock, and we were exhausted. I had no energy to be rearranging furniture at that point, but I somehow needed to rig the bed with one side up against the wall so he couldn't fall out. Plus, it was a twin bed, so unless I pushed it against the wall, the chances of one of us falling out were pretty good. Needless to say, I dodged his elbows and knees the entire night. "Cripes, kid," I thought to myself, "you sure move around a lot! It's like being in bed with an octopus!"

The next morning I began to prepare for a shower. Jay informed me he was still "scared" of the unfamiliar surroundings, so I poured him a glass of water and sat him on the kitchen chair facing the bathroom.

"Honey, I'll be right in here," I said, pointing to the shower. I would literally be just steps away. "Here, I'll even leave the bathroom door open." I smiled and kissed his cheek. The shower had one of those frosted glass doors — so you can sort of see a figure inside, without any detail. While I was showering, I could see the figure of his body standing right outside the door.

"Sweetheart, what are you doing?" I questioned.

"Don't worry, Mom," he answered in his little voice, "I know you have your private parts in there with you, so I'm only looking at your feet!" And he was; he was sitting on his knees, staring at the floor. I almost fell over laughing.

John and I tracked down Dr. Kretschmar first thing, and she was concerned but not alarmed by the CSF results. "We'll just wait and see. We'll retest him sooner than we normally would. Let's just keep going and see what happens." We had no choice. We had to wait and see.

To Infinity and Beyond!

Our trip to Naples, Florida, to visit my in-laws couldn't have come at a more perfect time. I was feeling very skeptical about the spinal fluid issue, and to be hundreds of miles away from the hospital was just what I needed to get things off my mind. The boys were excellent the entire trip, even on the flight. Jay thought being in a "real live airplane" was the coolest thing ever. As the plane took off from Boston, Jay, doing his best Buzz Lightyear impression, yelled out, "To infinity and beyond!" The entire plane full of passengers started laughing.

John's parents' rented condo was beautiful, right on a golf course. We went to the beach and the pool, took long walks, and ate to our hearts' content. My in-laws spoiled us with their hospitality and generosity. The weather was perfect — high 80s every single day. The only glitch was that neither one of the boys would sleep in the pack-and-play, which my in-laws graciously lugged down for us. So we ended up sleeping four in a bed. So comfy!

Charlie got a little fussy toward the tail end of the flight home. I decided to walk him up and down the aisles, trying to distract him. During one lap, I grabbed a paper cup for him to play with. As I was carrying him back to our seat, I stopped to regain my footing and grabbed onto the seat of a sleeping male passenger. Just as I stopped, Charlie lost his hold on the cup, and it went flying through the air, landing, I swear, upside down smack-dab in the sleeping man's crotch! Let's just say, it couldn't have "cupped" a certain area of his anatomy more perfectly.

I gasped. Not fully realizing what I was doing, I turned my head in embarrassment, and reached down to retrieve the cup off his lap. Just then, the man awoke to see me hovering over him, reaching for his crotch! I turned six shades of red, grabbed the cup (I have no idea why) and raced back to my seat, refusing to get up again until every passenger was off the plane. I was mortified beyond belief! The two guys sitting with the sleeping passenger were laughing hysterically, and I was laughing so hard, while trying to hide my face, I couldn't even get the words out to explain to John what had just happened.

Chapter 11
Waiting to Exhale

....

Phase Two Begins

Charlie's late February inpatient chemo went fine with the exception of needing to spend four hours receiving blood the night before we left. But as soon as we got home, all hell broke loose (again). Charlie got very, very sick — vomiting, diarrhea, nausea — you name it, he had it. He was also extremely lethargic, which he never was before, even after chemo. We spent Saturday in the Emergency Room, and an extra three days in the hospital clinic. No one could figure out what was causing this. Over the course of our stay, they ran a series of tests, including tons of blood work, testing his stool samples and his urine and taking an ultrasound of his liver, kidneys and spleen. They took X-rays of his head and chest too. You name it, they tested it. Fortunately, they couldn't find anything wrong. It must have just been a virus his body couldn't shake because his immune system didn't have any reserves after chemo.

Finally, after waiting a few weeks to connect, Dr. K finally sat down with us to discuss "next steps" for Charlie. I was hanging onto the slim chance that maybe, just maybe, she'd shock us by saying she thought Charlie was cured, and he'd be finished with his treatments.

"Well," she smiled, "I've got some news I think you'll be happy with. After this week's inpatient chemo, I think we'll take him off the Baby POG protocol."

"Really?" I said, as my heart skipped a beat.

"What I think we'll do is put him on CPT-11 as an outpatient," she said, awaiting my response. I sunk in my chair. This wasn't the news I was gunning for. "Now listen, it's not that bad. CPT-11 doesn't have any of the side effects that his other chemos have. The only major side effect is diarrhea, and we have something to give him if that happens."

John was excited. "Great. What's the outpatient protocol look like?"

"Well, you'll come into the clinic every third week for five straight days in a row, but the best part is, you don't have to sleep here! And the bonus is you don't have to come in for counts every Monday; you can have them drawn at home by the VNA. So, you'll have two full weeks at home, without any planned trips to the hospital." She sounded like she was giving out a prize.

"Awesome!" John exclaimed.

"How long will he be on this chemo schedule?" I asked somberly.

"About a year," she answered. She must have seen the discouragement on my face.

"Ugh," was all that came out of my mouth as my head drooped.

"Look, we'll start out assuming it's going to be a year, but if he cruises through, maybe we stop mid-way, who knows?" she said. "I can't be 100 percent convinced he's cancer free right now; maybe he is, or maybe there are malignant cells hiding somewhere. And since we aren't able to radiate him, I'd lean more toward making sure we're doing what we can to prevent the tumor from growing back," she said firmly.

"I'm psyched," John said, smiling at me. I was crushed.

I honestly wasn't surprised that he wasn't done with treatments, but hearing the words "another year" hit me like a ton of bricks. Another long year of chemo sounded just horrible. John was excited, but I got a bit weepy. Just looking at Charlie's tiny little body and realizing that it needed to undergo one more year of chemo was tough for a mommy to swallow.

"Hey," Dr. K chimed in, "the best news of all, with CPT-11, Charlie will grow hair again, and it won't fall out!" Now *that* was exciting news. I tried to envision what he'd look like with hair. He hadn't had any significant amount of hair since he was six months old. And although we never thought he looked "that bad," he still looked like a kid on chemo.

That was it. Her decision was made. We were looking at another year of chemotherapy. I tried to look at the bright side, but really wasn't up for it at that moment. We'd all be fine. If anyone could handle it, Charlie could. And I would just continue to pray that our life could move forward. We'd manage.

Believe me; I had constant reminders, especially during clinic visits, that things could be a lot worse. And I also knew how much better off we were now than last year at the same time. I didn't want to wish our lives away. I didn't even want to wish the next year away. Our boys weren't going to be little forever, and we wanted to treasure this time with them. So, I just wished and prayed for a smooth, safe and uneventful year. And now that we knew what the year ahead had in store for us, we were admitted for three days of scheduled chemotherapy.

Mommy's Very Own Pity Party

As always, my dad joined us bright and early on Tuesday morning. He found us in Charlie's favorite spot, the windows to the world on the 7th floor overlooking the heart of Chinatown. I was standing staring out the window as Charlie got himself tangled up in his line. My dad leaned over and kissed my forehead.

"How'd last night go?"

"Okay," I answered softly, continuing to gaze out the window.

"Did you talk to Kretschmar yesterday?"

"Yup," I replied, feeling the lump swelling in my throat. I couldn't look at him; I fixed my eyes on the view out the window, trying to stay composed.

"And what did she have to say?"

"Another year," I whispered, and with that, I burst into tears.

"Okay, okay, we can handle that. Look how well we've done this year," he said, pulling my head into his chest.

"I know," I sobbed, "and it will be outpatient, so that's good. It's just…it's just another year of our lives, another year of this crap running through his little veins," I sobbed, shaking my head. I hated falling apart on my dad, because I knew it must be terribly painful for him to see me this way. But he was my father, and I couldn't hide how I felt.

"Deirdre, listen, he's gonna do fine. Just look at him," he said, as Charlie turned around smiling. "You didn't think he'd be done anyway, did you?" he asked gently.

"No. I know, but I was just hoping…I just wanted her to say he's fine, go home, have a nice life. To hear the words 'another year' just *killed me*." I tried to wipe the tears as fast as they were coming down my face but it was a losing battle. "I just want…" I cried, as I bent down to rest on the radiator, "I just want our life back…I want to be normal…I want our life to move forward…I just feel like we're being held back…I want the best for my kids and my family…It's just hard…It's hard to have your friends sending you money…To accept people's generosity like we're a charity case…It's hard to worry about paying the bills…It hurts to see Charlie spending his childhood in a hospital…It's hard to see your baby learn to walk while hooked up to a pole...It's hard to keep Jay's life normal...He deserves a normal life...It's hard, and it just, it just sucks and it hurts." At this point the words were just spewing out of my mouth.

"I went to college and got an education so I'd get a good job so my family could have nice things...and John, look at poor John, he works so hard every day...Then he comes racing in here...And he doesn't get any sleep...This just wasn't the plan I had for my life...I want our life back... I want to be a normal family again...I want my children to be healthy...I don't want to see my baby sedated anymore...or puking...I'm tired of this roller coaster we've been on...Sometimes I don't think I can handle it any more...I'm just sick of all of this...and I just want him to live," I cried, slamming my hand on the railing. Now I had my dad fighting back his own tears.

"Deirdre," he said sweetly, "we all want this to be behind us. And we'll get there. I know we will. And I know it's hard for you and John right now; it's hard for all of us. We all just want him to live," he said, choking on his words. I could see this conversation was crushing him.

"I just want our life back," I whimpered, wiping my eyes with my pajama sleeve. With that, Charlie got up from his seated position, and still attached to his pole, darted, like a bat out of hell, down the hallway. He'd had enough of our misery; he had places to go, and people to smile at. Enough of the pity party, Mom. Let's get moving!

Farewell to 7 Medical

On our big wall calendar, we labeled March as "March Madness Month." John wanted to celebrate Charlie's last inpatient treatment. "I don't want to jinx ourselves," I said hesitantly.

"We're not going to, trust me," John replied. So, as Charlie sailed through his last four days of inpatient chemo, we brought in 50 cupcakes and 24 shamrock cookies for the floor to enjoy. We made a big sign that read, "Thank you for taking such good care of me. Love, Charlie," and hung it up. We sent Jay to school with cupcakes too, so he could enjoy the celebration with his friends. He excitedly told everyone, "My brother doesn't need to sleep at the hospital anymore!"

On Thursday afternoon, I packed up all our overnight bags, pillows, gifts, balloons, cookie sheets, etc. and we headed out of our hospital room to say goodbye. All Charlie's doctors, nurses, cleaning friends and fellow patients lined up on either side of him all the way to the elevator to wish him well. He looked so adorable sporting his little varsity letterman's jacket. As he shuffled along, grinning bashfully with his eyes cast downward, he waved his little hand as high as he could over his head, looking like Prince William in a photo opportunity. It was as if he knew he had accomplished something pretty big. I had a lump in my throat the size of an orange. We had survived an entire year of inpatient chemotherapy treatments. That hospital floor was our second home. We hoped and prayed we were finally closing that chapter in our life, God willing, for good.

That night, our neighbors wanted to have us over for cake and ice cream to celebrate. Since I was always concerned about Jay and his feelings, I suggested that, instead of another Charlie celebration, we should celebrate Jay. We'd called it "Hooray for Jay Day" to let him know how special *he* was, and how proud we were of *him*! Jay was just beaming! We all sang, "For he's a jolly good fellow," as he blew out the candles on his cake.

Bumbles Bounce

The clinic had scheduled a visiting nurse to come the following Monday to draw Charlie's blood so we wouldn't have to go to the clinic until it was a chemo week. Ya-hoo! At least that's the way it was supposed to be. Well, Charlie had other plans. He'd been managing the carpeted stairs down to our finished basement for well over a month without any problems, but not today. I was upstairs and John was downstairs watching *Family Feud* reruns after working from 3:00 a.m. to 2:00 p.m., when Charlie fell, head first, down the entire flight of stairs. I could hear him hit the stairs and the wall the entire way down. With a huge thud, his little body slammed onto the landing just as I reached it. He was completely conscious, thank God, but it was evident by the instant lumps that he had hit his forehead in two places. He also had a small rug burn on his forehead and a small scrape on the side of his shunt. I scooped him up and paced back and forth trying to comfort him. We decided after about four minutes to call 9-1-1 just to have them check him out.

He was crying pretty hard. John and I checked his pupils, his limbs, and every other body part, all of which appeared to be functioning normally, but, given his situation, we just wanted to make sure. An ambulance and a fire truck raced down the street. Five rescue workers came dashing into the house, and the commotion came to a complete standstill when we explained Charlie's health issue. "We don't know a great deal about shunts or central lines. You should call his doctors," was all they said. "That's it?" I asked, glancing at John. "Can't you at least flash a light in his eyes to make sure his pupils are dilating properly?" He appeared fine to them. Then they left. Jay came up from watching *Toy Story* to check out the fire engine as it drove away, but other than that, he couldn't have cared less about the commotion going on in his dining room. I then called the hospital, as well as the pediatrician. All agreed, as long as he wasn't vomiting, he was okay. Five minutes later, Charlie fell asleep. This freaked us both out. John and I went back and forth for about three minutes. "Should we wake him?" "I don't know, what do you think?" We decided to wake him. It was 3:30 in the afternoon and he appeared completely fine once we woke him.

I was planning to take him to a healing service at church that night with my devoted friend Amy Hardcastle. At 8:00 p.m., just as I was putting his jacket on, he threw up all over me! This was four and a half hours after his fall. So off to the ER we went.

"Weren't you just in here two weeks ago?" the ER nurse asked, punching Charlie's information into the computer.

John and I looked at each other and just rolled our eyes. "We live here," John replied.

They ran a series of X-rays to check his shunt, and just observed his behavior for a few hours. John and I remained completely calm through the whole thing. It was as if this type of stuff didn't even faze us anymore. We actually got a bit giddy during the X-rays. We were laughing about something pretty stupid, and the technician gave us a strange look. As the ER doctor wrote the orders to release us, he said, "If this had been an adult, they'd be in bed, in pain for days." But not our Charlie. To him, this was a walk in the park.

Inquisitive Jay

"Mommy, why doesn't Charlie go to school anymore?" Jay asked the following morning, out of the clear blue.

"Oh, he's too little," I replied, trying to dismiss the question quickly. But my smarty-pants son wasn't going to accept that answer.

"No he's not, he used to go, and Colin goes," he continued. Colin was our neighbor who is only six days older than Charlie. I knew that trying to pull a fast one on Jay wasn't going to fly. So I began to explain.

"Well, Sweetie, Charlie might still have the boo-boo inside his head and it can still make him sick. And until the boo-boo is completely better, he shouldn't go to school because of the germs he might pick up there."

"Oh, okay," Jay said, and off he went.

The following Monday, after Charlie's blood work was done, and I was told his counts were up, I decided to surprise Jay at school by bringing Charlie in. It had been close to seven months since he'd been inside the building. The minute Jay spotted us, he dropped the toy he was playing with and put his hands to his face, MacCauley Culkin style. He raced over, tripping over a chair along the way, and screeched, "Mommy, Mommy, does this mean his boo-boo is all better?" I just smiled. He was only three, but he was so darn smart, and what a memory on that kid!

A Time to Reflect and Celebrate

March 21, 2001, was the one-year anniversary of Charlie beginning his chemo treatments. We believed that this date one year ago began our journey to recovery. We felt very strongly that Charlie had done so well for many reasons: his own inner strength and determination, through God hearing and answering our prayers, and because of the unsurpassed care he received from the staff at the Floating. We constantly reminded ourselves that it was one woman, Dr. K, who gave us the hope we so desperately needed. We wanted to show our appreciation to the entire clinic staff. They were our family, our friends, and our saviors. Although we complained a lot about being at the hospital, we knew the staff there was exceptional. The nurses not only took care of Charlie, they really loved him. He wasn't just a "patient" to any of the staff; he was a person, a human being, a little boy. The Child Life specialists were extraordinary at their jobs – always there to distract the children from their difficult procedures, involving the siblings in activities so they didn't feel left out, and always offering to sit with the child so that mom and dad could sneak away for a few minutes of relief. The staff had certainly put up with a lot of my frustration, so we desperately wanted to let them know how much they were appreciated. So on March 21, we ordered a special catered lunch for the entire staff and had it hand-delivered with this note attached:

March 21, 2001

To all our clinic staff friends:

The Capodanno family has had a heck of a year! But rather than focus on all the difficulties we've faced, we want to focus on the positives.

So we would like to celebrate! One year ago today, Charlie started his chemotherapy treatments at the Floating. Although he may still have a long way to go, we feel March 21, 2000, marked the beginning of his road to recovery.

Today, we also want to celebrate our friendship with all of you! We joined the clinic one year ago as a frightened family, not knowing what would happen next. Very graciously, and ever so gently, each one of you has helped to piece our shattered lives back together. No words can ever express our appreciation for all that you've done to help us through this incredible journey. You are all such gifted people; every one of you has touched our hearts in a way that will last us a lifetime. You go the extra mile to reassure us when we have concerns, and most importantly, your honesty and patience with us (especially with me!) means everything.

We hope that you will take a minute or two today to step back and acknowledge how you've made a profound impact on so many lives.

Jay and Charlie are our entire world! When I was pregnant with both, I always prayed to God that if He would bless them with good health (since that was out of my control), I would make sure they were always happy and safe. Well, both are very happy children, and we certainly do everything in our power to protect them. For some reason, God had a different plan for

Charlie's health. However, we feel that God gave Charlie the inner strength he needs to beat his disease. With his strength, the power of prayer, the love his family and friends surround him with every day, and your expertise and unwavering care, we believe with all our hearts he will survive!

We thank you for your guidance, friendship, honesty, patience, understanding and devotion to your patients. Thank you for not rolling your eyes when I ask the same question seven times in one day. Most importantly, thank you for helping our son's future look brighter every day. Lunch is on Charlie - Enjoy!!!

With love,

John, Deirdre, Jay and Charlie

How Do You Do It?

Throughout the entire ordeal, many people asked us, "How do you do it? How are you able to run a normal life given the situation you're in? How does cancer not run your lives?" The answer is quite simple: "Cancer can't run our lives because our *children* already do — and they sure as heck aren't going to let anyone else take over their job!"

Jay has always been very mild mannered and laid back. He just enjoys every minute of life, and is always concerned about others. We believe Jay became a very compassionate and caring child because of all the things he'd seen and been exposed to so soon. He saw what his little brother and the other children at the hospital went through. He cared about how they felt, and how they were doing. He knew our golden rule, "Treat others the way you want to be treated." And even at the tender age of three, he lived by this rule. He's always been exceptionally well mannered and respectful of others. And his eyes sparkle when he smiles.

The Charlie who used to be so sweet and happy went out with the sponge bath water at about one and a half years old. All of a sudden, he was Mr. Stubborn. And he always seemed to get his way.

One morning he decided to start his day at 4:00 a.m. In order to avoid disturbing Jay, John brought him down to the family room and fed him a bottle in the dark while cuddling him on the couch. Usually, John was able to coax him back to sleep. Not this time. He began screeching and pointing at the floor. John picked up a magazine at his foot and gave it to Charlie, thinking that was what he wanted. Charlie tossed it out of his hand, and continued with his squealing and pointing. John placed Charlie on the floor this time. Charlie climbed back on the couch and lay down. John lay down next to him, and Charlie freaked out, continuing to point to the floor. John, who was exhausted and was inches away from ringing Charlie's neck, obeyed and went down on the floor. He waited five minutes, and when he thought Charlie was asleep, he crawled up next to him on the couch. Charlie shot up like a rocket, and again ordered John to the floor. Sad but true. Our 20-month-old forced my husband to sleep on the floor. I came down the stairs at 6:30, and there was John, spread-eagle on the carpet, while Charlie was snoring away on the couch.

"We're pathetic," I laughed. John didn't find it that amusing. We didn't want Charlie to be spoiled, but it was difficult not to give in to his demands, considering what he was going through. "I don't want to create a monster," I'd say to John. "Too late," he'd always reply.

Waiting to Exhale

Charlie began his outpatient treatments in April. Except for a major personality change due to the steroid he was given, all went well. And, in true Charlie style, instead of getting the most common side-effect from the new chemo, which is diarrhea, Charlie got constipated. Then, after a week, he'd had a terrible delayed reaction and was doubled over with diarrhea!

In mid-April Charlie had a scheduled MRI and LP. As always, we were stressed, but even more so this time because it was the longest break from chemo Charlie had ever had. In our way of thinking, if something were to grow, it would have done so during this time. Not to mention that two of our precious clinic friends, Caitlin and Timmy, both with brain tumors, had recently relapsed.

"Any word?" my sister asked anxiously as she called for the third time on the day we should have received the results.

"Nothing." I tried desperately to keep myself busy, but nothing seemed to work. I watched the clock and stared at the phone. If I went out, I rushed back. This went on for three days straight. In the back of my mind I always wondered, "Are they not calling because its bad news and they're waiting to have the doctor call?" You'd think after a year of this waiting torture we'd get used to it, but as a parent, you never do. And that will never change.

Finally, on Friday morning, I'd had enough. As usual, I waited until 8:31 to call. "Mary Jo, it's Deirdre, I'm going to start hyperventilating. Do you have any results yet? Please, don't put us through this over the weekend," I begged.

"Yes, actually, the results are right here. I'm surprised no one called you," she said. I shook my head in frustration.

"Let's see," she continued, as she flipped through the papers. My heart was pounding so hard that I thought it would pop right out. "The MRI looks great; no change, that's what we want to see," she began, "and the fluid is clear," she cheered. I could feel my throat tighten up.

"Oh, oh, that's so awesome. Thanks for the good news. Thank you, Mary Jo, have a good weekend; we sure will!" I said, hanging up before I started to cry.

About an hour later my dad and Bebe arrived, as they did every single Friday, to babysit so I could have some time to myself to run a million errands. Bebe had just come in, and my dad didn't have both feet in the door yet.

"I just got the results," I said quietly.

"And?" my father said, looking very serious.

"They were perfect, fluid's clear and the MRI was perfect!" Once again, my eyes filled. So did my dad's and Bebe's.

"Thank you, God," my dad yelled, shaking his fists above his head.

"We were so worried this time," Bebe added, sniffling. What all of us went through waiting for these results was incredible. I swear they took years off our lives!

Was Life Going to Be Normal Again?

May 2001 was the best month yet. Charlie finally had color in his cheeks, he was growing small patch of peach fuzz on the top of his head, some of which was actually covering his shunt, he'd finally gained enough weight to get him into the 25th percentile, and he was *full* of energy. And his little bum wiggled from hip to hip as he chased after his brother. His vocabulary was also improving, and he was actually putting two words together. We'd ask, "Who wants milky?" and he'd sing back, "I dooo!"

And, finally, after two harrowing months of trying the *Ferber* method on him in a desperate attempt to get him to sleep through the night, it worked. We were going on three straight weeks of uninterrupted sleep during the night!

On a ride into the clinic one sunny spring morning, I caught myself singing to the radio. I was shocked to realize it was probably the first time in a year that I had sung while driving down the Pike! I found myself wondering if I was letting my guard down. Was life becoming normal again? Well, as normal as it could be, given that our son was still on chemo? Could I actually allow myself to exhale? Could I lower my shoulders from that scrunched-up-to-my-ears position I'd been carrying them in, waiting for the sky to fall on us again? Would I be able to say to those people who continued to ask about his scars, "Oh, he used to have cancer." No. That was too extreme. He was still fighting his fight. He was not in remission. Well, not yet. But I'd continue to daydream of the day that I could say that. We'd get there; I believed it with all my heart. I just wanted desperately to feel that the worst was behind us. And not having to go to the hospital for two straight weeks was rejuvenating!

"Guess what?" I whispered into Jay's ear one night while tucking him into bed. "It's the weekend. Do you know what that means?"

"What?" he asked excitedly.

"Daddy doesn't have to go to work and you don't have to go to school."

"*And*," he added, "no hospitals either, right?"

"Right!" I replied, giving him a high five.

"Ya-hoo! My family's going to be together!" he yelled with a smile from ear to ear. Gulp. Yes, he was right, and everyone in the family felt the same way!

Survivor's Walk

The Relay for Life is a 24-hour walk around the Franklin high school track to raise money for the American Cancer Society and cancer research. We walked on our church's team. On Friday night, they held what was called a "Survivors Walk." Although technically Charlie wasn't a "survivor" because he was still on treatment, the committee and we agreed that since he survived five surgeries, 15 months of chemo, MRI, spinal taps, and blood transfusions, he qualified as a survivor. He wore an adult Survivor T-shirt, since they didn't plan on having any toddlers walking. The shirt hung to his ankles, and dragged on the track as we walked, hand in hand, as a family.

It was completely quiet as we walked, with about 50 other people, around the pitch-black field. The only light came from the 7,000 luminary candles that lined the entire track. On the front of each luminary bag was the name of a person who had lost his or her life to cancer, or who was still fighting to live, or who had survived the dreaded disease.

It was an incredibly moving and emotional experience. The pride we felt that night seemed to burst right out of our hearts. We had asked our family and friends to make sure that as we walked by they cheered for Jay too. We never wanted him to feel left out, or that everything was about Charlie. So, as we rounded the corner where our crew of supporters was standing, Jay heard his aunts and cousins yell, "We love you, Jay!" He yelled excitedly, "Wow, Mommy, this is my first parade ever!"

One Good Yank and It's Out!

Unfortunately for Charlie, things like flying down the stairs on his belly, running feverishly down the hall while attached to his IV pole, and just generally yanking on his central line left it hanging on literally by threads after 15 months.

I had discussed it with his nurses many times, but was told they don't like to replace the lines unless it is 100 percent necessary, because it would require yet another surgical procedure for his tiny body. "Ann Marie," I said to his nurse at the clinic, "his line is dangling out of his chest! We're going on vacation in a few weeks and I don't feel comfortable being so far from the hospital with his line in such bad condition. Plus, it could easily pull out, and then what would happen?"

"Well, if it snapped at home you could use the clamps we gave you to secure it until you got here," she replied.

"Well, if I'm holding the clamp, who's driving the car to the ER?" I said half jokingly and half sarcastically. "I know you guys aren't big on replacing the lines unless it's absolutely necessary, and in this case, I think it is!" She pulled up Charlie's shirt and checked the line.

"You're right, that doesn't look good. One good yank and it is out," she said, shaking her head.

"Yeah, and I don't want it to pull out at home, in the middle of the night or something. It's in his heart, right? Does that mean he'd bleed all over the place?"

"No, no," she laughed. "When it pulls out, it literally pulls out of the vein."

"Great; so it's an open wound just waiting for infection to set in?" I was being relentless.

"Okay, all right, let me have Mary Jo look at it since she knows Charlie's line better than I do," she said, leaving to find her colleague. Mary Jo appeared momentarily.

"Mary Jo," I said, "this line will be the death of me. Look at it, it's dangling out; you can see the cuff, and that can't be too good!" I insisted.

"Oh, you're right. Well, let's page the surgeon and see what he has to say."

Finally I felt like I was getting somewhere. I really wanted that line *out*! I was petrified that it was going to get infected. And if the surgeon allowed, Charlie would finally be able to get an Infusaport, which is a line under his skin, so there wouldn't be any external tubing dangling from his chest. That would mean no more dressing changes, which would cut my nursing duties in half. He would finally be able to get completely wet, after having nothing but sponge baths since he was six months old — and even the best scrubber in the world couldn't get this kid squeaky clean with a sponge bath!

We waited about 10 minutes for the doctor to arrive. He was new, and we'd never met him. He entered the room and I didn't even let him speak.

"Okay, here's the situation; he's got a Broviac that is dangling by a thread from his chest. I'd say it's a huge risk for infection. You can actually see the cuff, and with one pull, that sucker's out! Look at it! How dangerous is that! It needs to be replaced immediately," I stated matter-of-factly, holding Charlie's shirt up to expose his entire chest.

"Wow, that's a major disaster waiting to happen!" the surgeon said, with a look of shock on his face. "Is this allowed to happen here?" he asked, pointing to the stitch holding the line to Charlie's chest. "I'm sorry, I haven't introduced myself. I'm Dr. Gilcrest; now who are you? Do you work here in the Hem/Onc clinic?" he said, extending his hand to me.

"Me?" I said, surprised by his question. "Oh no, no, I'm the baby's mother," I laughed, realizing he thought I was one of the nurses.

"Well, you're good. You sure know your stuff, Mom," he laughed. "Let's get it done. What's good for you?" We walked back to his office and scheduled the surgery for three days later. That was it. That's all it took. I liked this guy a lot! He was a take-charge, just-get-it-done kind of person. A real parent pleaser. And as we hoped, Charlie had the Infusaport implanted in his chest, allowing him to do so many things he'd never been able to do before.

Here We Go Again

Following his surgery, Charlie had a scheduled MRI and spinal tap. It was the Friday before the long Fourth of July holiday week. I called the clinic begging them not to make us wait too long for the results. The nurse promised me she'd find something out for us before the day's end. Minutes later, the portable phone rang. Only it wasn't Cathy or Mary Jo, it was Dr. Grodman. I closed my eyes when I heard his voice. When the doctor calls instead of a nurse, you know it can't be good. John, my dad and I were out front watching the boys ride their bikes.

"Hello, Dr. Grodman," I said, staring blankly at John. I turned around and paced slowly up and down my front lawn.

"Well, there's been a problem here. Seems there was a mix-up with the MRI. They compared this week's MRI to one taken last year, so it's an invalid reading. I'm trying really hard to have the scans read again, comparing them to the appropriate scan done a few months back. Now, that could take some time," he said, promising he'd try to get results from the MRI for us as soon as possible. "The other news is that, unfortunately, they see some abnormal cells in Charlie's spinal fluid." My heart completely sank.

"Oh God, don't say that," I said, as I closed my eyes.

"Now, I know this is disturbing news for you, but please don't panic until Cindy (Dr. K) has a chance to review the reports with the pathologist. Unfortunately, she's on vacation for the next two weeks."

"*Two weeks!* You expect me to wait patiently and live normally for two weeks to find out about these cells?"

"Look, I don't know as much about these cells as she does. I know she's never had a great deal of concern about them before, and I know she's the better person to shed some light on this. I'll let her know she needs to get in touch with you immediately, and in the meantime, I'll get on those MRI results as soon as possible. Hopefully I'll have an answer for you today," he offered. That was 3:15 on Friday. No one ever called back that afternoon. So I called at 8:31 a.m. on Monday morning. "Oh, the scans look great, no change," I was told by Mary Jo.

We still had to sweat it out for another week and a half until Dr. K finally returned from her vacation. She had a million messages on her desk to call me, which she did.

"I'm freaking out about this!" I yelled. "Why are we seeing these cells again? What are they? Is there a test we can run to find out if they are in fact malignant? If our lab can't determine it, is there any other lab we can send them out to that can?" I was firing the questions at her before she could even answer.

"No, to the best of my knowledge, there isn't any other lab that could do anything differently than ours does here. I'm going to suggest we just repeat the LP and see what it says."

"When?" I asked anxiously.

"Let's do it as soon as possible," she answered calmly. Which is what we did. And the fluid came back clear.

"See, its fine now!" Dr. K cheered. "I discussed the situation with the pathologist and she said that any time they detect anything suspicious or abnormal, they need to report it. It does *not* mean it's malignant. Look, they could be dead cells destroyed by chemo. Even your spinal fluid could have some abnormal cells in it. It doesn't mean it is cancer," she tried to assure us.

"I don't know," I said, not feeling comfortable or confident with what she was telling me. "Sometimes we see this, sometimes we don't. It just doesn't make sense and it scares me."

"I'm not worried about it, I'm really not," she said as she left the recovery room.

"Why does this have to happen?" I asked John. "It's as if just when we feel he's out of the woods and his scans are all looking great, we see these suspicious cells just to remind us we're still in this battle. I want answers. I'm going to find a lab, or a doctor, or someone who digs deeper into these tests."

"Honey, if she's not worried, we shouldn't be either," John said.

I knew she was an expert, and I knew she was one of the best brain tumor specialists in the country. It wasn't even that I was doubting her, but I needed to do what I promised myself I'd do right when Charlie was diagnosed – whatever was in my power to make sure we left no stone unturned.

On a Mission

So that afternoon, I began my newest mission. I called the main number at a well-known cancer institute in New York and asked for a doctor I had heard was a brain tumor specialist. By pure luck, the doctor was available and got on the phone with me immediately. He sounded very young and was very gracious. I gave him a five-minute dissertation about Charlie's situation. I was beside myself with joy when he informed me that he had actually known of four children with CPC over the last eight years.

I explained, in detail, my concern about the spinal fluid.

"Well," the doctor agreed, "I can understand your fears. And no, I honestly have never had an issue with the CSF with any of our patients. And given that I'm not treating Charlie, it's difficult for me to speculate. But I'll tell you one thing; you're in the best possible care with Cynthia Kretschmar. She's one of the best there is." This made me feel incredibly good. He continued, "I'd be happy to review Charlie's scans and fluid next time you run the tests. Feel free to send them down."

"Okay," I said hesitantly. "I might regret asking you this, but I'm going to ask anyway. Of the four cases you are aware of, did any…did any of them...make it?" I bit my lip waiting to hear his response. My heart was pounding with anticipation.

"Oh yes, yes. A few did very well. A few are long-term survivors, and, unfortunately, a few didn't make it." So there were survivors! I swung my fist in the air, turning my eyes to the ceiling. "Feel free to call back anytime. But again, in my opinion, you're on the right track with Dr. Kretschmar, and given the fact that it was a total resection of the brain, and that you haven't seen any growth, you're doing very well." I was glad I made the call. If nothing else, it sounded reassuring. I didn't get an answer to my spinal fluid issue, but I'd keep working on that.

Heartbreak Over Caitlin

The summer was not without heartbreak for us. We lost beautiful little Caitlin, a precious five-year-old girl who had a brain tumor. Caitlin was very special to us. We had the pleasure of sharing a room with her a few times during our inpatient treatments. She had the spunkiest personality, and was just a hoot. Her mom would allow her to pack her own suitcase for her inpatient treatments. And the ensembles she'd pack would usually include a sequined miniskirt, Barbie high-heels and fluffy pajamas. She was a living doll. Due to the location of her tumor, she was cross-eyed, and bald as a cue ball. But she was the most gorgeous little girl we'd ever met.

Because she didn't have an appetite, she was hooked up to nutrients about 15 hours a day. Her mom had bought a little suitcase on wheels, pink of course, and placed the IV food and fluids in it, and Caitlin wheeled it around herself. This child never complained. She had a little Minnie Mouse voice, and she just adored Charlie. And every single time she saw us she'd immediately ask, "Can I tickle Charlie's toes?" She *loved* to tickle his toes — and he loved it too. She was just about the bravest little person I'd ever met. Never in the year we knew her, given all that she had to endure, did I ever once hear her complain or see her fuss. She never did. She'd come to the clinic, or she'd be up on the inpatient floor, and she always smiled and was constantly teasing the nurses.

One morning when we were in the clinic, she was in an isolation room because she had a fever. Her mom had gone to get some lunch. Charlie and I were out in the waiting area playing. As usual, the clinic was extremely busy. Out of the blue, we could all hear Caitlin screaming, *"Help...Somebody...Cathy...Help!"* She sounded desperate and in trouble. Every nurse's face went blank. Our nurse Cathy dropped everything and raced to Caitlin's aid; a hush came over the clinic waiting to hear what had happened. *"Caitlin,"* Cathy yelled, "you almost gave me a heart attack! I thought something happened to you."

Minutes later, Cathy exited Caitlin's room with a smile on her face, shaking her head. "What happened?" I asked with concern.

"That little monkey, she was screaming because she dropped the VCR remote control," Cathy laughed. That was our Caitlin. Always keeping everyone on his or her toes!

Caitlin and Charlie actually had MRIs scheduled on the same day back in April. We spent time in the waiting room with Debbie*, Caitlin's mom, as we waited for both kids to come out of the lumbar puncture procedures. "How's she been doing?" we asked. We hadn't seen her since she ended her treatments a few weeks earlier.

"She's feeling great, which always makes me nervous," her mom said anxiously.

Regrettably, Caitlin's mom did receive horrific news following that MRI. Caitlin had new tumor growth, this time in her spine. It had never appeared in her spine before. There were at least three spots. Her mom was devastated. We saw her the next week in the clinic. "I'm so sorry, what do they say, what are the next steps?" I asked, with tears in

*Name changed to protect privacy.

my eyes. "Maybe a stem-cell transplant, I don't know," her mom said, shaking her head. "I just don't know, I just don't know if I can put her through any more."

"How's she doing?" I asked.

"Oh, well, I had to tell her that it was back, and she asked me if she was going to die," Debbie* said. With that, I closed my eyes and shook. A five-year-old shouldn't be asking her mom if she's dying. This wasn't right, it wasn't fair, and it was cruel.

"There's got to be some next steps?" I asked, wiping my eyes.

"Well," Caitlin's mom said bravely, "I called my church, and we're going to be able to have her receive her first communion *and* her confirmation in the next week or so. According to a nun we know, she needs to have received both sacraments in order to get to heaven."

"What?" I said, feeling numb.

"Yeah, that's what the nun said." I had to turn away. This poor mother in her mid-twenties was in the process of planning for her child to leave this earth. I couldn't bear to listen to it.

"You can't give up, you can't. There's always something. What about another opinion if you think you don't want to do what they're suggesting here?" I started in.

Debbie* just shook her head in disbelief.

With that, I scooped Charlie up in my arms, pushed the doors open from the clinic, walked down the hall hugging my baby, and just wept. "Five-year-old girls aren't supposed to ask their mommies if they're going to die...she should be in school playing...her mommy shouldn't be planning for her death!" I cried, pacing the halls.

Caitlin's disease seemed to progress quickly as the doctors and her family tried to make some decisions as to what to do next. One Thursday morning I was in the clinic with Charlie for chemo, and John ended up surprising us. I was so glad. It had been a long week, and he offered to

---

*Name changed to protect privacy.

stay so I could have at least a half-day break from the place. I left around noon. When John returned home late in the afternoon with Charlie, he looked concerned.

"What's up, what happened?"

"No, no it's nothing with Chooch. Actually, right after you left, Caitlin showed up with her mom. She was pushing Caitlin in a stroller. She couldn't walk and she didn't look good, and everyone, Cathy, Mary Jo, all the doctors, were racing around, and they all looked pretty nervous. I don't know what happened. I could hear her mom saying, 'I don't know what's wrong with her, I don't know what's wrong,' then they wheeled her off on a stretcher." We said lots of prayers that night for Caitlin.

Charlie and I arrived the next morning for chemo, and Mary Jo checked us in. "How's Caitlin; did she get admitted?" I asked anxiously. Mary Jo finished scrubbing her hands, turned the faucet off, and looked at me sadly.

"I'm sorry," she said quietly, obviously overwhelmed by what she was going to tell me. "She didn't make it."

"No, don't tell me that," I moaned. "What happened? Why?" I was calm. No tears. I was just shocked that this beautiful princess lost her life last night here in a hospital bed in ICU. My heart was breaking; breaking for Caitlin who would be so missed; breaking for her mommy, daddy, and two brothers; and breaking because another precious child with a cancerous brain tumor had succumbed to this despicable disease. Caitlin was the fourth brain tumor child we knew who had died over the last year. The odds were stacking up.

Chapter 12
Moving On!

....

The Big Two – With Attitude!

On August 26, Charlie turned two years old! We had about 30 kids, his team of nurses, our parish priests, and a slew of family and friends over for a backyard cookout. We once again rented a moonwalk, and each of the kids enjoyed creating their own puffy paint commemorative hats and t-shirts. As my dad stated, "This backyard was overflowing with love for that child!"

The night before the party, I once again sat down and looked at the pictures of when Charlie was born. I slowly flipped through the album reliving the first six months of his life. It took only about four seconds before I was reduced to tears. If it had been Jay's album I was looking through, I'd be thinking, "Wow, it seems like just yesterday he was born." That's not the case with Charlie. It felt as if he'd already lived a lifetime. He'd only been here on this earth for two short years, yet it seemed like forever. He'd gone through so much, and yet, by God's grace, he was still here. As I went through the pictures, it hurt me so much to realize that in all of those newborn pictures, he had a massive tumor in his brain and he never cried or complained. Never. He was a happy little baby, always. Heck, he even slept through the night back then.

I shuddered for a second. In a way, it was a very eerie feeling to look at the pictures. I came to the picture I'd taken of him just the day before he was rushed to the hospital. It's a picture of him, in his PJs, spinning in his Exersaucer. He had a slight smile on his face, but in his eyes, there was a strange, glassy look. That was the last picture of him before our world turned upside down. I stroked the picture for a minute, and I found myself apologizing to it. "I'm sorry I didn't know," I said, weeping. I closed the book as if I'd just finished a chapter in time, and placed it back on the shelf with all the others.

September 11, 2001

It was a very clear morning on September 11, 2001, as Charlie and I raced down the Pike to begin our second day of chemotherapy for the week. Charlie was gazing out the car window when the song I was singing along to on the radio was interrupted with Brian Gumbel's nervous voice announcing that a plane had hit one of the two World Trade Center towers in New York City. I turned the volume up to listen more carefully. With a gasp, Gumbel went on to say a second plane had struck the other tower. Instantly, this went from sounding like a freak airline accident to a deliberate act of terrorism. My heart sank. I adjusted my rearview mirror to get a better look at Charlie, who gave me a huge smile. "Unbelievable," I said out loud, "here we are trying to save your life, and sick people are out there destroying other people's lives."

Once we arrived at the clinic, it was all anyone was talking about. It just seemed too unreal. I walked into the back room where people were huddled around a TV. Minutes later, on live television, we watched the first tower collapse. That was all I could watch; it was just too inconceivable and too terrifying to believe. I grabbed Charlie and left the room. I brought him out to the play area and tried not to listen to what everyone was saying. I didn't want to hear it. I didn't want to know that something so terrible could happen in our world. I desperately just wanted to finish Charlie's treatment for the day and get out of the hospital and out of the city and rush to the safety of my home and my family. But at that moment in time, did any of us feel safe?

At one point I heard someone say that both flights had originated from Boston. This is when I began to get really nervous about the situation. My very dear friend Terry flew out of Boston to LA on a weekly basis and I was terrified he may have been on one of those planes. I began to pray that he was okay. I used the clinic phone to try to reach some other friends who might have known if he was in the office or not, but by then the Hancock Tower, being the tallest building in Boston, had already been evacuated. The clinic was crazy with people calling to cancel appointments. "Are you going to stay?" one mom asked me. "I think we should get out of the city. The traffic is going to be horrendous, and the hospital will probably start getting overflow from New York."

"Well, I'm not leaving until he gets his chemo or we are told to leave," I said.

We were in and out of there in about three hours. There was no traffic at that point, because everyone who was able to leave the city had already left. I picked up Jay at day care and raced home. Once inside our house, we watched, like the rest of America, as the terror, devastation and destruction of September 11, 2001, unfolded before our eyes. I was literally sick to my stomach for days as we continued to watch, and I continued to worry about my friend. It took me two days to find out he was not on any of the planes. But I honestly didn't feel better until

I reached him by phone myself. Our hearts broke over and over as we learned how many precious lives were destroyed that dreadful day.

As did everyone in our country, we, as individuals and as a family, felt scared, angry, sad, distraught, and very vulnerable. For days, our eyes were fixated on the television and filled with tears. Our hearts ached as the magnitude of this national tragedy began to sink in. But at the same time, it gave us a new perspective and a new way of looking at life. We were once again reminded of how precious life is, and how fortunate we are. None of us knew what to say or do. And I remember commenting to John that it had been days since I'd seen anyone smile.

We were a nation in mourning. The following evening, we joined our neighbors outside to light candles of remembrance. "Mom, is it Halloween time again?" Jay asked, as we stood on the sidewalk quietly talking with the people who lived next door.

"No, Honey," I said, kneeling next to him. "We're standing together with our candles to remember the people who died in the plane crash," I tried to explain.

"Oh, can we pray for them tonight?" he asked sweetly. I scooped him up in my arms and kissed his cheek. "Yes, Honey, we will," I said with a lump in my throat. You'd never think in our lifetime we'd witness anything like this, but there we were, shoulder to shoulder with our neighbors mourning a terrible national tragedy. I saved all of the magazine issues over the next few weeks – *Time, Newsweek, People* – and placed them in the boys' "treasure boxes" so they will know just what happened on September 11, 2001, the day our nation changed forever.

Justin – A Hero at Age 13

Two days after the national tragedies, we suffered a personal one. Our dear and brave friend Justin Beardsley, at the young age of 13, lost his life. He had battled a brain tumor for six years. He was in a wheelchair due to a stroke he suffered during one of his surgeries. The most terrifying thing was that, as a result of years of chemo and radiation, he had developed leukemia. He died of respiratory failure while preparing for a bone marrow transplant.

Justin was unique. Not because of all he had endured in his short life, but because of the way he chose to live his life here on earth. We'd become very close to Justin's family, and his loss had a profound impact on us. He was another hero who lost his life during that tragic week in September.

After suffering through the tragedies of September 11 and of Justin's heart-breaking death, John and I decided we needed to get away from the news, the television, the radio, everything. After Justin's funeral, we decided to escape with the kids down to my sister's summer home on Cape Cod. We needed to remove ourselves from all the sorrow. We spent two days just hanging out with the kids, going out for meals, running on the beach, throwing rocks into the ocean, and snuggling with each other. I think it helped us sort things out in our own minds and regain control of our lives. We needed to feel a sense of safety, security and comfort again.

Too Many Children Were Losing Their Battles

We returned from the Cape Sunday night, and at 8:31 Monday morning, I called the clinic to set up a meeting with Dr. Kretschmar. I'd grown increasingly edgy about Charlie's situation given the fact that we'd lost Caitlin and Justin within a few short months of each other, and I wanted to discuss our plans for Charlie's care.

I was on the verge of tears when we met at the clinic later in the day. "Dr. Kretschmar, I'm scared. No, I'm terrified. Look at what's been going on here, with just the brain tumor kids. Timmy relapsed, Caitlin relapsed and died, Justin got leukemia from the chemo and died from complications; I don't know what to think anymore!" I said, choking on my tears. "And," I said, trying to choose my words so that I wouldn't fall apart completely, "Charlie and Justin were the only ones on the same combination of chemos."

She nodded in agreement that my fears were valid. "Look," she began, "I wish I could tell you what you want to hear, that Charlie will be fine. I wish I could." She closed her eyes for a moment and carefully contemplated what she was going to say. She knew that I clung to her every word, and I knew she was speaking from her heart. "I just can't, because I don't have the answers. Yes, Justin's leukemia was a result of years, and I mean years, of chemo and radiation. You have to remember that – he had radiation along with the chemo. Justin amazed us all that he lived so long. His body went through so much, and he just kept defying all the odds. And yes, it's the same chemos as Charlie, but Charlie hasn't had radiation. That's very important to remember." She smiled, trying to appear reassuring. "I understand your concerns," she went on, "and I know we will need to make a decision soon regarding Charlie's treatments and when to stop them. I feel if we get him two years past surgery without any changes, his chances increase 90 percent."

I could feel my eyes pop out of my head. "Really?" I sniffled. "So... so if by this February nothing has changed, and he continues to progress, his chances of survival would be that much better? Then we can take him off treatment?" I was shocked by what I was hearing.

"Yes, I believe that to be the case," she confirmed, smiling. "Who knows, maybe we'll stop at Christmastime. Let me think about it and get back to you. I want to look into it further."

"Well," I asked hesitantly, "how do you decide when the right time to stop is?"

316

"You guess," she replied matter-of-factly as a half-grin crept across her face. Now that didn't sound very precise at all. But if there was one thing we admired and appreciated most about Dr. Kretschmar, it was her honesty. She never lied, and never tried to sugarcoat anything with us. She told us the truth — there were no secrets. And we never wanted her to not share something with us; we wanted to know everything there was to know about our son.

When John arrived at the clinic later that afternoon, I filled him in on my conversation with Dr. K, who kindly offered to meet with us both so he could hear exactly what she had told me and ask any questions he might have.

"A lot of people have asked me this question, so I'll ask you," John said, looking uncomfortable about what the answer might be. "Some people ask if he's considered to be in remission. Would you say he is?"

"Well, yes," she answered.

For the second time that day, my eyes nearly fell out of my head, and I caught my jaw before it hit the floor. She could read my excitement, and she raised her hand.

"Now, technically, he is in remission, but remission means different things to different people," she began. "Remission is a term usually used when talking about leukemia patients, when cancerous cells have not been detected in their blood in a certain period of time. So, in Charlie's case, we haven't detected any malignant cells in his spinal fluid, and we haven't seen any changes in the two spots on his brain since July 2000. So, technically speaking, he is considered in remission. But," she said firmly, "this doesn't mean we can say he's cured." She emphatically made the famous quote-unquote signs with her fingers.

"Okay," I thought, sinking back into my chair, "that comment sure brought me back to reality. But maybe she has to say it..." Then she went on to remind us that we didn't have nearly enough information on CPC to go by. We don't know if it's a type that is likely to come back or not; we have absolutely no idea. There weren't any statistics to compare. So for a few minutes, we were on a high when she used the term "remission" – I loved hearing that R-word – but, as the roller coaster ride continued, we were again reminded that we were fighting a disease we hardly knew anything about.

"Well, that was kind of good news, right?" I asked John, after Dr. K left us. "I can't believe she used the word *remission*, can you?"

"I know. That's awesome! And to think he might be done in five months; that's the best."

Jay's Obsession with Dying

Right before Jay turned four, he became obsessed with dying. I had no idea how to handle this. It isn't listed in any of the parenting books I have, and there's no brochure you can pick up at the pharmacy. It started right around September 11. The kids at day care were talking about the people who "died in the plane crash." That night, he came home and began digging for answers to lots of questions. "Why do people die? Is heaven a safe place? How do you get to heaven?" I wanted to answer as honestly and as gently as possible, but it was a constant struggle. To answer his questions about the people in the plane crash on 9-11, I told him that their plane had an accident and hit the building. Now all those people were safe in heaven. But we'd always continue to pray for them and their families who were still here on earth so that they wouldn't be so sad.

Well, that covered September 11, but then he'd start in with children we knew from the clinic who had died of cancer; children like Julia, Caitlin and Justin. One fall afternoon, we were out in our backyard playing on the swing set. "Mommy, where did heaven go?" Jay asked with a concerned look on his face. I looked to the sky, which was clear and blue. Jay, like most children, associated the clouds with heaven. And on this clear, cloudless day, he didn't know what happened to heaven.

"Oh, heaven is way, way above the clouds. So high up, we can't even see it," I informed him.

Jay continued swinging back and forth, then, staring straight up to the sky, he let out a yell: "Hellooo Justin! Hellooo Caitlin!" His smile turned quickly to a frown.

"What's wrong, Sweetheart?"

"Mom, they didn't answer me. Can't Justin and Caitlin hear me?"

"You know, that's what's really cool about heaven," I replied. "Yes, I believe Justin and Caitlin can always hear you, even though you can't hear them because they're so far up in the sky. But I know they can hear you, and it makes them happy to know you're thinking about them."

Jay had known Justin and his family the most. Justin had been in a wheelchair, which Jay was always curious about. He'd continually ask, "Do Justin's legs work now in heaven? Does his body work again? Is he safe? When is he coming back?"

These questions were so painful to hear, and equally challenging to try to answer. "Yes, Sweetie, I do believe Justin's legs can finally work again now that he's in heaven. You see, Justin died because his body was very, very sick." I needed to choose my words carefully because his brother, Charlie, was also sick, and I feared he was worried about Charlie dying. I also didn't want to say he died of cancer, because he'd heard us referring to Charlie's cancer in conversation.

"Justin's body was so sick that it wasn't able to ever get better. Even with all the medications. His body just wasn't working right anymore. God took Justin to heaven so that he could be all better forever," I explained, trying not to show too much emotion, otherwise I would have fallen apart.

"But when's he coming back?" he asked softly.

"Well, Honey, I don't think he'll ever be coming back. And that's the really hard part. Because his mommy and daddy and sisters miss him so much. And that's why we pray to God every night asking Him to take care of Justin and his family."

We didn't go around our house talking about the kids at the clinic dying, as if it was normal dinner conversation. We kept it between John and me as much as possible, when we were alone. But Jay was always wise beyond his years, and even in what I considered a "coded conversation" among adults, he figured out what we were talking about. And since the children who died were in the same hospital with his brother and were "sick" too, he probably feared his baby brother might die also. I avoided bringing up the subject for a few days once the "Can we talk about dying?" slowed down. But when the questions started up again as I was tucking him in at night, I finally got the courage to ask him.

"Sweetheart, are you scared that someone you know might die?"

"Nope," he answered, twisting the arm of one of his stuffed animals.

"Honey, it is okay to ask questions and to talk about things, because that's how we learn, by asking questions. And you know that you can talk to Mommy about anything, right?" I said, stroking his light blond hair.

"I know I can. I don't have any questions. But why do people die again? How come their bodies stop working?"

So he never came out and asked about Charlie, thank God, but the questions continued, usually two or three a week. It made me sad that at such a young, tender age, he'd already known children who had died. He was so young and innocent. Kids his age just shouldn't have to deal with heavy, painful subjects such as other children dying.

Everyone Wrapped Around His Finger

Charlie continued to develop as a normal, demanding, impatient, but comical, cuddly, cute-as-a-button two-year-old with a really bad hairdo. After many discussions, and forever giving in to his pleas, we finally decided it was time to get rid of the *bubba* (his bottle). He loved his bubba, not so much because of the contents, usually his beloved milk, but because we continued to feed it to him as if he were still an infant. Some people thought we were nuts for continuing to feed him like that; others thought we were rather cruel to even consider taking it away. In any case, we had vowed not to let Charlie become a spoiled little monster, regardless of his circumstances, and so out went the bottle, cold turkey. Well, little Mister Smarty-pants figured out how to get his way, and refused to drink unless we held the sippy cup for him, like a bottle. "What a little nudge," John laughed. So no matter where we were, we held his sippy cup for him as if it were a bottle. And he'd scream for it, but instead of saying "cup," he'd yell for "miiilk, miiilk!" He sounded like a kitty meowing for milk. He'd do this all the time; in the car, in bed, you name it. And like the suckers we were, we'd give in every time. The old cancer crutch prevailed again!

This drama went on for about three days. On day four, we happened to have an appointment with Dr. G at Children's for an 18-month, post-surgery follow-up. My sister had come in with me. So there we sat in the neurosurgeon's office, discussing with her how spectacularly well Charlie was developing. I was very honest, to a point.

"We're thrilled that his motor skills are fine, but we're a bit concerned about his speech. He's very social, extremely active," and on and on I went like a very proud mommy. Then I tried to casually slide in, "Oh, and um, well, we just took him off his (I spelled out b-o-t-t-l-e so Charlie wouldn't hear me say the word) and, he still, um," I said, clearing my throat, "he, uh, still sleeps in our bed." I smiled sweetly and turned to look at my sister rolling her eyes in embarrassment. The doctor began to respond, when all of a sudden, Charlie started meowing for his milk.

"What, what's he saying?" she asked, looking at him strangely.

Pretending for a second that I hadn't heard Charlie, I hesitated and shot a look at my sister, who at this point was biting her bottom lip to prevent herself from laughing.

"Oh, um, that, he's saying he wants his, um, milk," I replied, grabbing the sippy cup from the diaper bag. As the doctor started telling me in a very delicate and professional manner that we had to stop babying him, Charlie started crawling up on my lap, meowing for his milk. I tried to hand him the sippy cup, and he deliberately let it drop to the floor. I picked it up, and hoping that the doctor wouldn't notice, I held the sippy cup up to Charlie's mouth by balancing it with only my thumbnail. She was graciously explaining that, for his own good, we needed to stop doing everything for him; and yet, there I was, right in front of her, with Charlie on my lap, feeding him his sippy cup like a bottle. When she finally figured out what I was doing, she stopped talking and grinned. I think she was rather amused by the whole thing. I wasn't. I was mortified.

"I hear everything you are saying, and you're right; I do agree with you," I said, feeling my face turn red. "But it's so hard not to give in to him after what he's gone through. I guess I'm making excuses. Well, no, I'm not. It's not an excuse. He has gone through so much, so that is why he is still babied." The doctor wasn't giving me a hard time at all, but still, I felt I needed to defend my actions. I wanted to say, "Walk a mile in my shoes, and I can guarantee you'd do the same," but I didn't. In a way, we were both right. She didn't want us to do everything he wanted us to, and I just wanted to make my baby happy.

So we left the meeting agreeing that we would reconnect with Early Intervention to reevaluate speech therapy options. We also agreed, and

John and I did stick to it, that we'd put our proverbial foot down, and after three distressing days, Charlie finally started holding the sippy cup on his own. But he still slept between us in the middle of our bed, every single night!

Too Cool for School?

The Barn Yard had graciously offered us an open invitation for Charlie to return to day care any time he wanted to, assuming, of course, that his counts would be up and that there would be no known illnesses floating around at school. I would need to stay in the room with Charlie due to state regulations on the required teacher/student ratio. I decided I'd try to take him in once a week during the weeks he wasn't on chemo. We'd go in just for three hours in the morning to let him interact with the other kids. He really needed to learn to socialize and play with children other than his brother.

The first day seemed to be going along smoothly, until he realized that he couldn't do whatever he wanted, whenever he wanted. "Hmm," I thought, "this is gonna be an issue." At school, there was structure. They read stories at a certain time, snacked at a certain time, rested at a certain time. Little Choochie wasn't used to any structure at all. When it was story time, he wanted to climb on the climbing structure. When it was snack time, he wanted to climb on the chair instead of sit on it.

It was evident Charlie was behind the other children in many ways. It was kind of like observing through one of those one-way mirrors as a monkey tries to socialize with humans. It's not that he was untamed; he just didn't understand everything the other kids understood because they'd already learned daily routines and tasks at day care. For example, all the little kids use Dixie cups at snack time to have their milk. I thought, well, let's give it a whirl. He's never used a Dixie cup before (cripes, we'd weaned him off the bottle just days before), but what the heck; it's a small enough cup. I poured him some water; he grabbed it, put the wrong end of the cup to his mouth, and proceeded to pour the entire thing down his shirt. So we decided this was something we'd need to work on at home.

At first some of his antics were amusing, and they definitely set him apart. But as the day progressed, I grew more concerned. During the late morning "free play" time, the children broke up into their little cliques (yes, there are cliques even at day care), and Charlie was left by himself, just checking out various toys. Not a single child approached him to join in their activities. This was very disheartening to me. After a few minutes of watching him play alone, I did what any loving mom would do: I went over to one of the children and tried to bribe him to go ask Charlie to play. "Luke," I said, trying to negotiate with a two-and-a-half-year-old, "if you go ask Charlie to play trucks with you, I'll bring you a special pudding on Thursday!"

Bad Mommy, Bad Move

John and I did something really, really bad during Charlie's October MRI. Okay, I did, but I forced John to collaborate with me. We were informed that the only MRI time that was available for him in October was at 2:30 p.m. on a Wednesday. Because he was unable to eat or drink twelve hours before a scheduled MRI, this was going to be pure torture for all of us. So the day before the MRI, I called a few nurses, because sometimes you'll get one who'll tell you it's okay to feed him up to eight hours before. Actually, six months earlier, John had accidentally fed Charlie a fist full of Cheerios before a scan, and the anesthesiologist said as long as it was six hours before, it was still "safe."

Even though everyone I talked to that day told me *not* to feed him anything after midnight except water, I caved in to Charlie's cries at about 8:00 the morning of the scan.

"This is cruel and inhumane!" I said, shaking John to wake him up.

"Huh?" he mumbled, rubbing his eyes.

"I can't do this; it's just ridiculous. He's starving. What if I give him half a fruit bar, what do you think? The scan isn't for another six hours."

"Go ahead, if you want to," he said, still half asleep.

"No, no! I'm not making this decision on my own. Should I give him something or not?" I said, standing over him. What I was really doing was getting him to agree with me so that if, God forbid, something happened to Charlie, I wouldn't blame just myself. We both knew it was wrong, but agreed to feed him.

"Fine, I agree, give it to him!" John said, placing a pillow over his head. It was six hours before the scan. I gave him half a fruit bar. He had until 8:10 to eat it, and that was it.

When we arrived in the MRI waiting room, I had the deer-in-the-headlights look the whole time. I felt as if I had "I fed my son" written across my forehead. But John and I kept our little secret. An anesthesiologist we never worked with before came down and asked when the last time Charlie had eaten. I lied. "Last night," I said, staring at the floor. But the guilt was eating away at me.

"Actually," I said, clearing my throat, "let me ask you, because we've heard different answers. Some people have told us it's midnight the night before the scans, others say its six hours prior. What is your opinion?" I thought for certain she could see my heart pounding.

She shook her head. "Oh no, *never*. It's absolutely midnight the night before." She went on to say how incredibly dangerous it is to have anything in the stomach during the tests. The anesthesia could make him nauseous and vomit, he could choke on his vomit, and the vomit could go down into the lungs. If something else went wrong, they'd need to put a breathing tube down his throat, and on and on she went. We, of course, knew all this; we'd heard it a hundred times before.

She left the room, and I started sweating.

"Should...should we just tell her?" I frantically asked John. "Stupid fruit bar," I grumbled.

"Honey, look, it's now 3:30, the scan was supposed to start over an hour ago. You fed him..." John began.

"Wait! *We* fed him, remember?" I sounded like a five-year-old.

"Whatever," John said, rolling his eyes at me. He wasn't going to argue with a crazy woman at this point. "He ate almost eight hours ago. He'll be fine."

When I entered the MRI room with him, my hands were sweating. I started in with my rituals. I said my Rosary, and prayed like a madwoman to God, St. Therese, St. Jude, St. Anthony and our guardian angels. Of course, this time I was not only praying for good test results, I was begging that he wouldn't throw up that fruit bar! I was at the edge of the chair the entire time watching his chest to make sure he was still breathing. Well, little Chooch did fine. No vomiting, nothing. I learned my lesson, though; I'd never do that again. MRIs are stressful enough!

This MRI procedure had its funny moments. I had actually brought a pair of scissors with me to cut Charlie's unruly hair! I figured I'd take advantage of the fact that he was under sedation, since fully conscious, he wouldn't let anyone near his head with scissors. And he was in dire need of a haircut.

Immediately after his spinal, the nurse raced out of the room and said, "Now's your chance, grab the scissors." So there I was, cutting Charlie's hair with the help of the anesthesiologist! We had a nurse hold his wobbly head upright, and I did my best (which was pretty awful) to cut some sort of style into his mop of hair. This was no small task considering he had an oxygen mask around his face and head. Well, as usual, he came out of the anesthesia in a very bad mood, but we couldn't stop laughing because he now resembled Captain Kangaroo. With all the scars on his head, and the shunt, his head was cowlick-central. There really wasn't anything we could do. At least he finally *had* hair!

Giving New Meaning to Stressful Holidays

Although we had a relaxing and filling Thanksgiving, the month of November was extremely stressful for us. John and I continued to talk at length with Dr. K to determine when to stop his treatments. We knew full well that although chemo continued to kill the malignant cells, it also continued to damage the healthy cells in his body. The thought of the secondary cancers, such as leukemia, continued to consume my thoughts, especially after Justin's death. We'd been told numerous times that the chances of Charlie getting leukemia were very low, but let's face the facts here, everything about Charlie is rare. Rare should be his middle name. Heck, his cancer is so rare that only 10 to 20 kids in the country are diagnosed with it each year. And it's rare that any of them survive. So telling us it's rare that he'll develop leukemia really didn't do a lot to ease our concerns.

Dr. Kretschmar was leaning toward February to take Charlie off chemotherapy, and then she thought maybe Christmastime. Gulp! That was only one month away. To hear her say it made my heart pound out of control. She said she'd like John and me to think about it and get back to her with our decision. I must have made a strange face, because she immediately responded.

"What, what is it?"

"We...there is no way...I don't think *we* can make that decision. How can we decide?" I said, with a horrified look on my face.

"Well, why don't you two discuss it, and we can talk about it again the next time you're in for treatment; is that fair?" she replied graciously.

"Sure," John answered her. With that, Dr. K left the room.

"Is she nuts?" I asked John. "How are *we* supposed to come to a conclusion on when to stop his treatment? She's the expert, not us! She's got to tell us! We can't decide. What do we know?" I was annoyed. I really wanted her to have made up her mind, but she hadn't.

Could It Be Genetic?

After worrying sick the entire month over how we'd make the decision on when to stop Charlie's treatment, the phone rang. It was a man I worked with at the advertising agency seven years ago. I had learned that his dad worked in oncology research in New York. A mutual friend had put me in touch with him again, and I'd shared with him Charlie's history, his diagnosis, his development, everything I thought would be helpful if his father could find out any further information regarding CPC.

"Hi, Deirdre," he said in a low voice. My heart dropped, but I tried to stay calm.

"Hey, hi, hi, how are you?"

"Well, ahhh, I wanted to get back to you on a quick conversation I had with my dad about Charlie," he continued nervously.

"Well, what did he say?" I interrupted.

"He said, well, he couldn't believe Charlie was still alive," he answered quietly. "Because, um, people with CPC usually don't live past a year after being diagnosed." He was being as gentle as possible as he delivered this news, but there was no easy way to say this kind of stuff. "Actually," he went on, "he was familiar with CPC, which I was surprised about. So that's good." He laughed nervously and cleared his throat. "He wondered if you guys knew anyone who had survived CPC?"

"Well, no, personally we don't. But we don't know anyone else with the disease." I was trying to continue to clean the kitchen as I spoke to him, but my hands started shaking, so I gave up.

"Has anyone mentioned to you that CPC might be in the genes?" the man asked. With that, I dropped the towel I was holding and slumped into the kitchen chair, taking a huge breath.

"No, no one's ever said anything about that. Why, what did your dad say?"

"He said it's in the lining of the genes. They actually have laboratory rats in his lab with CPC, and they believe it's in the genes."

I shook my head. "Well, I'll have to look into this with his doctor. I do have another child, so this is; well, pretty terrifying to hear." At this point, my head was racing – what about Jay?

"Oh, and I did ask him the question you had about stopping the treatment because of the fear of secondary cancer. He said he'd be more concerned that the brain tumor would grow back than he would about the leukemia issue," he continued. "I don't know if this information is helpful or not. But keep in touch if I can get any other questions answered for you, okay?"

"Thank you, that sounds good," I replied, hanging the phone up as my hand shook. "In the genes? Does this mean genetic? Hereditary? What the hell?" I said under my breath. By now, my entire body was trembling. For the most part, this information wasn't anything we hadn't heard before. We knew people usually didn't live past a year after diagnosis, but this part about being in the genes was horrifying to me. I have two children. John and I created two babies together; did this mean that Jay was in danger of having this disease?

John was in the playroom having a dance-a-thon with the boys when I walked down the stairs. The lights were off, and the kids were dancing around with red and green flashlights, shining them on the ceiling. The music was blaring (as usual for my husband).

"Who was that on the phone?" John yelled.

"My friend whose dad works in cancer research," I said, feeling a lump in my throat.

"Oh yeah, what'd he say?"

"Well, it wasn't the most positive conversation, but for the most part, it wasn't anything we hadn't heard before. Oh, except that they have rats there with CPC, and that they think it's in their genes. And he'd be more worried about the tumor coming back than the leukemia issue." John could tell I was nervous.

"Good, good to know. We need all the information we can have to fight this," he replied, grabbing me by the waist and attempting to dance with me. "Honey, this guy doesn't know us, he doesn't know Charlie. Yeah, it's great he may know more about his cancer, but it doesn't mean any more than that. Don't get all bummed out, please." He twirled me around and dipped me backwards. Then off we went, dancing with our boys.

Information like this always knocked me down a peg. Just when things looked bright on the horizon, it seemed we'd always get tossed some grim new information, just to keep us wondering and worrying. Still, we *never* allowed ourselves to focus on the most horrible information we had about Charlie's condition; we never focused on the statistics. That's why we went with Dr. K. She was treating *Charlie*, not just a patient with CPC. And we always, *always* believed, since day one, that if only one person in a million could survive this disease, that one survivor could and would be our Charlie. It wasn't blind faith; we believed it with all our hearts, and with every breath we took.

I decided to tell Dr. K about this new information during the next clinic visit. I confessed to her that I had been in contact with another doctor in New York. I felt like a wife who'd cheated on her husband. Dr. K didn't seem bothered by it in the least. But she was totally blown away when I informed her that he said it could be in the genes.

"I've never, in all my years, heard this. What is he basing this conclusion on?"

"I don't know. Rats, I guess, lab rats." I felt embarrassed by how it sounded. "Look, we value your opinion above anyone else's. Obviously, you are Charlie's doctor, you know him and his case, and so we listen to you. If you tell me not to freak out about it, I'll try not to. We just want to be on top of things."

She shook her head. "I don't believe there's any relevant information to support the theory that it is in the genes. Show me the chromosome, and I'll give it some consideration. Mrs. Capodanno, please, try not to freak about this."

"Okay, I won't," I answered. But that was a lie.

Smarty Pants!

Charlie had an appointment with the neurologist at the Floating in late November. He only had to see the neurologist once a year, which was just fine with us, since all of us who see Charlie daily, knew he was developing normally. The neurologist is one office away from the Hematology/Oncology Clinic. We were actually getting chemo that day, but surprise, surprise, it wasn't ready when we arrived, so there we were with the neurologist.

Rather than waiting for the doctor to ask the same obvious 100 questions, I started rambling on about all of Charlie's achievements. "He can count to ten, he can identify three colors, he can say some of the alphabet, he can follow directions, says about 75 words, identifies objects, blah, blah, blah."

The neurologist seemed impressed. She opened one of those "My First Word" books and flipped to a page filled with pictures of fruit. "Charlie, where's the apple?" No response.

I grabbed him and placed him on my lap. "Chooch, where's the apple?" I ask sweetly in his ear. Nothing. Charlie didn't so much as bat an eyelash.

"Okay, Charlie," the doctor asked, "where are the grapes? Can you find the grapes?" Dead silence.

I butted in again: "Choochie, come on, you know which ones are the grapes. Show us the grapes, Charlie." Not only did he not respond, he had this total "duh" look on his blank face.

"Okay, let's try colors. Charlie, what color is the banana?" she asked, searching his face for a reply. He just stared at the book.

Jay and John were with us and were sitting on the exam table. I looked at John, pursing my lips with a half smile. "He knows this stuff, I swear!" I told the doctor. "Charlie, what color is the banana?" I asked, with a hint of annoyance in my voice.

Just then you could hear Jay trying to throw his faint voice over to his brother. "Chooch," he said through his teeth, "it's yellow. Chooch, the banana's yellow." John laughed and covered Jay's mouth with his hand. Then we all just started laughing.

"Nothing like making old Mommy out to be a liar, little boy," I said, tickling him. With that, he finally giggled. I swore to the doctor I wasn't lying, and she laughed. "Oh, this happens all the time. He's not familiar with his surroundings, he doesn't know me. It's fine. I know he sees doctors all the time. I'm not at all concerned."

The "What If" Games

December was a difficult month as well. My mind constantly wandered: "What should we do? Should we take him off the chemo? If we did, would the cancer instantly return? If we continued to treat him through February, would it be too much chemo? Would he end up with leukemia?" These thoughts haunted me, consuming every waking minute, especially when I was alone. "What if we make the wrong decision?" I would panic. I'd reduce myself to tears. "How are we going to make this decision?"

What was worse, I would bounce back and forth between two horrible possibilities: "If we keep him on chemo until February and the cancer eventually returns, would we just be prolonging his life two extra months? Would more chemo increase his chances to get the leukemia?" On chemo, at least it appeared that the cancer was gone — it was a safety net for us. But what if, once the chemo stopped, it returned?

I again called the clinic and asked Cathy to have Dr. Kretschmar give me a call. I waited and waited. When I didn't hear from her after three days, I called back. "Cathy," I pleaded, "does she realize I'm stressing out about all this?"

"I know. I've asked her to call you, but she said she'd rather speak to you in person when you come in for chemo on Monday, okay?" Cathy asked sweetly.

"Ugh. I wanted to talk to her before the weekend, but I guess I'll wait until Monday. I'll be a wreck, you know."

"I know you will, Mrs. Capodanno, I know you will. But I just don't think she's made any decisions yet either. Try to have a nice weekend, and we'll see you bright and early Monday morning," she chirped.

"You know you will," I replied, hanging up the phone.

We arrived at the clinic Monday morning at 9:30 and Cathy greeted me with her usual gracious smile. "Good morning, Capodannos!" she yelled. I rolled my eyes at her. She knew I had business to attend to that day. The night before, John and I agreed that if Dr. Kretschmar really wanted us to make the decision, we wanted to take Charlie off the treatments. We were more concerned about the leukemia at this point. And, more important, we wanted his little body to finally have a rest from all of this. Cathy waved me down the hall.

"Does she know I need to talk to her today?" I asked impatiently.

Cathy smiled again. "Yes, Mrs. Capodanno, I put it right in her book; she knows. She's in the report meeting until eleven, as you well know, then I promise I'll make sure she sees you right away."

At 11:20 a.m., Dr. Kretschmar walked through the clinic doors. She gave me a smile, and then just walked on by. Cathy motioned me into one of the exam rooms, and after a few minutes, Dr. K walked in. She shook her hands in the air at Charlie, sneaking over to tickle him. "Hey, Charlie, how's it going?" Turning to me, she said, casually, "Cathy said you wanted to talk to me?"

"Yes, I want to talk to you. Last time we spoke, you were going to give some consideration to taking Charlie off chemo before Christmas. Well, this is the last week of treatment he has before then. I really was hoping you could shed some light on your decision, if you've come to one yet," I said, settling back into the rocking chair while Charlie got himself tangled up in the IV line.

"Oh, well, okay, let's do first things first. Let's examine Charlie, and then we'll chat," she said, grabbing her stethoscope. Was she trying to put this off, or what? I could feel my palms begin to sweat. I hoisted Charlie up onto the exam table. She did the usual: checked his ears, eyes, throat, heart and reflexes. (Kids on chemo rarely have any reflexes left in their knees.) "Gee, as always, he looks terrific," she beamed. It was obvious; she really had a thing for Charlie. She crouched down to be at eye level with him. "You're doing great!" she laughed. She helped Charlie down from the table, and pulled a stool underneath her. "Okay, let's talk. What do you want to discuss?" Now I was anxious and annoyed.

"Well, have you made any decision yet, regarding taking Charlie off treatment?" I asked nervously.

"Like I said last month, I wanted you and your husband to discuss this and let me know what your thoughts are."

"Dr. Kretschmar," I began, clearing my throat, "I…we…we want you to tell us what we should do. No, that's not totally true…we really want to take him off treatment, but we're scared….we don't want to be the ones to make that decision…because, well…" I felt a lump in my throat swelling and I desperately tried to remain composed. "Because what if we say to take him off, and he relapses or something terrible happens?" I said in a frail and wounded voice. "But I know if John were here, which he was planning to be, he would say he wants him off. I'm just really scared."

"I completely understand what you're saying. And, as a doctor, I want parents to be involved in the decision-making process as much as they can be. Some parents don't want my opinion at all; in fact, they want to have total control of their kid's treatments. I understand your fear that if you two decide and things go wrong, you'll have that guilt of making the wrong decision. Listen, regardless of our decision, if he's going to relapse, it's going to happen." Nothing was more painful than hearing statements like this. But I tried to comprehend exactly what she was saying. "Really, if it's going to happen, it will to happen, whether it's now or in February."

Her words turned like a knife in my chest. This is where I usually started losing control of my emotions. I hated these reality conversations, but I knew she had to be honest with me, as painful as it was to hear. "Look," she said, "if we went until February, how many more treatments

335

would that be, five, six? I don't believe that five more treatments are going to make that much of a difference. I really don't."

"I know, but..." Feeling my eyes begin to well, I turned my head and glanced down at Charlie, who was playing with some wooden beads. I cleared my throat once again, choosing my words carefully: "Would it buy us more time with him? I mean, if he were to relapse, it would at least have given us more time with him..." I choked on my words. It was a very painful question to ask. I'm not sure if she realized I was crying; I couldn't look up. "I mean, can chemo just keep the cancer at bay for a while; maybe just keep it from spreading, but it's still viable? Could it still be there?" I was so afraid to hear her answer.

"Well, yes, it could," she answered.

I closed my eyes and my body shook. "Like with Caitlin and Timmy, there was no sign of any cancer in them whatsoever for twelve months, and then only after three weeks coming off treatment, their cancer was back in full force. Did the chemo just keep theirs at bay?" I just wanted to understand how they could have appeared in remission, when in fact, they still had cancer.

"Yes, I'd say that's what happened with them," she answered directly.

I shook my head back and forth. "We're just so afraid...We don't know what to do; there's the issue of the secondary cancers."

"Well, I'm not as worried about that because, remember what I told you, almost all the kids who came down with the secondary cancers also had radiation. Charlie, knock on wood, didn't have any radiation. That's a huge plus," she added, looking for a positive response from me.

"Look," I said quietly, "like I said, I know John and I want to stop, but we want the final decision to be yours. Obviously, it goes without saying, we know you don't have all the answers, and we know you don't hold a crystal ball in your hands. But let's face it, we're not the experts. You are.

And as the expert, and as his doctor, we want you to have the final say. So if you say we'll stop, then let's stop."

I locked eyes with her, but remained silent.

"Okay, look. Even if we decide to stop, I wouldn't do it without another scan. When is his next scan scheduled for? Do you know yet?"

"December 19," I answered.

"Okay, here's the plan. We give him this week of chemo, and scan him on the 19th. If everything is fine with the scans, that's it. This will have been his last week of treatment. Deal?"

I nodded my head in agreement, but did not verbally respond. I was too afraid to give my approval.

Was This the Final Treatment?

The week was pretty uneventful, which was always a blessing. We hardly knew any of the families in the clinic those days. All of our friends we started treatment with were now either off treatment, thank God, or, tragically, had passed away. Charlie and I spent most of the week at the arts and crafts table painting Christmas decorations. I must say, I loved doing this; it was very therapeutic for me. There I'd sit, at the kiddies' table with all the little kids, painting to my heart's content. I think that by the end of the week I had painted at least eight decorations. Charlie couldn't have cared less about the painting; he'd just pick up the paint container and dump it all over the place.

My sister, fortunately, was able to hang out with us for two days that week, which was awesome, and she would bring us lunch – McDonald's for Chooch and salads for us. One day we were eating our salads as I continued to perfect my artwork, painting a wooden stocking with sparkling red glitter paint. Charlie had just finished eating his cheeseburger when he started to cough, and instantly, out of the blue, began throwing up uncontrollably. I raced him to the barrel, and he just kept on going. It was Thursday, so I was wondering if it was the result of four days of chemo. But that didn't make sense, because he rarely got sick on this chemo anymore. "Cripes," I thought, "now they're going to want us to stay at least another hour to hydrate him."

At first, I thought maybe the nurse hadn't noticed he'd vomited, and I was sure as hell not going to tell them. But it didn't take long before they noticed. "Oh no, Charlie, what happened?" she asked sweetly.

"He coughed while he was eating, so I'm pretty sure that was all it was," I answered quickly. Which was true, but I doubted that's what caused it.

"Really, do you think that was it?"

"Yeah," I replied. Let's face it; we never, ever wanted to be in that hospital one single second longer than we had to be. As nice as they all were, and as pleasant as they all tried to make it there, I wanted to leave the minute I got there. And I was *not* going to stay to hydrate him — I knew he was fine. If I thought there was an issue, we'd stay.

Fortunately they let us go. But later that night, as we were all about to head out to dinner with friends, Charlie started coughing again, and again a vomiting episode ensued. This time, I caught the vomit mid-air in the cup of my hands. I'd actually perfected the talent of catching vomit. After a year and a half of it, I was awfully good at it. Gone were the days when seeing my son vomit made me cry. Now, it was nothing out of the ordinary.

I could see our friends' car headlights in the driveway.

"Chemo?" John questioned, bringing over a towel.

"Guess so, but it's an odd time to have it. Who knows? Well, for better or for worse, we have a scan in two weeks." I opened my hand for John to wipe it down.

Nosey Jay inspected the mess. "Eeeww, gross, is that mac and cheese?"

"Jay, that's nasty!" I laughed. Funny though, this was the same child who, months ago, whenever his brother started throwing up, would swan dive onto the couch to block his eyes and ears. Now it didn't faze him in the least. Now he was actually curious about its contents!

I waved to our friends and told them to meet us at the restaurant. Long gone were the days when we wouldn't leave the house after Charlie got sick. It didn't faze him or any of us in the least anymore. Charlie was 100 percent himself right after vomiting; he didn't appear sick or uncomfortable at all. He flipped his jacket on over his head and back, which was his new trick, and walked over to the door. You see, it was normal to have our child throw up one minute and head out to the Bugaboo Creek restaurant the next.

On Friday morning, we entered the clinic for what I was praying would be our last chemotherapy treatment ever. But I didn't mention it to anyone in the clinic. It wasn't something I was planning to shout from the mountaintops. Although I'd love to, I knew better. We'd seen way too much there, too many relapses, too many kids beginning treatments from square one again, too many little ones who had died.

"Please, Jesus," I whispered to myself, "please let this be the last treatment."

I thought I should mention the vomiting to Mary Jo as she was hooking up his line, and I noticed that she gave me a puzzled look. "Well, there is a bug going around. Hmm. Let's see how he does today. He seems fine."

"*Gawd, Peez Kurrr Me!*"

I'd exhausted the arts and crafts table by early morning, so I grabbed Charlie and took a long walk around the entire hospital. We visited the 7th floor, went down to the lobby, swung up to the playroom and chatted with all our friends – the cleaning staff, the room service staff, the nurses, everyone who knew us.

And of course we stopped for a moment at our favorite spot, our Windows to the World. It was a clear, beautiful December day in Boston. My mind wandered back to the many, many mornings we watched the pitch darkness of the early morning hours turn into rush hour traffic. It had been ten glorious months since we had slept there.

I checked the timer on the IV pump; we had about ten minutes left with this final bag of chemotherapy so I sat on the floor to be at Charlie's eye level. "Woo-woos," Charlie cheered, as an ambulance raced by. He so loved that window. It was actually very entertaining. The ER entrance was right below the window, so we'd see a number of ambulances each time we sat there.

"I spy a mailman!" I yelled pointing to a mail truck. "Boy," I thought, "we've spent hours in front of this window. And we've seen so much. Charlie's learned a lot of words just by staring out this window."

"Meeeal-maan!!!!" Charlie repeated.

I got up on my knees to check the timer again. Exactly five minutes left.

"Dear God," I said out loud, slowly assuming my cross-legged position on the floor. "Please, please, God, let this be it. God, please, this has *got* to be it...the last chemo to ever enter his precious body, ever!"

I stared up at the bag of chemo dangling from its pole. It was as if the liquid poison was dripping in slow motion. Drip. Drip. Drip. My eyes traced the flow of liquid dripping from the bag, flowing down the line until it disappeared under Charlie's shirt. Charlie was watching me, quietly, which was extremely unusual for him. Realizing the daze I was in, I grabbed my little boy and plopped him down onto my lap. I whispered very slowly into his ear, and he repeated clearly in his own toddler voice:

"God..."

"Gawd..."

"Please..."

"Peez..."

"Cure..."

"Kurrr..."

"Me...."

"Me! Charlie!"

He bounced up and down on my lap excited that he was able to repeat every word. I lowered my head. To hear him asking God to cure him was beautiful and emotional and innocent. I could feel the tears begin to well again and I buried my face in the nape of his neck.

Beep...Beep...Beep. The pump began signaling. "That's it, little man. That's it. Let's go get you unhooked, God willing, forever!"

I lifted Charlie off my lap, wiped my eyes, jumped to my feet, and scooped him up in my arms. Grabbing the pole with my free hand, we raced back to the clinic. Beep. Beep. Beep. The pump was announcing once again that we were done. My heart was pounding.

"All set?" Mary Jo asked.

"Yup, we're all set," I answered quietly.

"Hey, this is it, right?" she asked, smiling.

I looked around the waiting area to see if anyone heard her, which was impossible, because her voice was as quiet as a mouse. "Well, um, yeah, we sure hope so. But, I'm not saying anything," I answered. I'm *never* at a loss for words, I wear my heart on my sleeve, and I'm the first to share any good news with anyone who will listen. But this was different.

It just didn't seem right to be jumping for joy. We still had to get through the scans, and then, who knew what else.

"Is this it?" one of the Child Life specialists asked as we waited for the line to flush.

"God willing. We hope. We're keeping our fingers crossed. Say a prayer," I said, putting on our jackets. With that, we left the clinic without really saying goodbye.

You'd think after five straight days of chemotherapy Charlie would be exhausted. Not this bound-and-determined little two-year-old. He raced down the long hallway toward the garage, with his little clipped-on mittens swinging wildly from his jacket sleeves. "Slow down," I'd yell, to no avail. Everyone smiled at him; he's just so darn cute.

"I wish I had that energy," an elderly man laughed. Little did he know Charlie had just finished a full week of chemotherapy.

We came to the dreaded urine-soaked stairwell. I tried to carry Charlie up the seven flights of stairs. But he was in his stage of full independence and wanted no part of being carried by his mommy. He screeched and squirmed and wiggled right out of my arms.

"I dooo it! I doooo it!" he bellowed.

And then it began; the long, smelly hike up the repulsive stairwell. Of course, Charlie dragged his hands up the filthy railing the entire way, which turned my stomach. I could hardly wait to retrieve the antibacterial wipes from my back pack!

He never stopped once, not the entire way up. And he had to count each step: "1, 2, 3, 4, 5, 6, 9, 11!" He was so very proud of himself.

"How can you not be tired?" I asked, shaking my head.

Once we reached the top, I stopped to catch my breath.

"Door, door!" Charlie yelled, trying to open the door to the garage.

"Hey, buddy boy, this is a parking lot; slow down and hold Mommy's hand." I grasped the nasty doorknob with my shirtsleeve and pulled.

Charlie squeezed through the doorway and dashed away. "*Charlie Capodanno*," I yelled, "hold my hand!"

"No. I go home," he said with a laugh, dodging my grasp.

Okay, so I can't carry him, he won't hold my hand; maybe this kid's getting a little *too* independent. I was walking right beside him, but I was still getting dirty looks from a woman waiting for the elevator. "I pick and choose my battles," I said, winking at her.

Finally we arrived at the car. I unlocked the door and tried to pick Charlie up to put him in the car seat. "No," he squealed. "I doooo, I doooo!"

"Come on, Chooch, it's been a long week for both of us. I'd really just like to get home," I pleaded. But he was insistent on climbing into the seat by himself. This, of course, took a good five minutes, but he was so determined. He grunted and groaned, and at one point, he got stuck between the passenger's seat and the car seat. "Let's *go*, Chooch," I said impatiently.

Finally, after what seemed like forever, he plopped himself down into the seat. "I did it," he cheered. "*Mama, I did it!*" He was sporting a smile from ear to ear.

I bent down to be at eye level with my precious son. An enormous sense of pride rushed through my entire body. I leaned over and kissed his cheek.

"You sure did do it, Sweetie-pie. You sure did!" I realized I wasn't talking about climbing into the car seat.

My two-year-old son had endured 21 months of chemotherapy, six surgeries and survived Stage Four brain cancer. He was alive.

"You are Mommy's hero, Charlie Capodanno," I said with great admiration.

Chapter 13
Believe in Miracles

....

Staying Preoccupied

We had a week and a half before the scan. I did my very best to keep myself distracted, trying to focus on Christmas rather than the test that would determine our future. But, regretfully, Charlie began vomiting and with great reluctance, we ended up back in the hospital. It was the last place on earth I wanted to be.

Dr. K came in to check on us. "What are you doing here?" she asked.

"Ugh. Don't ask. It's the *last* place I want to be...oh, no offense." She squeezed my shoulder sympathetically. "Please don't make us stay," I pleaded. "I promise I'll get him to keep something down and get him hydrated."

She laughed. "Well, a lot of the kids have had to be admitted with this stomach bug. Let's see how his electrolytes look before we decide. In the meantime, I want the nurses to hydrate him for at least two hours."

Fortunately, his electrolytes came back fine. "I promise, I'll get some Pedialyte into him, I swear. Please let us go home." Obviously, I'd do anything that would make Charlie feel better. If he were dehydrated, I'd stay. It had been ten months since we'd slept there. Now, within three days of perhaps being off treatment for good, we might have to stay.

"Okay," Cathy bargained, "his electrolytes are fine now, but if he keeps vomiting and can't keep anything down, you'll have to come back."

"I know. You know I know! I have an idea. How about we have the VNA check his 'lytes at home tomorrow?"

"Deal," she said.

The stomach bug lingered for days, but miraculously, his counts, including his electrolytes, were fine. He finally seemed to feel better two days before his scan.

The day before the MRI was spent reattaching the Christmas tree ornaments that Charlie kept removing from the tree and hiding throughout the house. During the evening, Jay raced upstairs after watching *The Grinch* video. With Charlie trailing behind him, he asked if he and Charlie could go out front for a minute.

"Honey, it's starting to get dark and cold. Why do you want to go outside?"

"Please, Mommy, just for a minute; I gotta check on something," he pleaded. "And I need to bring Charlie with me; we'll be just a second."

"Where are you going?"

"Just right there," he said, pointing to the bushes right in front of our house.

"Okay," I replied. Grabbing Charlie's hand, the two of them raced out the front door giggling. I watched, like a hawk, from the family room window. As they stepped back from the house, Jay grabbed Charlie by the arm and pointed to the roof. A huge smile consumed Charlie's face. I opened the front door, and before I could utter a word, Jay yelled with joy,

"Yes, yes, we do have a chimney! Ya-hoo!" He had just seen the Grinch climb down the chimney, and seeing ours confirmed in his innocent little mind that Santa had an entryway.

Because it was peak season for UPS, there was no way John would be able to take the morning off to be with us for the MRI. Fortunately, my sister volunteered to join me. MRIs and spinals are emotionally draining and absolutely nerve-racking procedures, and Charlie always came out of them like a bear, so it was helpful to have an extra set of arms to help calm him down. But mostly, my sister joined me just to be there for support. I never considered myself to be superstitious, but this was the first scan ever that John wasn't able to join us for, and it made me more nervous.

"I just don't like this," I said. I was pulling apart my dresser drawer trying to find my rosary beads. I couldn't find them, and it was making my anxiety rise to new heights.

"What...what don't you like?" John asked.

"I don't like that you can't come. You've always been there; this is the first time you won't be there. Now I can't find the rosary beads that were blessed by the Pope," I answered.

"Kel will be with you, and you can certainly handle things," he reassured me.

"No, I don't mean that. I don't know; I'm nervous that so far all the scans have been good, and you've always been there. This time, you won't be there."

I raced into Charlie's room, frantically pulling apart his drawers, then back to my room, where I finally found the beads in the bottom of my "collect-all" basket. Phew! Well, at least that made me feel better. If I had neither John nor the rosary beads with me, I'd be a disaster.

My father called. "Is your sister still going with you tomorrow?"

"Yup, I'm picking her up at six-thirty," I answered, anticipating what he was going to say next.

"Well, don't worry. I'll be there in the morning, too. Where's the MRI room?"

"Dad, you don't need to come in. We'll be fine. They don't let too many people in the MRI area, and they probably won't let a third person in the recovery room. And I'm stressed enough as it is," I explained. I knew very well that his mind was made up, and that he wanted to be there. Needless to say, it's never a pleasant experience for any of us to see Charlie in such a lifeless state, under sedation. "It's no fun to see Charlie lying there like that," I added.

"Deirdre, I've seen him in a lot worse condition, trust me. I'll be there. It'll be fine. What time will you get there? Where should I meet you?" He had a dozen questions for me, none of which I had the energy and patience to answer. Ugh, another thing to stress me out – worrying about my father.

I hung up and immediately called my sister. "I swear, Kel, I can't handle him being there if he's going to get upset or anything. I can't deal with that tomorrow," I started in.

She tried to reassure me. "He'll be fine, don't worry about it. I'll handle Dad," she said.

The morning of the scan, I woke up, or I should say I got out of bed, at 5:00. I hardly slept a wink. I spent most of the night tossing and turning, and praying frantically. As always, Charlie was unable to eat or drink anything after midnight. I was anxious that he would be upset and hungry, so I held off waking him up until right before we had to leave. We had to be at my sister's house, which is about fifteen minutes away, by 6:30 to be at the hospital by 7:30.

I woke Charlie at six, and fortunately, he did not seem to be too hungry or thirsty. While undressing him, he started to fuss. And when

I applied his "magic cream" over his Infusaport, he knew he was headed to the hospital, which upset him. I did my best to keep his mind off the cream by telling him we were going to pick up Auntie Kel. This piqued his curiosity and immediately cheered him up.

My sister did her best to distract me on the ride into Boston, making small talk about a job she was being offered. But my mind was elsewhere.

The Stress of the Scan

Charlie remained awake for the entire ride, which surprised me. He was content, which was a blessing, since at this point he must have been really hungry. But the minute we pulled into the hospital parking garage, he sank into his car seat and started to cry. He knew exactly where we were and he hated it. We were supposed to have Cathy Downing access his Infusaport in the clinic at 8:00.

It was exactly 7:30, and we checked in with MRI as we had been instructed. But lo and behold, the technician informed me that Charlie wasn't on the schedule until 12:30. I could feel my face turning red. I looked at my sister and rolled my eyes. I took a deep breath. And as calmly as I could, I informed the technician that the appointment for this MRI was made well over a month ago, and we were never notified of a change. My child had not eaten since eight o'clock the night before, and he was hungry. I did not have time to sit around the hospital until noon, and there was no way we were going to make Charlie starve for another four hours.

"Well, it's not his turn," the technician replied.

"Yes," I began, hearing my voice rising, "it *is* his turn, because he was on the schedule for *now*! He is two years old, which is why he always has the first morning appointment!"

My sister was doing her best to distract Charlie by building a Lego building with him in the waiting area. "Look," the technician said, pointing to the schedule book, "Charlie's at 12:30." I pointed to the 7:30 slot, which of course was covered with eraser marks. You could see the faint imprint of Charlie's name, but another name was written over it. Gone were the days when I would have gotten teary-eyed over a situation like this. I went from being frail, to being diplomatic, to being downright demanding.

"*Who* handles this schedule? I want to talk to them *now!*" I said with smoke coming out of my ears. See, this is what killed me every time. I mean, as if an MRI wasn't stressful enough, to come in and have them tell me Charlie was bumped without notifying me just pissed me off to no end.

"She'll be here in a minute," the tech said, disappearing behind a set of doors.

"*Can you believe this?*" I yelled. "This is *exactly* what drives me over the edge!"

"Well, I think you're handling it very well. I'd be swearing my head off at this point," my sister replied.

Seconds later, the anesthesiologist who knows me very well (and still liked me) came around the corner.

"Oh, thank God you're here. Listen, I don't know what's going on, but a month ago, Charlie's MRI was scheduled for today at 7:30. Now the tech is trying to tell me he's been bumped to 12:30, he hasn't eaten, and there is no way I'm making him wait until noon. No way! We were never informed of any switch, and we're here now!" I was ranting and raving like a nut.

"Fine, let's just get it done," he answered matter-of-factly.

"You're awesome! Thank you! How can you stand me?" I asked, smiling.

"Well, you're here, I don't see another child waiting to be scanned, obviously no one told you not to come in, so let's just get it done."

The technician came around the corner. "It's not Charlie's turn; another baby is supposed to be scanned," she began.

"I don't see another baby here, do you? Charlie's here, he's ready to rock, so let's just get it going," the doctor answered her abruptly. Case closed.

Regrettably, due to this whole mix up, about a half hour was wasted, so we didn't have time to bring Charlie up to the clinic to have him assessed. I was comfortable with the anesthesiologist doing it, but Charlie wasn't. When we sat down to remove his clothing, he started screaming and crying. He fought my hold on him with every ounce of energy he had. It was so painful to hear him cry like that in fear and frustration. The doctor wasn't hurting him; Charlie just wasn't familiar with this stranger who was about to jab a needle into his chest. Usually, they gave him a little Versed, which is a drug to take the edge off, before they gave him the full-blown sedation. But since Charlie didn't appear overly hungry or fussy, the doctor and I agreed to skip the Versed in hopes that he'd come out of the sedation a bit less cranky.

Normally, I would hold him for a few minutes, and he'd slowly, usually with a fight, drift off to sleep. This time, the doctor injected the Propofol into his line, and in the middle of a scream, he coughed hard twice, and his head jerked backwards and his eyes immediately shut. It scared me. "Is he all right?" I asked nervously.

"Yup, he's all set. That's how the Propofol works without the Versid first."

"That really scared me; I didn't like that at all." My voice cracked as I looked up at my sister's face.

"Poor Chooch," my sister said with tears in her eyes. It's just so hard to watch him in that condition. Motionless. Head tilted back, arms dangling to the sides. Just awful. My sister rubbed my shoulders as we watched them work on Charlie's limp little body. Once they were done, the nurse waved me in. I'd never met her before.

"Rumor has it, you don't let him out of your sight, Mom," she laughed.

"Nope, I don't," I said with pride.

The MRI went off without a hitch, and at the very last minute, Charlie began to cough, which startled me. Of course, the anesthesiologist was in the room in two seconds, and checked the sedative, giving the vial a squeeze to put Charlie "under" again, since we still had the lumbar puncture to go. "We're all done with the scan," he informed me. "Just need to bring him across the hall for the LP. Dr. Pelidis will be right down."

I always stayed out of their way as they removed Charlie from the scanning table and back onto the gurney. Out of the corner of my eye, I could see my dad in the hallway, trying to give me a wave. I smiled at him, but did not leave the room until the technician and the nurse scooped Charlie up, shuffled him back out into the hall, and placed his limp body on a waiting gurney. They whisked him instantly to the other procedure room for the LP. I was not allowed in there with him, but I respected that decision because I knew how important it was for the room to be completely sterile when they gave him the spinal.

I walked over to see my dad and sister, and within seconds, I realized my dad was crying. This is exactly what I feared would happen. I turned and gave my sister a look. "I know," she whispered in my ear, "it just upset him to see Charlie like that; it's hard for him."

"I know, but I can't deal with this right now," I answered quietly.

My dad strolled down the hall for a few minutes, and then reappeared. He came over and kissed my forehead. "Sorry, it's just so hard," he said, sniffling. "It's been a while since I've seen him like that."

"I told you, Dad. This isn't pleasant, and I don't want you to be upset, 'cause then I get upset."

A burly man in a white lab coat emerged from the viewing room. He had a very welcoming look on his face. Without thinking, I raced over to him. "Sir, excuse me, do you work in radiology?" I asked anxiously.

He gave me a big smile. "Yes, yes I do," he answered politely.

"Well, sir...I, um..." (I had no idea if he was the technician, or a doctor, or what. He could have been a student in the radiology area for all I knew.) I could feel the tears welling in my eyes and a lump swelling in my throat. Without realizing it, I grabbed hold of the man's wrist. "Is there any way...I mean I can't...we really can't wait three days for these results. They could hopefully, um, change our life...and, it's Christmas, and I'll go out of my mind worrying and waiting," I said, realizing that at this point I was squeezing the man's arm extremely tightly. I just kept on rambling, "Could you maybe, um, just maybe ask if someone could review those scans soon...so we can maybe have a merrier Christmas?" I stopped, staring directly into his eyes. He just had the sweetest, gentlest smile.

"I'll take care of it for you right now," he answered, and with that, he was gone.

My sister asked, "Who was that? He was so nice; all smiles."

"I have no idea." My tension was turning into excitement. "But he said he worked in radiology, and when I asked if he could push the scans through, he said he would."

Our Christmas Wish Comes True!

At home, Charlie bounced back that day like he hadn't been through anything out of the ordinary. He and Jay were racing around the house, playing tag and hide and seek, and just being loud, reckless boys. It was about 5:45 p.m. when the phone rang.

"Hello, Mrs. Capodanno," the voice said pleasantly. I instantly knew it was Cathy. My heart sank because unless she had news, or she was returning my calls, she never just called to check in.

With all the noise the kids were making, I had to place my hand over my ear to hear her better.

"Cathy?"

"Yes, it yours truly. Well, Missy, I don't know who you know in radiology, but I've got some news for you," she chirped. I walked into the living room and immediately dropped down on the edge of the couch, staring blankly at the lights on our Christmas tree.

"*What?*" I swallowed hard. "What do you know?" I asked, feeling my heart leaping right out of my chest.

"Well, the scans are already back, they're perfect, and his spinal fluid looks great! How's that for good news!"

"What...what do you mean? So everything's fine? The scans are fine, and so is the fluid?" I asked, spontaneously shaking my knee. I was trying to comprehend exactly what she had said.

"Yup, everything looks great. You sure know the right people," she laughed, "because whoever you spoke to down in MRI made sure you'd have the scans read today. When does that ever happen? And here's the even better news," she went on. "Little Charlie is officially *off treatment!* So I'm going to give you the next two weeks off. Enjoy every minute of your holidays, and I'll call you in two weeks to arrange a time to discuss your 'off treatment' schedule. How does *that* sound?"

The words "off treatment" were swirling around inside my head. I placed my hand against my forehead and began rubbing my temple trying to comprehend what I had just heard.

"I can't...I can't believe you're saying those words. But they sound so awesome." I was silent for a moment.

"Mrs. Capodanno?" Cathy questioned.

"Oh...I'm so sorry. I think I'm just in a bit of shock, I really do. I don't know how to react. Oh my God, I just can't believe it! I used to daydream all the time about when we'd finally be off treatment...." my voice trailed off.

"I know it's a lot to take in. This is big! Well, Merry Christmas, Capodanno family. Call if you need anything. You know where to find us, right?" Cathy said joyfully.

"Yes. Thanks so much, Cathy. And thanks for calling us tonight; you should be on your way home."

"I just wanted to make sure you had your news tonight!"

"Cathy, thank you; I mean, really, thank you for *everything*. I hope you know how much we appreciate all you've done for us. And I know I haven't been the easiest mother to deal with..." I began to well up. "And thank you for giving us this wonderful news. Merry Christmas," I said, fighting back the tears.

"You don't need to thank me. I'm just as happy as you are. Merry Christmas!"

I sat frozen on the couch. I didn't feel like jumping up or down, I didn't feel like crying, I didn't know exactly what to do, or how to respond. I just sat, just staring at the lights on the Christmas tree, hearing my little boys buzzing around doing a number on our hardwood floors with their toy trucks.

"What a Christmas gift," I finally said to myself. "Off treatment... my baby's finally off treatment." I dialed the number to page John, and he returned the call instantly. Because he was calling from his cell phone in the UPS truck, he could hardly hear me, and he was yelling.

"*Honey?*"

"Yes, listen, the results came back and everything is clear," I said with little inflection.

"*What?*" The noise of his truck was too loud for him to hear me.

I yelled into the phone, this time with excitement in my voice. "*I said the tests are back, and they're clear!*"

"Already? They're back already, and everything's fine? Awesome! That's *awesome!* I knew he'd be fine." I could hear his voice crack a bit. "That's my boy!"

"And Cathy said he's off treatment!" I shouted

"*What? He's off what?*"

"*Off* chemo! He's done! No more chemotherapy!"

"No *way!* That's *awesome!* That's *great!* I'll be home soon. Give those boys a kiss for me. I love you, Honey," he said sweetly.

"I love you too, and I love our little family," I replied.

I called my dad and Bebe. Bebe answered pleasantly.

"Hi, Bebe, it's Deirdre. We got our wish. The results are back already. Everything's just perfect," I said, and for the first time, the shock seemed to be wearing off and I started to choke on my words.

"Oh, my God, Sweetheart, that's just, just wonderful news," and she began to cry.

"He's off treatment...no more chemotherapy...can you believe it?"

My dad called when he returned from the store.

"Hi there," he said in a shallow voice trying desperately to stay composed. "Tell me *exactly* what the nurse said, please." He wanted to savor every glorious word. I repeated verbatim what Cathy told me, and, of course, with my dad, I had to repeat it several times.

"God answered our prayers for sure. No question about that! I'm just thrilled; thrilled for you and John, thrilled for Charlie and Jay. I'm thrilled for all of us. We couldn't ask for any more than this. Thank You, God!" he proclaimed.

After I hung up the phone, I wanted to scream it from the mountaintops and get on the phone to call everyone I knew, especially our loyal supporters who'd been following Charlie's ordeal via e-mail from the very beginning. What had started out as a way for me to vent my fears and frustrations to a handful of good friends had been transformed into an e-mail distribution list of well over 150 people across the country, and as far away as France and Scotland. Some of these people were close friends, others were complete strangers. Yet every month, through my "Charlie Updates," I'd share with them Charlie's troubles and triumphs, and my joys and deepest fears. I decided at that moment I needed to send an e-mail blast to everyone.

It was about 6:00 p.m. and many of them would still be at work, but we knew they were all just as anxious about the results as we were. I wanted to spread our joy immediately to absolutely everyone I could.

I was no longer naïve. I knew full well that we still had a hard road ahead of us. I completely understood that we were going to live with this fear hanging over our heads for the rest of our lives. We were fully aware of all the "what ifs" and "what could happens," too. But at that very tender and fresh moment, I wanted to rejoice. I wanted the world to know what Charlie had accomplished. My son had survived cancer. I know some cynics out there, including other parents from the clinic whose kids had relapsed, would think I was crazy for feeling this sheer elation, but I really didn't give a damn. We'd made it so far. We witnessed a true miracle unfold right before our eyes, and I was going to let everyone know it! I sat down, and without even considering what I'd write, I poured my heart out in this e-mail:

Well, my friends and family, our Christmas wish came true! Charlie
underwent his MRI and lumbar puncture this morning, and for the first time
EVER we received the results the same day, and, as we had all been hoping

and praying for, his spinal fluid was "clear of any malignancy" and the scans of his brain and spine were fine. This is exactly what we wanted to hear! I had to have his nurse repeat the information to me a few times, just to make sure I was hearing her correctly!

The most exciting thing she said was, "I'll call you in a few weeks to discuss your 'off treatment' schedule - meaning when we'll have to go in to have his line flushed, and to schedule another scan, etc. Off treatment sure has a wonderful ring to it, doesn't it? This is truly amazing. Our life has literally revolved around having chemo treatments every three weeks for close to two straight years. Heck, I don't know what I'll do with all this extra time!

Needless to say, we are so overjoyed, elated, and maybe a tad overwhelmed! (Oh, yes, and of course, a bit scared, but we won't focus on that right now.)

We just hope and pray that this part of his life as a cancer patient is behind us. Sure, we will live with this fear for the rest of our lives; Charlie will continue to be scanned forever. But we just hope that the cancer will never, ever return to his body. Many of you who are reading this e-mail have walked in our shoes, and we know all too well all the "what ifs" that hang over our heads. But you know that, right now, we need to focus on how far Charlie has come. Look at all the odds he has defied, all the hurdles he's overcome.

Please know we do not use the word miracle lightly. For all of you who have been through this entire experience with us, and know full well how high the odds were stacked against him, how grim his survival rate was, how rare his cancer is, and that John and I were told he "wasn't going to see LAST Christmas" if his cancer progressed, the fact that he is still here racing around on this earth really IS a miracle. There is no doubt about it.

Charlie's story has touched many lives. And it DOES give us all a reason to believe in sooooo many things: to believe in hope, even when that's all you have left; to believe in the power of prayer and positive thinking, because we've all witnessed our prayers being heard and answered; to believe in inner *strength, even when it's so hard to find it sometimes; to believe in the will-power of a six-month-old boy who needed to be tied down to his hospital bed after eight hours of brain surgery because he wanted to get up and go; to believe in brotherly love, because it carried this family through our entire journey; and of course, to believe in miracles...because you've all witnessed one!*

Thank you all for being there for us, especially today with all your prayers and positive vibes! You'll never fully understand how your unwavering love and support has carried this family through our entire journey.

We hope you all have a happy, safe, and peaceful holiday - and thank you for sharing in our joy! God bless you all! Oh, and PLEASE keep Charlie in your prayers.

Love,

Dee

As I went to click the send button, my hand shook. Almost instantly, I began receiving heartwarming responses to my e-mail that proved to John and me that Charlie's story had touched many lives and many hearts, and that his strength and determination were inspiration to so many. In total, we received well over a hundred responses. It was clear from the gratifying notes that Charlie's journey had not only touched others' lives, but had changed them as well. His young life had made a difference; his battle was not in vain.

A New Year – And a Whole New Life

January 2002 was an amazing month for our family. Our holidays were joyous and we were surrounded by our family and friends, all of whom attested to the fact that their Christmas wishes had also come true. It's what we'd all been praying for – and all we could ever wish for.

Not having to go into the clinic for chemotherapy was just about the best feeling in the world. But it was scary, too. The elation was wearing off a bit, and I began to feel uneasy. Removing Charlie from his chemo seemed so final. For the first week, I had the fear of "what ifs." Still, I tried to relish the fact that our lives seemed normal again, for the first time in a very, very long time. And it was amazingly good to feel like regular people again. Honestly, it seemed unreal. But the fear of the sky falling again was always tucked in the far corner of my mind.

We had our official "off treatment" appointment with Dr. Kretschmar in late January. I was hoping she'd say something like, "Congratulations, good job, good luck, come back and say hi in a few years." But no such luck. She did the usual exam and chatted about how great Charlie looked.

"Oh come on, what do you think?" I pleaded with her. "I know you can't say anything I'd hold you to forever, but how do you feel about all this?"

"I always had a good feeling about Charlie," she said, allowing a huge smile to consume her face. This brought immediate tears to my eyes. Not just because it was *exactly* what I wanted to hear, but because I knew this woman well enough to know she'd *never* say anything that she didn't mean. *Never.* She doesn't say things to make anyone feel better; she knows not to do that.

So to hear her say those words made my year! She was the *only* person who had ever given Charlie any chance at survival. She was our glimmer of hope. She believed in Charlie, just like we did. I remember her words, clear as day: "We don't focus on the statistics; we focus on your child."

As we gathered our belongings to leave the clinic, Charlie turned to her and without any prompting at all, gave her a big wave and said,

"Tank-oo." This caught me completely off guard. It was as if he was saying, "Thank you for saving my life."

"Ohhh," I said, placing my hand to my heart. "That's got to make you feel good."

She winked at me. "It sure does."

"Would it be okay if I gave you a hug?" I asked hesitantly. I wasn't sure if she was the affectionate type, but I wanted to hug this woman, and thank her for giving my son his life back.

"Oh, sure, of course," she said, extending her arms.

"Thank you," I whispered softly in her ear as I embraced her.

"My pleasure," she replied, giving me a squeeze.

As we were leaving the clinic, Priscilla, the parent consultant, gave us our "off treatment" package, including a book entitled *Childhood Cancer Survivors* (gulp!) and the official "Make-A-Wish" application. I was all excited. To me, this gave some finality to things. But as I flipped through the book on the ride home, I realized it was all about looking for the signs of relapsing, the horrible long-term side effects of chemo, and all that yucky stuff. So I decided not to read any further. I was not in denial; I knew quite well what the signs of relapsing were. And I sure as hell didn't need to spend my nights reading up on them just as my son ended 22 months of hell! Lord knows, my mind plays enough tricks on me. I didn't need a book to give me any more wacky ideas!

The "Make-A-Wish" brochure had me in tears in three seconds. Imagine a program designed to grant wishes to children with life-threatening or terminal illnesses, and your child is eligible. Try reading *that* without falling apart. We wanted to choose something not just for Charlie, but for Jay too, since he'd endured so much over the last two years.

The most moving experience that month was being asked by Father Tom to update the children at our church who had all been praying for

Charlie and following his progress for the past 22 months. Father Tom and I agreed we'd let the little ones know that God was listening to them, and that they were being heard and answered.

I crafted my speech so that the young children could understand. With John, Jay and Charlie by my side, I read the words to the entire congregation at the 9:00 a.m. children's mass:

Almost two years ago we were in the hospital with our baby Charlie, who at the time was only six months old. Doctors told us that Charlie was very sick with a disease known as cancer, which was in his brain and spine. Charlie would need an operation and lots of medication, known as chemotherapy, to try to make him better so that he could live.

It was very hard for us to tell to our oldest son Jay, who was only two years old at the time, that his baby brother had a boo-boo in his head, and that Charlie would need to spend lots of time away from him in the hospital.

Our family knew that it would take more than all the medications and the operations to cure Charlie of his sickness. And we knew that the only person who could really make him better was God. So we called everyone we knew and asked them to please start praying for Charlie. We needed to let God and all the angels in heaven know that we really wanted Charlie to stay here with us on earth. Because we love him so very much.

I immediately called Father Tom to ask if our friends at St. Mary's could pray for Charlie. He said you all would. Charlie's Grampy even went to every church and Catholic school he could find across Massachusetts to pass out pictures of Charlie, and asked if all the children could pray for him. Grampy really believed that if God was going to hear any prayers, it would be the prayers of the children. So hearing you all pray for Charlie here at the nine o'clock Mass always made our hearts feel better.

Well, today we are here to say thank you to all of you for your prayers. And to let you all know a little secret. God was listening!

We know He was listening to all our prayers because just before Christmas, we got a very special gift! It wasn't wrapped in paper and bows. And Santa didn't bring it down the chimney. Our gift came as a phone call. Charlie's doctor called to tell us that Charlie's latest test results were in and they were clear. It looks like all the boo-boos in his head and spine are gone. And after 22 months, he is now officially off his chemotherapy treatments! So our Christmas gift was the gift of life for Charlie! And this precious gift was given to us by God. He answered all our prayers.

Although you are all very young, some day you might hear someone tell you, "God doesn't give you any more than you can handle." Well, when Charlie got sick, we didn't know how we'd be able to handle it. We didn't know how we could handle the struggles of caring for a child with so many medical needs, and didn't know how we'd handle watching him go through the difficult treatments. And we didn't know how we'd handle keeping Jay's life happy and normal, which we desperately wanted to do because he deserved a happy childhood. But what we soon learned was that we never had to handle anything alone. We believe with all our hearts that God made sure we were constantly surrounded by caring and loving people like all of you, your moms and dads, our devoted family, supportive friends, and our amazing neighbors. Even complete strangers - all who reached out to help us. You all made sure we always had food in our refrigerator, that our house was clean, that Jay was still driven to school every day, and that we had shoulders to lean on when we needed support. You see, it was through your love and prayers that we gained the strength we needed to handle our challenges.

We also believe that when God was creating Charlie, He made him extra strong and brave so that his little body could stand up to all the yucky medicines and six operations. Charlie is our little engine that just keeps on chugging up the hill! And God created Jay to be such a caring little boy, with a huge heart, who always watches out for his baby brother, and is always concerned about all the other children at the hospital, whom he prays for every night.

We always had our faith in God, even when the doctors told us Charlie might never get better. We always believed a miracle could happen. If there is a lesson to be learned through Charlie's story, it is that with God's love, anything is possible. Trust in God; He's always by your side. Always keep your faith alive in your heart. Remember to say your prayers, because you know God's listening. And say "Thank You" to God every day for your blessings.

We thank Him every day for ours, and for giving us all of you. Your prayers helped our miracle happen. And your love and support carried us every step of the way. For that, we will be forever grateful.

Cancer is a very unforgiving disease that doesn't give up easily. If you could, please, please continue to keep Charlie in your prayers, because we want to make sure the boo-boos never, ever return to his body again! Thank you and God bless.

Quite surprisingly, I made it through the entire speech without crying, although my voice did crack a few times. It was an incredibly moving experience to be standing in front of our congregation as a united, whole family. I tried desperately to remain focused so that I would not fall apart. I occasionally caught a few glimpses of the boys as they attempted to sit quietly on the altar steps. At one point, Charlie stood up and walked down the steps and over to his grandfather in the third pew, just to check in with him. He then marched himself right back up, arms swinging the entire way, to sit next to his brother. It was easy to see, as I delivered my speech, that there wasn't a dry eye in the crowd.

We were not claiming victory in our speech. We know that we live with the fear of Charlie's cancer returning at some point. But at that moment in time, we wanted to let everyone who'd been on our side, praying for our Charlie, know that all of our prayers were not only being heard, but answered.

I turned to Jay and grabbed his hand; John scooped Charlie up into his arms, and we walked back to our pew. I could hear the clapping and cheering, but I couldn't look up. It was a tremendously overwhelming and humbling experience. It wasn't until I reached the pew and sat down that I realized everyone was giving us a standing ovation.

The Messenger

During the last week of January, I decided to pay a visit to a woman named Debbie, whom I had met at the first healing service I'd brought Charlie to at St. Mary's. She was at the service where I asked the Father Ainello to pray over Charlie and he said he'd envisioned a small face that would be healed.

I'd never visited her place of work before, nor did I even know where she lived in town. In fact, aside from her dropping off a medal at our home right after Charlie was diagnosed, we'd only seen each other at Mass and had spoken a few times on the phone. But I thought she was just a really special person, and I admired her strength and faith.

Actually, I had invited Debbie to a Pampered Chef party at our home a few days earlier. I had started selling Pampered Chef kitchen tools in early December. My brain was basically turning to mush and I needed an outlet – something to get me out of the house a few nights a week; something interesting to focus on that was just for me. Most important, something that would help supplement our income again.

Fortunately, my little Pampered Chef business totally fit the bill. I set my own schedule, chose my own hours, met some really nice people, talked with adults again, and, to my surprise, earned a very good salary.

Plus I earned an entire new kitchen full of fantastic cooking tools. It was very good for me socially and mentally; I loved my new career.

When Debbie called to say she would not be able to attend my Pampered Chef open house scheduled for the weekend, we had a nice chat. She said Father Tom had told her that Charlie had been taken off treatment. "We're thrilled and terrified all at the same time," I shared with her. We ended the conversation by agreeing to get together once she returned from her Florida vacation.

Two days later, I decided out of the blue to stop in at her office, which was in downtown Franklin. I thought I'd drop off a Pampered Chef catalog with her to see if she'd be interested in placing an outside order, although we hadn't discussed that idea during our conversation.

When I arrived at her office, she wasn't there, so I chatted with her brother for a while. He too was a cancer survivor. After staying for about 10 minutes, I gave her brother the catalog, and was headed for the door when I heard a car door shut. "Oh, wait up, that's her now," he informed me, looking out the window. I walked over to greet her at the front door.

"Deirdre, Honey, I can't believe you're here," she said, with her eyes as wide as the moon. I was surprised by her reaction, but I thought she was just happy I had stopped in. "Honey," she continued, grabbing my hand, "I was going to call you today, and now you're here. You won't believe this; come into my office."

"What is it?"

"You won't believe this," she repeated. "After our conversation on Wednesday, I wanted to send Father Ainello an update on Charlie, which I did yesterday. I wrote him a brief e-mail to let him know how well Charlie was doing, and that he was off treatment, and that it appeared he was cured."

"Wow," I began, "that was so nice. Do you think he remembers Charlie?" It had been over a year and a half since he'd met him.

"Honey, no, listen to me," she said, shaking her hand in front of me. "He wrote me an e-mail back *last night* and his exact words were, 'Thank you for confirming this. Christ told me he'd be fine.' Deirdre, can you believe that? And here you are in my office *today!*"

I was stunned. I couldn't answer her right away. "Oh...oh my God, that's unbelievable," was all I could utter. "I believe in this, you know. I believed the minute he said he saw 'a small face that would be healed' that he was talking about Charlie. I totally believe God told him Charlie would be fine. Oh my God!"

Hearing his response to the news about Charlie confirmed my belief that we'd made the right decisions in taking him off treatment. I believed my baby was healed. He was going to live. He was a miracle from God.

There was a reason I went to Debbie's office that day – to receive this glorious message. Debbie had given me the message; only it was not from her, it was from God.

A Profile in Courage

Whenever we were asked how we managed to survive 22 months of fighting for our child's life, we'd respond the same way: "We gathered our strength from Charlie." Charlie was only six months old when he was diagnosed. He hadn't even learned to walk or talk and yet he had chemotherapy racing through his tiny veins. Even as a newborn, long before he was diagnosed with cancer, he showed us his amazing strength and determination as he struggled with his inability to lift his head up on his own. He never gave up, never cried or whimpered or wavered over it. He just kept on trying with all his might.

After struggling for weeks, he finally succeeded. Although his head wobbled and bobbled, he managed to balance it on his tiny shoulders. We could tell that he was almost as proud of his accomplishment as we were of him. Little did we know that the weight and pressure of the enormous tumor in his head, and the excruciating pain it undoubtedly caused, were more than likely the reason why he was unable to gain enough strength and control to hold his head upright. His willpower astounded all of us, even the most skeptical doctors. Let's not forget, he literally needed to be tied down to his hospital bed after eight hours of brain surgery, even though he was in visible pain and unable to open his eyes because he wanted to get up and move around.

And even after being diagnosed, he persevered and never showed any signs of pain, frustration or weakness.

He was bound and determined not to be held back. He had places to go, people to see, and things to do. When he was in the hospital, he'd be awakened throughout the night. The chemo would make him violently ill. The sedations would leave him wobbly and weak. But each new day, he'd wake up with a smile, and within a matter of minutes, he'd be squealing and pointing to the door — he wanted to get out of the room and start greeting his friends up and down the halls of the hospital. He was always on the move, always on the go, never stopping to feel sad, or bad, or even angry. He didn't have time for that. He fought nap time and bedtime every single day and evening. He would never succumb to sedation without a fight. He didn't want to rest, for fear he'd miss something exciting. He had no patience or time for being sick or weak. It was not his nature.

So this is where we gathered most of our strength from — Charlie. I along with many others learned more from him in the first year of his young life than many of us will ever learn again in our lifetimes. He has more courage than any adult I'd ever known. So even when I was having a pity-party for myself about how hard it was to live such a crazy life, and how stressful it was to watch him go through all this, it would only take a glance at Charlie for me to realize I shouldn't be complaining. He was the one in pain. He was the one suffering. He was the one with cancer and chemo in his body, not me. And he handled it all, every bit of it, with tremendous determination, and confidence, and bravery. And he was less than two years old. He was still here on this earth, still breathing, and eating, and laughing, and developing. That's all it took for us to realize all that we had. His little face, his heartwarming smile, his long, beautiful eyelashes, were all we needed to see us through another day or get me over another hump. My baby boy is a brave, courageous, witty, fresh, strong-willed little man.

And Jay played a significant role in keeping us grounded. Through his three-year-old eyes, we saw all that was good and innocent. He was so patient and understanding and cooperative. Sometimes he was too smart for John and me. We learned quickly we couldn't pull the wool over his eyes. And with each passing day we realized what a kind, loving and thoughtful child he was. He was incredibly sensitive to the needs of others, especially his brother. And Charlie absolutely worships the ground Jay walks on. They share a bond I can honestly say I've never seen between two young siblings before in my life. Jay is Charlie's protector, teacher and best friend.

The sense of pride I have for both my children just pours out of me. I can't help it. Although they're only now two and four, they're wiser than I am in so many ways! I thank God for the blessing of my two sons every single day!

Where Does Life Go from Here?

Through the entire two-year experience of Charlie's battle with cancer, people from across the country and from all walks of life would make the same comment: "I could *never* have gone through what you guys did. I couldn't deal with it, I couldn't have survived." I can't tell you how many times people have said this to us. But John and I would always give the same reply: "You'd do the same; you'd do whatever it took to save your child's life." We had the choice to sink or swim. We were not going down without the fight of our lives. And it was true. It would have been very easy just to crumble and allow cancer to destroy us. In fact, it might have been the easier, more logical choice. But it didn't take more than a glance at both our boys for us to make the conscious decision to fight, not only for Charlie's survival, but to provide our sons a happy, semi-normal life, and to preserve the quality of life for our family. And quite honestly, we were no different from any of the other families at the clinic. When faced with a crisis, as one mom in the clinic put it, "You just deal." We're the first to admit, we're nothing special.

We rose to the occasion, but we didn't do it alone. We give so much credit to every single family member we have, and to our neighbors, friends, day care providers, and even complete strangers who reached out to help us maintain our own stability as we fought to save Charlie. And of course, we gathered every ounce of strength we could from Charlie, and from our unwavering faith in God. Without our faith and divine intervention from heaven, the outcome would never have turned out in our favor.

Life Lessons Learned and Taught

Obviously, John and I learned a great deal, and grew tremendously, living through an experience like this. I heard a person on the radio one afternoon who had written a book promoting the idea that we are all in charge of our own destinies. I agreed, to a point. There are things that we do have control over, and for the most part, our own happiness is one of them. But, let's face the facts here; we don't have control over everything that happens in our lives. I believe 100 percent that God has a plan for all of us. So in that respect, certain aspects of our destiny are in His divine hands.

I'm not a big fan of the expression "What doesn't kill you makes you stronger," but I do believe that with every life-changing experience we endure, there are lessons to be learned. Some lessons come easily and others may rock our worlds and shatter us to pieces.

Given what I learned and lived through during Charlie's illness, here is some unsolicited advice I would like to give to anyone facing life-threatening challenges or obstacles that seem too difficult to bear:

1) *Believe in your gut instinct.*

2) *Find courage in the inner strength you possess even though you may never have realized you have it within you.*

3) *Resign yourself to the fact that there are things in life beyond our control.*

   As the classic Reinhold Niebuhr prayer goes, "God, grant me the serenity to accept the things I cannot change; the courage to change the things I can; and the wisdom to know the difference."

4) *Keep faith alive in your heart and try to understand that God has a plan for all of us.*

5) *Do not listen to statistics. We are human beings – not numbers on a chart.*

6) *Be your own advocate. You're not on this earth to win a popularity contest – ask questions, push for answers, seek other opinions, ruffle feathers when necessary.*

7) *Realize that falling to pieces and having mental break-downs can be tremendously therapeutic, cleansing, and very rejuvenating.*

8) *Flip the bird to your illness every now and again; let it know you will not let it dictate your life.*

9) *Accept the help and generosity of others. To you, it may be humbling or even feel like a sign of weakness. But for those who love you and might otherwise feel helpless, the opportunity to help you will actually be your gift back to them.*

10) *Let go of the "why me/why us" banter. This wasteful mind-chatter only steals your energy from staying focused and positive.*

11) *Believe in the power of prayer.*

12) *Find the dark humor that surfaces during a crisis, and try to remember to laugh.*

13) *Remind yourself to breathe.*

14) *Remember that there is always someone worse off then you. Sad, but true.*

15) *Hold on to hope as tight as you can.*

16) *Never doubt for one moment that if the "chances of survival or recovery are one in a million" there is no reason why you can't be that "ONE"!*

17) *Believe in miracles.*

Will we ever stop worrying about Charlie's health? Never. Will there be moments when I gaze upon my precious son's head and wonder, "Is something brewing in there?" I'll do it constantly. Will his monthly and yearly MRIs and check-ups ever be stress-free? I strongly doubt it. You see, once cancer has afflicted you or someone you love, you'll live with that lingering fear forever.

I was asked to speak at a "survivors' reception" during a Relay for Life fundraiser in our hometown. The goal was to share Charlie's story to inspire all of those there that evening who were battling the disease. My speech was in two parts. First, I wanted to let the audience know that miracles do happen, and that you CAN survive cancer, as my two-year-old son had. My second intention was to reinforce the message that we as individuals and as a united country should never rest until we find a cure for this despicable disease.

Do we have any idea what tomorrow brings? For better or for worse, we do not. But today feels just fine! And after living through this experience, we've learned to take everything one day at a time.

We will never forget the children who lost their lives to cancer. This book is dedicated to those angels in heaven. Their precious young lives have had a profound impact on my family. We learned from their strength and determination never to give up. Coley (age 3), Julia (age 5), Caitlin (age 5), Emily (age 6), Timmy (age 7), Brandon (age 9), Justin (age 13), and Leanne (age 16), you will never be forgotten. You have captured a place deep within our hearts, where you will live as innocent, beautiful, brave children forever. You were called home to heaven for a very special reason that is still hard for us to comprehend here on earth. But we feel your presence and protection every day. For you are our guardian angels in heaven. May God hold each one of you tightly in the palm of His hands. You are loved, and you are missed.

Epilogue

August 2007

It has been over five years since I started writing this book. And I can say with honesty and enthusiasm, life is so good! I have two amazingly beautiful, healthy, happy, fun-loving children who bring me so much joy and keep me on my toes every day of my life.

Jay remains the most loving, compassionate, mild-mannered and thoughtful child I have ever known. I've been approached by so many people who have complimented me on what a fine young man he is. He is creative, smart, very funny, athletic and intuitive. Some of his nine-year-old passions include writing and illustrating his own books, scripting his own songs and rap tunes, collecting sea glass, shooting hoops, riding his bike and "jamming" with his little brother and the neighborhood kids on the drums and electric guitar. At this stage, Jay is toying with the idea of becoming a singer/actor and a professional basketball player when he grows up. He is a friend to everyone, and he is the first to offer help whenever it is needed. He is incredibly patient and understanding, especially with Charlie, and will oftentimes compromise just to keep the

375

peace. He has been Charlie's greatest teacher and is always encouraging Charlie to tackle challenges head-on. Given all he had to endure at such a young age, Jay is wise beyond his years, and yet he still remains a happy, well adjusted, gifted boy who is loved by every person who knows him. I am just so honored to be his mommy.

And what can I say about my little Choochie-ma-goochie? By the grace of God, Charlie has been in remission for five years. For anyone who has dealt with cancer, this is a tremendous milestone! My little man is entering the second grade, although he wishes the summertime could last all year long! I have never met anyone who loves life like Charlie does. "Is it going to be a sunny day today?" he asks me every single morning. He has an incredibly outgoing personality and a sunny disposition, and people just gravitate toward him. He is like the mayor of his school; everyone knows Charlie! He does require one-on-one time at school with various teachers, aids, and therapists to help him through the learning challenges he faces, which may or may not be a result of the tumor, and the long-term effects of chemotherapy. He wears hearing aids since one of the chemotherapy formulas knocked out his hearing, but he only wears them in a classroom setting. And guess what? We couldn't care less! He is the most adorable, huggable, hilarious, athletic, and charming little person, and he can make just about anyone melt with his gorgeous hazel eyes behind those long eyelashes. He is a true entertainer in every sense of the word, and loves having an audience around him. He idolizes his big brother and follows him like a puppy dog. He wants to be a professional basketball player or rapper when he grows up. Charlie is a very special little boy, and I love him to pieces.

As far as Charlie's health goes, the MRIs have become less frequent. When Charlie first came off treatment, we were still doing scans every three months, which then went to every six months, and are now just once a year. We will need to make the decision whether to continue with the MRIs or not to do them any longer (gulp!). At this writing, I think we will probably do one more this December, which will mark six years in remission, and then we will not do them any longer. Charlie does not remember so much as one minute of his treatments, the hospital stays, or the blood transfusions. Within the last year he has asked questions such as "What is cancer?", "Did I have cancer?" and "Did I almost die?" When another first grader made fun of Charlie's height, he stuck right up for himself and said "Who cares how tall I am, I had cancer and I survived!" That's my boy! And when he said it, his big brother was standing directly behind him beaming with pride. Charlie does understand that the MRIs require him to "go into the tunnel" and they are very upsetting to him. But he is always very brave.

And how am I doing? Well, it is with great hesitation and a very heavy heart that I have to admit that after eight years of marriage (to the day, in fact), and eleven months after Charlie went into remission, John decided to end our marriage. I was completely blindsided. Shocked. Devastated. Charlie was only three and Jay was two weeks shy of his fifth birthday when John made this decision completely on his own. And there was no changing his mind. My heart was once again shattered into a million pieces and I didn't know if I had the strength to overcome yet another crisis in my life. To protect the innocence of my children, I will not elaborate any further. As always, Jay and Charlie were my priority and my reason to move forward. Regardless of what was happening between me and John, we both reassured the boys that they were loved and adored by both their parents, and that would never change. And we stand by that commitment to this day.

But fear not! Although it took me a solid year and a half to once again build a backbone after my divorce (thanks, once again, to my devoted family and friends), I successfully managed to get back on my feet financially, mentally and physically and I can say with pride and confidence that Jay, Charlie and I have rebuilt a wonderful life together! Single parenthood has its own handful of challenges. At times, it can be very exhausting, but can also be incredibly rewarding as well. John is still involved in the boys' lives, and he and I have made peace, and get along very well. We have two exceptional children, so we must be doing something right!

I made the conscious decision to sell our much-loved home on Crossfield Road. Although we had created many beautiful memories at that house, there were also just too many painful memories there as well. I wanted to start a fresh, new life for just me and my boys. On my own, I built a beautiful new home across town in Franklin. I am a director at Kel & Partners, a marketing services company founded by my sister Kel and her life partner, Ginny (www.kelandpartners.com), and could not be in a happier, healthier (but sometimes hectic) and more grounded place in my life.

And I'm happy to say, I found love again. For the last four years, I have been in a relationship with a thoughtful, kind, caring man named Danny. I have known him since I was 16 years old working in the bakery department at Roche Brothers' Supermarkets. Danny came back into my life when I didn't know if I could ever love or trust another man again. My guard was up and I was undoubtedly overprotective of my heart and of my children. But Danny, in his gentle way, helped me to overcome my fears, and has become a very special person in my life.

There are days that I could pinch myself that I am so happy and my life is so complete. And there are days when I just can't conceive what we went through with Charlie. Through my many life-changing experiences, I have learned a lot and I try not to take anything for granted. I thank God every day for the life He has given me and for my many blessings.

Author's Acknowledgements

Where Would We Be Without Your Love?

There are no appropriate words that I can conjure up to truly express my deepest and heartfelt gratitude to every single person, from across the country and around the globe, who reached out to offer their love, support and prayers as my family faced this incredibly challenging and terrifying journey. It would take another ten pages for me to acknowledge every person individually and I'm afraid I might accidentally leave someone out. But let me use this forum right now to thank those of you who lent us your shoulders to cry on, cooked and cleaned for us, sent us donations and overwhelmed us with gifts, cards, e-mail, letters and phone calls of encouragement, prayed for us and delivered a steady stream of positive thoughts and energy our way each and every day for two straight years. God works in mysterious ways, and I can honestly say He hand-selected each and every one of you to give us the strength we desperately needed as we fought the battle of our lives. Because of the love and support we were surrounded with, my family and I were able to stay focused on what was most important, curing Charlie of his cancer, and just as important, allowing us to provide Jay with the happy, "normal" childhood he deserved.

I do wish to take this opportunity to thank a few select individuals who were my own personal saviors during Charlie's illness, as well as during the other tragedies and triumphs I have endured over the past eight years of my life:

To my dad, Paul Carey: Your unwavering love and devotion to your children and grandchildren is awe-inspiring. I just can't imagine the pain you felt watching your baby grandson and your own daughter suffering so. Your heart was just as broken as ours, and yet you remained strong, not for yourself, but for us. You have been a constant support for me, especially during the three years of hell I went through. Without your willingness to help in every way possible to see me through the darkness, I would have been lost.

To my mom, Joanne Carey: You taught me through your own life experience how to face adversity head-on, to not go around a hurdle but to thrust myself over it, to never give up on anything that was worth fighting for. As a single mother, you made uncountable sacrifices to devote your life to making your children's lives the best they could possibly be. And now I am walking in your shoes. You raised us to believe that everything happens for a reason, even when we couldn't understand why certain things happened to us. Mom, you were a gorgeous, loving, thoughtful, creative, generous, funny, talented woman, and I can honestly say that the best qualities I possess, I got from you. Kel, Brendan and I believe in our hearts that you are having a ball in heaven with God and all the other angels!

To my sister Kel: I think it is safe to say, you have saved my life more than once. You have always been more than just a sister to me. You also took on the active role of being my mother, my best friend, my therapist, my protector and my biggest cheerleader. You were my lungs on the days I literally could not find air to breathe. You were my ears when I just couldn't bear listening anymore. For three straight years, you gently unfolded my crumbled body from a fetal position when my heart just couldn't handle any more pain. You'd picked me up, dusted me off, and pushed me to refocus time and time again. I leaned on you for absolutely everything that life tossed my way. And you were always there for me. Always.

To Bebe O'Donnell: The love you possess for your grandsons is so endearing, and they just adore you. Thank you for always being such a special part of this family, and for making me feel like no favor was ever too big to ask. You certainly deserve a tremendous amount of praise for your role in helping raise Jay and Charlie to become the sweet, thoughtful and kind boys they are today and for being their #1 fan.

To my brother Brendan: I thank you for showing me how to stay strong and to find the courage deep within me to persevere even when life is unkind, and to bear the days when I just don't know how much more I can take. You may not see it within yourself, but to your family who loves you and admires your bravery, you are a silent warrior and an exceptional human being.

To my sister-in-law Ginny: Where would I be without you? You are a gift to this family, and you're one of my best friends. Because of your presence in my life, my world is a better place. And it is a testimony to your endless guidance, love, encouragement and patience that I am the happy, healthy person I am today!

To my niece Julia, and nephews Shaun and Patrick: You were all very young when Charlie was sick, and I thank you for sharing your mom with me at a time when I needed her by my side the most. Charlie, Jay and I adore you, your mom, and Ginny and Trey more than anything in this world. It is an honor to be your Auntie. I'm so proud of the beautiful, caring and loving people you've grown to become.

To "Money and Papa" - Frank and Joan Capodanno: Thank you for the outpouring of love and support you gave my little family through all the challenges we faced. I always found such comfort knowing that when we could not be with Jay, he was with his "Money and Papa" in his own room at your house, being showered with love and affection, treated like a prince, playing with the trains and Hank the Hulkman. You have always made Jay and Charlie feel as if the sun rises and sets just on them. And they adore you so much.

To Jill and Matt Petrie: Jill, you are a sister to me. Matt, the boys think you are the king of all uncles. I'm not sure how we would have been able to navigate through our life as successfully as we did during such tenuous times without you there by our side. For every tear we shed and every joyous cheer we raised, you were feeling every single emotion we did. Thank you for being a constant source of unconditional love and support.

To Douglas and Suzanne Capodanno and Beth and Rob Mejia: Each of you had your own lives in full swing with your children, careers and responsibilities, and yet the minute Charlie was in trouble, you dropped everything to be by our sides.

To our beloved **Dr. Lilia Cuozzo and Cathy Pellegrine, and the entire staff at Dedham Medical Associates:** Thank you for treating our family like we are part of your own. We would have been lost without your guidance, patience and support. Dr. Cuozzo, if you didn't push for that CT scan and introduce us to Dr. Kretschmar, I'm not sure Charlie would be alive today. You were always there to take our calls and to gently guide us through this whole ordeal.

To Dr. Liliana Goumnerova: How do I say thank you to the person who saved our son's life? We were broken parents when we had to release our beautiful son into your care. Now Charlie is a happy, healthy, functioning, athletic, intelligent little boy because of your amazingly gifted hands. You will always be our hero.

To Dr. Cynthia Kretschmar: If you hadn't come into our lives, I shudder to think where we would be today. You are a remarkable and gifted woman – brilliant, caring and truly exceptional! You were the only glimmer of hope we had, and we clung to your advice and expertise every step of the way. Thank you for seeing Charlie as a human being, a person, a little boy, and for being gentle and forthright with us throughout the entire journey. My family credits you for helping cure Charlie of his disease from a medical standpoint, but just as important, you ensured we were providing him the best quality of life as he battled his cancer. We love you very much, and owe you our lives. You have dedicated your life to finding a cure and treating children with cancer and we praise you to the high heavens.

To the entire staff in the Hematology/Oncology Clinic at the Floating: We were thrust, obviously against our will, into the world of pediatric oncology. Our lives were shattered, and we were blinded with fear. Every member of your team helped us physically and emotionally piece our fragile lives back together again. Thank you all for your love, wisdom, empathy and exemplary care. I am in awe of what you do every day to save children's lives; it is very humbling. Mary Jo and Cathy, I have to thank you both so much for putting up with me and gently educating me as I blindly entered the world of pediatric cancer. You were my lifesavers.

To every doctor, nurse and staff in every department at the Floating Hospital for Children/Tufts New England Medical Center: God bless you all! To our friends in MRI, Radiology, ER, Psychology, ENT, Surgery, Anesthesia, Pre-Op, the PACU, Day Surgery Recovery and every department in between, we owe you a debt of gratitude you may never fully comprehend. Each of you played a key role in Charlie's survival, and for that, we will be eternally grateful. And to the entire medical and nursing staff on 7 Medical (especially our primary care nurses Chris, Heather, Mary Beth, Jamie, Christine, Tonra, and my guardian angel Carol), we love you all so very, very much. You provided our family with the best possible care, and we credit each of you for helping save Charlie's life (and keeping me from swan-diving off the roof).

To all the doctors, nurses and staff at Boston's Children's Hospital, especially our incredible nursing team on 9 North (including Christine, Lisa, Jill and CeeCee): You were a godsend to us at a time in our lives when we could hardly function as human beings. Thank you all for your incredible, gentle and loving care you provided to our precious child. We also want to thank you for your endless advice and words of encouragement, your tender hugs, gentle mannerisms, expert guidance, and unending understanding. Children's Hospital will always hold a very special place in our hearts, a place that we will never let go.

To Kristin Carroll, Donna Susi and Patricia Harnan: You girls will never, ever truly understand how much I appreciated your Monday night inpatient visits. Trust me, those anticipated visits were what kept me sane and thoroughly distracted during our very long, lonely ordeal.

To my dear friend "Auntie" Amy Hardcastle: I don't think I'd be alive today if I did not have you as my friend. You are my saving grace, and I came to count on you for so many things. You opened your heart to us and showered my family with your unwavering love, thoughtfulness and generosity, and were a constant ray of sunshine and hope even during the darkest hours. And I will never forget how you and Bob came over to put my Christmas tree in the stand and helped decorate it when the boys and I were left to endure that first Christmas alone.

To Kristine Powers: You were the unsung hero throughout this whole experience and beyond. God sent you and Kevin to Crossfield Road for a reason, and I am so grateful He did! You went above and beyond what any neighbor, friend and teacher would ever do. You became like a second mom to Jay, and he always felt safe and comfortable in your care. Colin and KJ also played a key role in Charlie's survival, and I know our four sons will remain close friends for a lifetime, given what they went through together at such young ages!

To Anne and Rob Gilberti: You were the backbone for this family. You were always there every time we needed you, day or night. You offered hugs, prayers, and shoulders to lean on every day. You cooked us dinner every Monday night for two years straight, fed our dogs (I bet with great reluctance, about which you never so much as hinted) when we couldn't be home, took care of Jay at a moment's notice, cleaned our dishes, shoveled our driveway; simply put, whatever need we had, you met. And you did it all out of the goodness of your hearts, never looking for anything in return.

To all of my friends on Crossfield Road, my Cloverland Family (Jane and Paul McCarthy, Barbara and Paul Messina, Kevin and Carol Delehanty, and Jimmy and Kelly Foxx, you've all seen me through every personal tragedy and triumph I've experienced through my life – and still love me just the same), **and all my friends at Hill, Holliday, Carat Freeman, Roche Brothers, Harvard Pilgrim:** God made sure that we did not face this crisis alone! All of you sprang into action to help us spiritually, financially, and emotionally. Thank you for your kindness, your generosity and the unique ways you let us know we were so loved and that you were rooting for us and Charlie! And thank you for rising to the occasion to love and support me through trauma number two when my marriage ended so abruptly, and I once again needed to reconstruct my backbone to rebuild a new life for myself and the boys.

To our friends at St. Mary's Parish, Father Tom Walsh and Father David Goodrow: Thank you so much for raising your voices to God and asking Him to cure Charlie and give us the courage and strength to move forward each day. Because of the power of prayer, we were blessed with watching a true miracle unfold right before our eyes.

To Helen Mullen: You are an angel here on earth. Thank you for answering all of the hundreds of pediatric oncology questions I threw at you, and for answering God's will to devote your life to helping sick children and their family's battle cancer.

To the Petrucci family of Westwood: Joe, Nancy, Maria, Nanci-Jo, Tina and Joey: You became our extended family and we fully credit you and the entire Barn Yard staff for providing Jay a secure, loving and stable environment every day, which allowed him to continue to grow and learn and thrive!

To the Petrucci and McGinnis Families: Thank you for sharing your beautiful angel Coley with us. Although her time here on earth was too brief, her energy, love of life, and courage helped us find the strength within ourselves to continue to fight our battle every day. Ann and David, although horrific circumstances brought our families together, a trusted and treasured friendship grew, and for that, I will be forever grateful. And even through your own trying times and impending grief, you and your entire extended family reached out to generously help Jay, Charlie and me out when we needed it most.

To Jack Connors: I am your biggest fan! Thank you for everything you've done for me and my family both financially and emotionally. I admire you as a businessman, a philanthropist, but mostly as a father. You have such an enormous heart, and are so incredibly kind and generous. For me, it is an honor to be able to call you and your entire family my friends.

To Terry Carleton: Thank you for helping take the financial burden off my family during a time when we needed to use all of our energy to fight for our son's life. You are definitely one of my favorite people on this planet, and I feel truly blessed to have you as a dear friend.

To Gina Gallagher: Thank you for giving me the inspiration to take this manuscript off the shelf after years of collecting dust, and to remind me that we moms of children with special needs and circumstances can help make a difference in the lives of others. Gina's book is called *Shut Up About Your Perfect Kid* –*www.shutupabout.com*– get your copy today!

And finally to all of my new friends in Brandywine Village and at Kel & Partners: Especially Katie Marino, Chris Regan and Jody Heaton for taking the time out of your own busy lives to help edit the manuscript. And to my dear friends: Kate Massey, Diane Coffey and Bill Kelly for reading the manuscript and encouraging me to self-publish. And I owe a very heartfelt thank you to my talented and beautiful friend Erin Johnson who designed the most beautiful and compelling book cover I could have ever asked for.

I love you all very, very much!

How Can You Make a Difference?

Reach out to the following organizations, hospitals and foundations and learn how you can make a monetary donation to help find a cure for cancer, volunteer your time or talent, grant a sick child a wish, or give the gift of life by donating bone marrow, blood and platelets.

Tufts-New England Medical Center
Floating Hospital for
Children's Cancer Center
750 Washington Street,
NEMC #231
Boston, MA 02111
1-617-636-5000
www.nemc.org

The Neely House at Tufts-New England Medical Center
750 Washington Street,
NEMC #0716
Boston, Massachusetts 02111
1-617-636-0716
www.camneelyfoundation.com

Make-A-Wish Foundation® of America
3550 North Central Avenue,
Suite 300
Phoenix, Arizona 85012-2127
1-800-722-WISH
www.wish.org

American Cancer Society
P.O. Box 22718
Oklahoma City, OK 73123
1-800-ACS-2345
www.cancer.org

Children's Hospital Boston
300 Longwood Ave.
Boston, MA 02115
1-617-355-6000
www.childrenshospital.org

American Red Cross
Donate Blood & Platelets
1-800-448-3543
www.givelife.org

Give Kids The World Village
210 South Bass Road
Kissimmee, FL 34746
1-800-995-KIDS
www.gktw.org

National Marrow Donor Program
3001 Broadway Street Northeast,
Suite 500
Minneapolis, MN 55413
1-800-627-7692
www.marrow.org

In loving memory

Nicole "Coley" Petrucci
December 15, 1999 – March 5, 2003

Our dream was for you and Charlie to dance together at your prom.
May your tiny toes be dancing joyously in heaven.

In loving memory

Joanne F. Carey
January 4, 1932 – August 1, 2003
My Mom
&
Nana Extraordinaire

She listened to her heart before any other voices.

About the Author

Deirdre Carey was born and raised in Westwood, MA. She graduated from Regis College in Weston, MA with a BS in Communications in 1989 and went on to pursue her dream of working in the fast-paced world of advertising. She and her two sons, Jay and Charlie, along with their beagle Hershey, now reside in Franklin, MA. Deirdre, a single working mother, is the Director of Client Services at Kel & Partners, a marketing & public relations agency based in Westborough, MA.

Deirdre enjoys skiing, biking, and cruising the high seas with her sons, reading her beloved People Magazine, and vacationing on Cape Cod with her family and friends.

Printed in the United States
94517LV00003B/46/A